2580

Systems Analysis
for
Business Management

Stanford L. Optner

*Consultant in Systems Engineering
and data processing, Stanford L.
Optner and associates; member
of the instructional staff, Engineering
Extension, University of California
at Los Angeles*

1960

Prentice-Hall, Inc.   Englewood Cliffs, N.J.

PRINTED IN THE UNITED STATES OF AMERICA

88122–C

To Ruth

Preface

Today, there is no general systems theory which has been applied to business. In almost all institutions, business is taught much as it always has been. It is among our most undisciplined areas of knowledge and has exhibited slow, uninspired improvement over the last fifty years. Our future business managers are being taught vocational skills in the absence of "think processes" which would equip them far better for reality problems. A "think process" in this context would be a tool of analysis or synthesis which would enable the competent executive to solve his problems with a high degree of reliability. General systems theory supplies such a vehicle.

The need for a general systems theory has become increasingly evident. Some companies are so large they are no longer understandable in the simple, descriptive terms of their formative years. As a result, corporate objectives frequently work at cross purposes with current policies. The typical executive is forced to attack his problems as if they were an endless number of special cases. What is needed are general concepts about the nature of business operations that would assist him to abstract the properties of an individual problem. A tool of this kind would make the problems of business more accessible to the analyst.

Our expanded industrial technological frontiers have not been reinforced by the development of large numbers of business trained, technically oriented personnel. Industry needs more men who have the combination of a good general education, business experience in more than one field, and supplementary training in some academic discipline. These broadly equipped persons would be well prepared to attack today's massive corporate problems. It is true that many companies send their executives back to school for short term refreshers or orientation in new fields. This activity undoubtedly increases managerial capability. However, the absence of general theories in business penalizes executives who would like to find a frame of reference through which they could do more effective problem analysis and decision making.

The superficially similar characteristics of systems have naturally led researchers to apply the tools of scientific disciplines in less disciplined fields of endeavor. Sociology, anthropology, history, economics, and political science are areas of study coming under the scrutiny of specialists who have exposure to more than one field of knowledge. These specialists are searching for general theories to improve the organization of knowledge about a particular area of study. For a pertinent example, my recent work in the area of city planning[1] has demonstrated the usefulness of the systems approach; reaction to this material indicates that systems analysis has some usefulness for professional planners.

My effort to attack the problem of a general systems theory in the business management field began in 1956 with the development of case material for an extension course to be offered at the University of California at Los Angeles. Subsequent to this, the opportunity to test the usefulness of a systems approach in business became possible in a variety of industrial problems which I encountered as a consultant. In addition to providing a useful frame of reference in complex problem areas, the systems approach became a powerful analytic tool in problem identification and problem solving.

This book, therefore, has a dual purpose: To contribute to a general systems theory in the field of business management, and to provide a practical means of understanding and applying the fundamentals of systems analysis in the business environment. In the former task, I hope others will join and carry this work forward in greater detail; as an early entry in this effort, this book has only begun to explore the possibilities of a general systems theory for busi-

---

[1] Stanford L. Optner, *Report on the Feasibility of Electronic Data Processing in City Planning, to the Department of City Planning, City of Los Angeles*, 1959.

ness. The work of others will increase the usefulness of the ideas I am setting forth.

The initial problem was, of course, to state the thesis. Chapters 1 through 5 are devoted to this end, concentrating on the elements and definitions, the fundamentals, and the method. The thesis has been stated both academically and realistically by frequent examples that come from the business world.

Chapters 6 through 9 are devoted to electronic data processing equipment. In a relatively few years, computers have caused a major revolution in data processing. Wherever data is to be processed, systems analysis becomes a major consideration. After the first rush of electronic dizziness,[2] it has become evident that the effective design of systems is still the fundamental requirement of successful computer applications. Computers have had a special impact on the growth characteristics of industry. The use of electronics has tended to force companies toward centralization of data processing, although decentralization is taking place in manufacturing, engineering and marketing areas.

The intent of Chapter 7 is to give the systems analyst a single source where a few examples of computer equipment can be compared in parallel. (There are several manufacturers whose equipment is not listed, and their absence from this chapter is not to be construed as a condemnation.) This cross section of available equipment describes many of the characteristics and differences in equipment and will be especially useful to practicing systems analysts.

It would be desirable to cover Chapters 1 through 9 parallel with the analysis of case studies in Part Two. Each case emphasizes one or more situations in which systems analysis contributes toward a more incisive understanding of the company's problem. The case study method works most effectively in a group. Because cases are explored through discussion, participants have an opportunity to draw on the range of each other's knowledge as the group discusses important issues. Cases have been designed to enable participants to express many possible solutions, although the fundamental systems problems may not be obvious. Cases must be thoroughly digested prior to discussion. Cases have been designed for teaching purposes, and

---

[2] A *Business Week* Special Report: *Computers,* McGraw-Hill Publishing Co., Inc., New York, 1958. (June 21, 1958 issue of *Business Week.*)

do not deliberately indicate the policy or practice of any company, corporation, or individual.

Throughout the preparation of text and finished copy, I have had the assistance and guidance of many people. Among these, I would like to mention my friend and colleague Jack K. Weinstock who contributed substantially to many of the basic ideas in this book and assisted in editing the manuscript. I am also indebted to Professor Wallace J. Richardson, Department of Industrial Engineering, Lehigh University, for his continued interest in this material during the years of its formulation, providing constructive review and critical comment. Finally, I must acknowledge the work of Michael Sundermeier of Prentice-Hall in editing, proof reading, and the hundred and one functions that take place behind the scenes to produce a readable text.

S. L. O.

Contents

PART ONE

SYSTEMS ANALYSIS

1

The systems concepts
in business

STRUCTURED SYSTEMS

Systems can be broadly classed as physical or nonphysical. Physical systems are a part of our everyday vocabulary; we are accustomed to refer to the combined tubing, electrical parts, accumulators, and pumps of a hydraulic mechanism as a hydraulic system, and we refer to complexes of equipment for a wide range of uses as electrical systems, broadcasting systems, telephone systems, transportations systems, and so on.

Scientists responsible for the development of physical systems in the last 200 years have pursued the part of the complex phenomenon which was simple to understand.[1] This emphasis has shifted in the last 50 years; many disciplines have begun to attack complex phenomena with the goal of determining what, if anything, can be formulated from its parts. This shift from analysis to synthesis means that somewhat less emphasis is now placed upon studying individual systems and more is placed upon predicting how a number of combined systems will function as a unit.

Experiments with larger, complex systems, at first unacceptable, have now become an important facet of scientific investigation. Such study has led to the hypothesis of a closed system. The closed system can be defined as one which is free of variation or disturbance. One of the ways to study such systems is through the concept of the "black box." The experimenter conceives of a simple machine into which he will introduce known inputs and obtain certain resultant outputs. These are noted in a format and completeness

1 W. Ross Ashby, *Yearbook of the Society for General Systems Research* (Ann Arbor: University of Michigan, Mental Health Research Institute, 1958).

that will describe only those results which are directly observable. The problem for the experimenter is then to

(1) deduce the contents of the black box;

(2) determine what was not deducible;

(3) test the rules under which the experiment was performed, to determine their validity or need for modification and further experiments;

(4) determine the limitations which were placed on the experimenter;

(5) determine the usefulness of the output.

The record of experiments would thus contain the following:

(1) the inputs which were used;

(2) the outputs which were recorded;

(3) the variations which were observed.

The experimenter, in seeking to learn something of the black box, examines his output in search of some force which is operating. This makes itself known through the statistical arrangements of output which he is free to rearrange, providing that, in doing so, he does not alter or introduce something which was not already in the record.

The goal in designing such experiments is to produce a condition which is non-varying in time. This results in a controlled or tight system. Ashby refers to these systems as information-tight since they are designed to admit no disturbance at input.[2] Such systems would thus have no gain, only decay while the process is in operation. Since the capacity of the black box is "finite," the frequency and volume of data to be introduced determines the amount of decay (data deterioration), which, in the absence of gain, can be measured through observation. These invariant systems have machine-like characteristics and are highly predictable.

Highly predictable systems of the type described, are typical of physical systems. These systems are structured, or designed, to operate in non-variant, highly predictable ways. Because system disturbance may be known to occur, the black box (the hydraulic system, the electrical system, and so on) is designed to function within statistically predictable limits. Black box components are

2 W. Ross Ashby, *op. cit.*

chosen with the same rigor, taking into account factors such as fatigue, stress, and reliability.

A pre-World War II characteristic of complexes requiring many component systems was the relatively independent design of each. Components were operationally compatible but design was not completely integrated with associated hardware. Each component system (called a subsystem) was designed close to some optimum (most favorable condition) in terms of the current level of technology. Thus, each subsystem might function adequately in terms of its own specific "mission"; but the end product in which components were installed fell far short of the optimum goal.

The design and development of ballistic missiles were projects requiring the use of complex subsystems. The scientists charged with the development of these projects required a new packaging concept. In weapons development, with hundreds of breakthrough requirements, technical staffs recognized the need for new propulsion techniques, new guidance mechanisms, new fuels, stabilizing equipment, armament, and countless other things. These requirements demanded, in addition, integration and unity of function in one package, a consequent complete specialization of purpose, and a heavy emphasis on the reliability and performance of the end product. These requirements were extended, moreover, to include the ground support equipment, materiel, and man power necessary to maintain and operate the end product. This, in brief, is the weapons-system concept of the modern day missile, where the nose cone is conceived as a *subsystem;* propulsion and guidance are *subsystems;* and the missile, its ground support equipment, materiel, and personnel are the *system.*

Note the parallel structure of this complex system and the experimenter's model. In the former case, the system comprised the following:

(1) the inputs and outputs
(2) the processor (black box)
(3) the experimenter

This man-machine combination was quite manageable in terms of size, compared to the missile system. And yet, if one were to deal with a subsystem of the missile—or one of the major assemblies comprising the subsystem—one would soon be at a level where the inputs, processor, and human factors would be more manageable, too. Systems of the physical type contain the intrinsic structural properties of the experimenter's model. However, the manufacture of components or systems admits a very large number of variables, mainly in the form of human factors. Some typical human factors follow:

(1) The engineers who design for production
(2) The materiel personnel who order parts
(3) The engineers who design tooling and call out manufacturing sequences
(4) The personnel who plan and schedule production;
(5) The operators who make, assemble, inspect, and test parts

The experimenter's laboratory model will seldom be designed to operate within the wide bounds of the complex subsystem. As near as one might come to this concept in the industrial world would be the pilot plant which functions as the economic and operational model for a future product. The goal in the industrial world would be to use the experimenter's model as the means of isolating individual phenomena, whose ultimate use may not be clear. The laboratory model might act as the means of eliminating certain possible courses of action. Systems which are designed to operate with humans will not qualify as closed systems.

INCOMPLETELY STRUCTURED SYSTEMS

I will use the term *incompletely structured* to describe systems of the industrial and business world; this tabular presentation will qualify the structured and unstructured systems for the present:

Property	Structured	Incompletely structured
1. Input	Invariant; no disturbance	Variable; many disturbances
2. Output	Predictable; statistically stable	Unpredictable; statistically unstable
3. Processor	Machine-like	Man, or man-machine

Incompletely structured systems are of two general types. The man-machine system noted above, an example of which was the missile system, is one. The other differs from this in that it does not necessarily contain a physical system. Such nonphysical systems are those in which the human being and his man-made institutions execute all of the processor's functions. Following are typical functions to be performed in nonphysical systems:

(1) Planning

(2) Investigation

(3) Designing, inventing, creating

(4) Classifying, sorting, calculating, summarizing, recording[3]

(5) Problem solving

(6) Decision making

Since there is no model which dictates that investigation should or will come first in every human action, in all of these examples, there is overlapping and much interchange. There is also no way of knowing how efficiently each phase of the above sequence will be implemented. Thus, when man becomes the processor of a system, his functions will be much more loosely executed than those of the machine in the physical system—we do not expect machine-like efficiency, reliability or accuracy. Some examples of nonphysical systems in which man may be the sole processing agency follow:

(1) Engineering
   a) Part number assignment
   b) Drawing control
   c) Prototype or production drawing release
   d) Change control
   e) Drawing room methods

(2) Administration
   a) Wage and salary review
   b) Labor and materiel requirements
   c) Purchase of manufactured parts
   d) Development of time standards
   e) Release of orders for manufacture

There are many, many areas not listed under Engineering and Administration which are examples of incompletely structured non-physical systems. There are, also, a large number of similar systems in Sales and Manufacturing. Generally, except in highly automated companies, the majority of systems must consider human factors.

There are some additional characteristics of nonphysical systems

3 T. F. Bradshaw, "Automatic Data Processing Methods," *Proceedings, Automatic Data Processing Conference, September 8 and 9, 1955* (Boston: Harvard University Graduate School of Business Administration, 1956), Chapter One.

which apply broadly to man's creations, such as business, industry, government, law, cities, and so forth; these are listed below:

(1) The potential of a large variety, quality, and quantity of related and unrelated inputs

(2) A large number of processors of finite capabilities, occasionally working at underload or overload capacity

(3) A large number of anticipated and unanticipated outputs

(4) Control mechanisms which operate with unequal efficiency, providing the opportunity for unequal applications and results

(5) All actions not measured with equal rigor and seldom reintroduced into the system to improve future performance.

These characteristics are operational in nature. However, there are some additional, general nonphysical systems characteristics which are not operational:

(1) These systems are generally in a qualitative (non-quantitative) state of development.

(2) Abstraction is at a very low level, and the bulk of available data is in descriptive, non-numerical form.

(3) Comparisons between systems reveal large numbers of superficial similarities (isomorphisms), most of which are poorly defined, uncatalogued, and whose causal relationships are poorly understood.

(4) The *self-organizing* (ability to be self-regulating) or homeostatic characteristics which occur, seldom appear in systems other than those which are highly generalized, and then only as mass effect.

It is now possible to complete the table which had only three elements at the outset, and now has five:

Property	Structured	Unstructured
1. Input	Invariant; no disturbance	Variable; many disturbances
2. Output	Predictable; statistically stable	Unpredictable; statistically unstable
3. Processor	Machine-like	Man, or man-machine
4. Control	Reliability approaches 100 per cent	Wide range of reliability
5. Feedback	Self-organizing	Outputs are not automatically reintroduced to improve performance

There appear to be five system properties, or elements. These are the attributes of any on-going process, structured or unstructured. It follows that when an on-going process is found, a system may be in operation and the analyst can proceed to define the attributes from direct observation.

The electronic computer has been specially designed to execute the general purpose data processing requirements of its users. Thus, it will be informative to step back, and look at the computer as a system.

THE ORGANIZATION OF A SYSTEM

Figure 1–1 shows the organization of a computer. Note there are three essential areas, input, output and the central processor. The

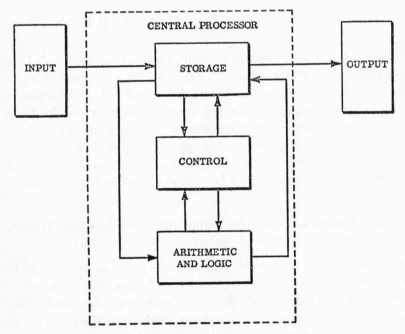

Fig. 1–1. The organization of a computer.

combination of input and output peripheral equipment with a central processor is referred to as a computer system. Thus, the electronic data processing system is based upon at least these three requirements:

(1) A means of getting into the central processor in order to do something,

(2) A means of getting out of the central processor after something has been done,

(3) A means of going about the business of doing something in a reliable, automatic way.

However, the processor must have the ability to reject improper raw data, inconsistencies or intermediate results that do not conform to the set of rules under which it has been instructed to operate. There must be, as an intrinsic part of this processor, a device that monitors its internal operations. This sets up the requirement for a fourth system element:

(4) A means of monitoring the processor so it will operate in a prescribed way.

There is still another system element, however, which hasn't been isolated. It is like element number one, in that it is a kind of input, but it is unlike number one because it is generated by the action of number two. This element is also related to number four in that it reports on the behaviour of the system. However, instead of monitoring the processor, element five reports output, bringing the results of the process back into the system so that corrections in future input can be incorporated. Thus, we describe the final system element as:

(5) A means of monitoring output, delivering the results of operation back into the system as input, to correct future output.

The computer is a physical (man-machine) system. It achieves its operational systems characteristics by its design. The computer is composed of transistors, diodes, switches, wires, tubes, and so on, which when energized will perform, under the direction of its operators, those functions for which it was designed.

Having referred to the missile as a weapons *system*, it will be useful to apply the recognized system elements, and see what they reveal. The missile in flight will have:

(1) A set of *Inputs,* coded signals, called a program, which will tell the missile what to do.

(2) A set of *Outputs,* the speed and direction in which the missile is travelling, which are the result of its program.

(3) A *Processor,* a computer or similar device which accepts instructions, processes them, and is the operating unit on which all system elements work.

(4) One or more *Controls,* the built-in program that has been designed to keep the missile on its course, and applies the rules under which the on-going process will take place. (There are many other controls, such as configuration, reliability, and so on.)

(5) A *Feedback,* the transmission of output data as another input, to correct any discrepancy between what the missile is doing, and what it should be doing.

A convenient way to look at this set of processes is borrowed from the way in which the computer system is organized (see Figure 1–2).

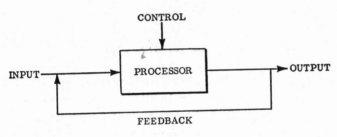

Fig. 1–2.

There will be frequent reference to this arrangement of system elements in the future. It will sometimes be called a module to emphasize how it reappears at many levels in the business organization. This module will be used to describe the attributes of a very elemental subsystem or a very complex, high level subsystem. It makes no exception of the type of data being processed or the type of processor being utilized. It provides a way of looking at the functional relationships which exist in any on-going process. As such, it becomes valuable as an objective standard. Since we know every system has certain elements, it follows that we can look for the system elements when we suspect there may be a business system in operation.

The missile in flight to the target was seen as a system. The systems engineer must learn in orderly steps of analysis, to look at business processes as systems. It is with this general frame of reference we can now begin to employ the systems approach in the business and industrial world.

THE FACTORY AS A SYSTEM

The first requirement is to look at an on-going business, out of the eyes of a systems engineer. The business enterprise must be viewed as a system. So the first logical question to ask is what are the outputs, always starting with output since it establishes the purpose for which the system exists. This question is easily answered, since the output of a manufacturing company, for instance, would be a salable product and a state of profit or loss which is the company's measure of effectiveness. In this example of the manufacturing company, if the outputs are a salable product and profit or loss, what are the necessary inputs? They may be numerous, but they can be generally stated as direct and indirect labor, direct and indirect materials and capital, in the form of cash, land, buildings, and equipment.

Note that the factory is the system under study, and that its place in the module is as the processor. In all cases, the system under study will be the processor. Only in a factory of a special configuration will it be possible to provide the functional relationships (processes) which will change the input from its original state into the required output. It will be extremely important to determine when the processor can or can not produce the output. This may happen either because the inputs are unsuited to the process, or because the processor is in some way unsuited to the inputs. This could also reflect inadequate control or feedback, as well. Unprofitable operation can be characterized as a business state that exists when system elements do not combine in an optimum way. The converse may also be stated. Profitable operations will exist when the business system elements combine in a way which approaches an optimum.

What are the controls which operate on the factory system? Certainly there are legal requirements to consider. For instance, in the case of a food products manufacturer, the Pure Food and Drug laws would apply. There are additional controls in the form of a minimum hourly wage or other federal, state, and municipal restrictions. These controls may be called external to the system in the sense that they apply with more or less equal rigor to all factory systems. Such external controls must be considered within the system boundaries if they apply to the system under study, and their use as a constraint must be reflected in the operations of the factory.

Controls can be considered internal to the system when they monitor the way in which operations are to be conducted. Any particular factory system under study will have policies, organization, and a plan under which it operates. These can be quite specific and have the ability to monitor the factory operation. At this point, we must assume the controls are numerous and precise enough to keep the system in profitable operation, something that will be examined in more detail at a later point.

Finally, we must determine whether or not there are mechanisms at work that operate like feedback in the missile system. Certainly one of the results of delivering a salable product to a customer is the reorder reaction. If the product has sold, it will be reordered; if it has not sold, there is less likelihood that it will be a candidate for reorder. The sum of the reactions of all customers to the initial shipments of a new product line are a very useful feedback. The factory may stop manufacturing slow moving items and concentrate on faster selling numbers. This may be a response to style, competition, climate, economics, or any other of a number of conditions or combinations of conditions.

What about the factory which ships parts that pass its final inspection but are rejected at the customer's receiving inspection? Here the feedback may be that parts are unacceptable because of the following conditions:

(1) Made from the wrong material
(2) Shipped too late; order had been cancelled
(3) Shipped too early; cannot use
(4) Out of tolerance
(5) Intended for another plant of this division
(6) Quantity greater (or less) than ordered
(7) Shipped with inadequate paperwork

Thus, it is clear that there are feedback mechanisms at work—a lot of them. The problem for the systems engineer is to design the system to take advantage of all the system elements. In doing this, he must assess which of the possible candidates for the systems elements are critical, since those which are not critical will not be used. The processes by which systems elements are isolated and their importance in the system operation analyzed will be covered in Chapters 2 through 5. Economy of system design dictates that there should be a balance between all possible system elements and those which are important in perpetuating the optimum system operation.

It is possible that a system will be designed with all the elements and still not provide optimum output. All system elements must be *reliable*. If, for instance, you are depending on individual purchasers to return a factory guarantee registration slip which is packed in every new appliance carton, you are willing to accept less than perfect feedback. If an incentive to return these slips were provided, the result might improve. *Accuracy* is a major requirement of effective system design. If a manufacturer plans his shippable inventory based on the level of store inventory, as many seasonal manufacturers do, the means by which he derives his knowledge of current store inventory can point him to bankruptcy as fast as it might place him in the forefront of his competitors. *Frequency* is an important system characteristic, since the updating (making current) of records should contain the minimum lag. In one week of daily information, a change in trend might be discernable—and ultimately provide the clue to a market reaction—but weekly data for the same purpose might be inadequate since it would take three or four weeks to identify a new trend. *Completeness* of data is mandatory for proper system design. Completeness does not necessarily mean that 100 per cent of the available input will be incorporated into system operation. Sampling techniques may make it possible to reduce input requirements, substantially. Sampling techniques must be geared to an individual problem. If the system is to be the sensitive device that assists in decision making, it will be essential that it return sufficient data to insure a high probability of success. These criteria of adequate system design pertain to all system elements. The factory as a system is illustrated in Figure 1–3. What

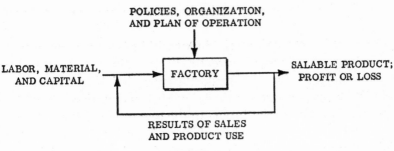

Fig. 1–3.

has been said so far is not specific enough to be useful, as yet; the model of the factory system is true of most factories. So it is clear that, in order to be very useful, the factory will have, first, to be restated as a specific factory making a specific product; secondly, it will have to be stated as the sum of its most important subsystems. Much as the physical components of a missile are interlocked in design and function, the subsystems of a business must be intimately interrelated. The goal for the systems engineer is to find the means of expressing this relationship with the over-all objective of optimizing the well-being of the company and the users of the product.

THE FACTORY SUBSYSTEMS

Because there is no specific factory under study at this time, we will make a general statement of an important subsystem common to any manufacturing plant, called *Production Control.* If Production Control is the processor, what is its over-all objective? Probably the overriding objective would be to maintain schedule. The schedule is assumed to be an optimal trade-off (exchange of values to come closer to a "most favorable" solution) from another subsystem called *Order Release.* This subsystem compromises all of the possible shipments with those that can be made within certain cost and time (working days available) restrictions. Thus, we are sure at the outset that a customer delivery schedule is one of the major inputs to our Production Control system. A delivery schedule implies the existence of a counterpart, closely related, to the production sequence of operation. Thus, we can be reasonably sure that the production schedule is a major input to the Production Control system.

The most important material input will be inventory status, telling the number of parts in process, in stock, in transit, on order, and short for each future manufacturing period. There must be a basic labor counterpart for the scheduled inventory status which was the primary material input. In the case of labor, it could be a labor load (long range schedule of direct labor requirements), or it might be a machine load (short range schedule of direct labor requirements tied to specific machine classes).

One important ingredient is missing: The technical package that tells what operations to do on each part, the sequence of operations, the tooling, the machine tools on which operations will be done, the dimensions, tolerances, machine finishes, and so on. Now we can organize these elements in a modular fashion (see Figure 1–4). Note

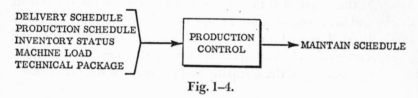

Fig. 1–4.

that our system module is incomplete because the control and feedback elements have not been described. Here are some of the important controls which should be operating in this major subsystem:

(1) Organization role of Production Control

(2) Master Schedule—the company's top level plan of operation

(3) Management decisions based on periodic reports

(4) Minimum lot sizes or other rules relating to releasing orders for production

(5) Standard practices, company policies, rules, and so on.

There are other controls working in this general system, and it would be essential to find them in a real-life situation.

Now for the feedback: One of the most valuable is the progress report which shows the status of work-in-process. Like the missile in flight which signals its flight path to tell where it is, the progress report does the same thing for the factory operation. Another document which tells more about the output is the performance report. Here, the standard hours for the parts which have been completed are compared to the actual hours expended, as a measure of efficiency and successful scheduling. The actual-hours feedback tells the number of hours which can be removed from the machine load when the updating process takes place. The budget fills the same role in keeping management advised on the state of dollar expenditures.

INTEGRATION IN BUSINESS SYSTEMS

There are five inputs in the model of the Production Control subsystem. The data and reports used as input to the Production Control subsystem, were outputs of other, more simple subsystems. Properly organized, the outputs would be constructed to integrate with the higher-order subsystems as inputs. Integration between subsystems is essential, since in practice it gives the following results:

(1) Reports are used for many purposes; special purpose reports are at a minimum.

(2) The need for reports is well established by their use in higher order subsystems.

(3) The timing, frequency, and contents have been specially designed to energize (activate) next higher order subsystems.

(4) The volume of data is closely related to the minimum requirements to transmit all information essential for higher subsystem decisions, but not in excess of this amount. Simultaneous updating of files affected by one input becomes possible.

Integration in subsystem design is the key concept of systems analysis in business. Integration of systems postulates the trade-off between the functional requirements of a subsystem with its immediately related subsystems. Integration in this sense also means the intercompatibility of subsystem design. Each subsystem becomes a black box when viewed by the systems engineer. Using the data at his command, the systems analyst observes the subsystem operation, looking at inputs, outputs, and the processing device (the black box) to determine whether or not each subsystem is making the desired contribution to the over-all system (the factory) requirements. The systems analyst must deal with the known facts to deduce the need for redesign of the system. Since this is not a closed, physical system, he will deal with more inputs, outputs, and a more loosely defined processor than that of the experimenter working under laboratory conditions. The statement of systems boundaries indicates how the systems analyst will deal with the design of an incompletely structured business system.

The dependence of higher order subsystems on more elementary, lower order subsystems for input must be reminiscent of the original description of the missile system (see page 5). Lower order subsystems are, in turn, dependent upon still simpler, more fundamental subsystems for input. The factory system is actually a tightly (or loosely) interlocked collection of subsystems. While its needs are more general and of wider range than that of the physical system, we can take some valuable clues from the analogy. The integration of physical subsystems should accent utility (need), economy, and unity of purpose. All of the factory subsystems are man or man-machine systems. The size of the factory and its product production rate and other factors will determine the exact balance of men and machines. The dependence on manual functions in business brings about the symptoms that have been associated with the unstructured system.

The first requirement in assessing a business system is to state the problem. This means that existing operations must be seen as systems and the systems engineer must decide the systems elements which are present and missing. This definition of the system under study would have us begin by looking at the whole or the largest part of the whole, whichever is more manageable and practical. Understanding the existing system operation will lead to the ability to state the systems requirements from which the design of the improved system will follow.

Having defined the properties of unstructured systems, it is appropriate to ask whether or not they can ever be better structured than they are in the best managed company. Parkinson's Law would tend to show that the mere existence of a business with its attendant, gradual personnel enlargement will invariably open the possibility of systems analysis to restore or improve the level of operations. As business grows, it will never be less complex in its goals and means of achieving them, only more complex. Both operations research and electronic data processing have had some impact on the need to structure business systems more efficiently. However, both have some limitations in the universality of their application and in the attendant costs. Small business enterprises make little use of these tools, yet their problems are relatively the same.

The usefulness of systems analysis is that it provides a much needed, objective frame of reference. Concepts such as systems integration are invaluable as a tool in problem solving. The systems approach supplies a number of principles such as the one relating to the system elements. These principles will make analysis and problem solving easier and more effective because they fill the need of providing basic and elemental ways of describing all business operations, regardless of complexity or type. Systems analysis in business is built on the premise that there are striking similarities between the way physical systems and business systems function. The principles of systems engineering suggest that we can learn something about the way an effective business system should operate by using as a tool the analogy to a logically designed electronic system. Systems engineering requires that business operations consist of a set of intimately related subsystems. The integration of subsystems is the key to effective and economic operation.

2
Describing the system under study

THE BOUNDARY CONCEPT

The system processor is deceptive in its simplicity. It is clear that a man or a machine can be called a processor for the purpose of analyzing a problem; but when the processor is the Production Control subsystem, it is not nearly so simple to say where production control starts and stops. Nor is it easy to say just what subsystems will be included, and what subsystems will be excluded. This is a matter of how the organization defines Production Control, and may be so subjective that it merely reflects an individual's opinion of what Production Control should be doing. The systems engineer defines the system under study by stating its boundaries. The use of a boundary concept makes it possible to define any on-going (non-static) process as a system. It further enables the systems analyst to look at the problem as a whole, and set up the framework for later looking at the parts (the subsystems) in something close to their correct relationship.

There are some statements that could be made about all production control systems. However, such statements would have to be very general and therefore of marginal value in solving a specific operational problem. In any real-life situation, objective recording of observable phenomena is requisite to understanding the process. A statement of systems boundaries is dependent upon an ability to define the system under study. This becomes the goal of initial investigation into the nature of the system. In attacking the system under study, the engineer makes only one *a priori* conclusion: The systems requirements will dictate how the system should be designed. A knowledge of the system requirements will follow from an understanding of the following:

(1) The activities which are associated with the on-going process

(2) The inputs which are processed in the system activity

(3) The outputs which are obtained as a result of system processing

(4) The way in which the on-going process is controlled

(5) The errors, deviations, and exceptions which have been marked as system malfunctions. Included in this category are the following:

   a) System malfunctions in time: that is, the time element necessary to introduce input or obtain output, feedback, or control inhibits the function of the system or its next in line subsystem,

   b) Cost malfunctions: that is, the costs to introduce input or obtain output, feedback, or control are greater than they were in the past; or the costs to sustain the system are intuitively determined to be higher than the value of the system operation itself.

A statement of the boundaries will, by determining the content of the system, place limits on the system to be studied. This is necessary since an ability to define the adjacent areas of a system will emphasize the integration problem. It will have the additional value of concentrating investigation in areas where evidence pertinent to the solution of the problem is available.

A boundary in the systems' sense restricts the scope of a problem to a size commensurate with the cost or time available for solution and the amount of detail necessary to understand the process. It is possible to view Production Control in many ways and change the boundaries accordingly. Management's view would tend to relate Production Control to the organization as a whole, and Management would tend not to see it as an operating unit filling a variety of minute, day-to-day needs. The operators or users of Production Control services would tend to think in non-organizational terms, perhaps only looking at one or two special functions performed for them alone. These statements are not necessarily contradictory—they only emphasize the range of definition possible for the processor. Thus, it is entirely right that the system under study be accurately described in terms of the role the processor plays, in a specific instance (see systems purchasers, Chapter 3).

A boundary of a subsystem will create a problem of manageable size. Systems which include many subsystems will, in proportion to the complexity of the organization, tend to be less easily managed or controlled. The ability to look at systems and subsystems with the same set of requisites, improves the ability of the analyst to maintain uniformity and consistency in the statement of objectives, criteria, and assumptions. This ability improves performance in problem recognition, problem identification, and fact gathering for problem solving.

The statement of boundaries will assist in determining whether an output can be produced, given either the processor or the input. There must be additional conditions which specify something about the behaviour of the missing elements, as well. For instance, if you are told that one measure of an effective Production Control would be a reduction in scrap—would you agree? This module is illustrated in Figure 2–1. One is quickly and inescapably led to the

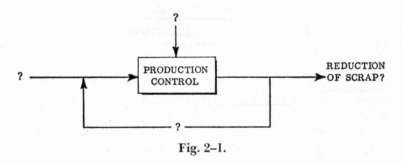

Fig. 2–1.

conclusion that there actually are some things one could do to achieve this desirable goal. Some of the possibilities are outlined below:

(1) *Input.* Improve quality of technical package, reducing scrap caused by
  a) inadequate drawings
  b) inappropriate tooling
  c) poor materials
  d) improper cutting tools
  e) improper feed, speed, depth-of-cut

(2) *Control.* Provide special rules and procedures designed to reduce scrap caused by
   a) inadequate supervision or in-process inspection
   b) wrong man working on the job
   c) improper operation of machine tools, hand tools, hand checking devices.

(3) *Feedback.* Find means of relating actual quantities of scrap to causes of scrap, bringing appropriate changes into the system to modify past scrap-producing practices by
   a) increasing standard hours allowance: operators generate large amounts of scrap attempting to meet or beat standards
   b) increasing lot size: scrap per cent shrinks as large quantities are processed; bulk of scrap occurs in first fifty pieces
   c) not permitting operators to make their own setups: substitute specially trained set-up men who will do more precise work.

However, the major factor in producing scrap has not been considered because this is actually the wrong subsystem. The module that should have been analyzed is illustrated in Figure 2–2. The

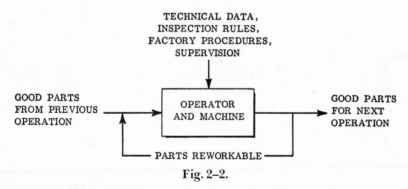

Fig. 2–2.

rule is to look at the processor most directly concerned with the problem. In this case, the systems analyst would study the fabrication process in the attempt to reduce scrap. Human error makes more scrap than machine error. Technical data, factory procedures, inspection, etc., are seen as controls over the on-going production process, not input (compare Figures 2–1 and 2–2). If the goal is to reduce scrap, one way is to apply controls and feedbacks, taking the part of the output which is not good, and rework it. This module more faithfully reflects how to achieve the desired goal.

It is now possible to deal with the problem of whether or not reduction in scrap can be considered a primary objective of a production control system. The answer is, no. There are some more or less
direct, and many indirect effects of production control actions
which tend to reduce scrap. However, reduction in scrap is really
more closely related to the machine, the machine operator, inspection, the technical package, etc. The system module must be analyzed to determine whether or not the system elements are actually
related in the way they have been postulated. It is especially important to test the processor to see if it is capable of producing the
output. The processor must define the boundaries within which the
on-going process will take place.

The ability to find the correct subsystem or to identify the proper
systems elements, emphasizes the art in systems analysis. As in any
other field, the ability to perform efficiently is to some degree a
result of the participant's training, experience and ability. Thus,
the business-oriented systems analyst can make a major contribution because of his knowledge of business operations, generally.
Knowledge of or experience in the system under study will speed
the analysis and identification of systems elements. In the absence
of such knowledge or experience, the systems analyst can rely upon a
knowledge of the properties of systems to aid him. An understanding of systems analysis will never replace a knowledge of the
problem under study, but it will provide an objective frame of
reference in which investigation and hypotheses can logically occur.

The system boundaries can now be defined for data processing
purposes as the following:

(1) A human: in this case, the work performed will be done manually.

(2) An electro-mechanical, man-machine combination: in this case
the work would be performed by men in conjunction with
punched card (tabulating) equipment, bookkeeping machines,
and so on.

(3) An electronic, man-machine combination: in this case, the work
would be performed by men in conjunction with a computer
and its associated complement of electro-mechanical equipment organized as a computer system to achieve certain predetermined ends.

The system processor can be defined for all other purposes as:

(1) Man-made objects or institutions: in this case, the system may be an inanimate object which has an on-going process which can be readily described by its system elements. Examples of this would be cities, government, and so on.

(2) Environmental: in this case, the system might be the topography of the land, the watershed and water uses, the land use, and so on.

BOUNDARIES OF ISOMORPHIC SYSTEMS

The isomorphic (superficially similar) nature of systems can be restated for subsystems such as Production Control. There are superficial resemblances among Production Control systems. Some multiplant manufacturers insist on the uniformity of systems design in their operating units, with some variability in the success of individual applications. The outstanding issue is to determine the conditions under which similar but not identical systems requirements may be adapted to operate effectively with the same system design. These are the necessary conditions:

(1) When both systems have the same "mission" or reasons for existence. *Example:* A machine shop and a sheet metal shop employ about the same number of people, operate as job shops, generate a comparable dollar volume, and organize their factory operations around service departments of the same type and size. If we look at these two, independent examples as systems, we might come to the conclusion that, despite the differences in salable product, both the business objective and the means to achieve it have been organized under the same boundaries. In this circumstance, an identical system design might be adopted with little or no change.

(2) When both subsystems have highly specialized data processing requirements. *Example:* A dress manufacturer and a furniture manufacturer employ about the same number of people. In the preparation of their payroll and associated quarterly tax returns it would be very likely that both could utilize the identical data processing system.

(3) When each subsystem is extremely simple in its processing role and is designed to receive input with no variation. *Example:* A

retailer of dry goods and a wholesaler of sports equipment re-order their stock when the stock level reaches a predetermined point. If the number of items to be controlled is approximately the same, it is conceivable that both companies could use the same number of personnel, the same system and perhaps the identical forms to record inventory facts.

(4) When control is outside the system, and operating on output, which becomes input to an adjacent system. *Example:* See Figure 2–3.

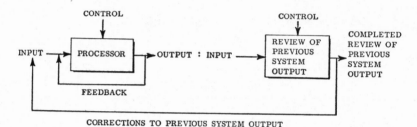

CORRECTIONS TO PREVIOUS SYSTEM OUTPUT

Fig. 2–3.

(5) When decision making is not included in the system operation (see item 4).

(6) When both systems operate well within time restrictions that preclude unequal deterioration or decay of data. *Example:* Two divisions engaged in different manufacturing activities are required to provide corporate headquarters with reports of monthly sales. All reports are due the fifth working day after the close of the month. Systems for generating data on monthly sales could be identical if they supplied the requisite data within the time restriction.

These conditions restrict greatly the universality of any one business system—and rightly so, since each organization has objectives which are somewhat different than any other organization.

FILTERING INPUT AND FEEDBACK

Even under circumstances where identical products are produced by the same manufacturer in different locales, environment acts as a filter altering to a considerable extent the nature of the system. Environment acts as a filter by allowing only certain input and processes, eliminating others. For instance, the labor pool in south-eastern United States is quite different from that in New England. The wage earner of the Pacific Northwest is quite different from his counterpart in the Southwest. Similarly, environment has a marked effect on the availability of the resources normally provided by capital. For instance, Tucson, Arizona, which has few factory buildings or facilities, must provide space to encourage immigration of new business. Los Angeles, with a wealth of facilities available, has passed the point where the Air Force feels it is desirable to continue to concentrate certain industry in its environs. Climate is, of course, a major environmental filter, as well.

The filter is a useful concept and is defined as *a man, man-made, or environmental factor which consciously or by its state of being, acts to admit certain system elements to the system process keeping others out.* In the area of systems design, it would be desirable to have filters which allowed the entry of all valid and valuable input, automatically rejecting invalid or valueless data. A way to show the filter in the systems module is indicated in Figure 2–4. As can be

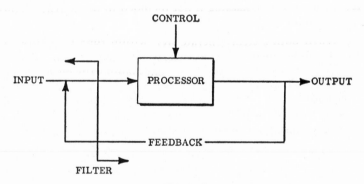

Fig. 2–4.

seen, the postulation (necessary existence) of a filter in a system actually infers certain subsystems which cut across input and feed-back, but which may lie outside or inside the system. The system processor acts as a filtering mechanism as well, producing only those outputs which can be created from specified inputs. Likewise, certain operations, such as one called *edit-input* (or *edit-output*), are filtering-type operations. Manual systems generally call for more filtering-type operations than those which are mechanized or auto-mated. In stating the boundaries under which a system will operate, the ability to recognize the existence or absence of filtering opera-tions, will be necessary.

It is now more clear why systems can follow no stereotype but are at best isomorphic. A host of environmental factors work against uniformity. Differences in management objectives are reflected in organization and operations. The design of a system is the solution to a problem of a specific management. For the systems analyst, the solution will arise out of the existing process and a knowledge of the systems requirements.

ILLUSTRATING SYSTEMS

The systems diagrams of Chapter 1 are typical analytic devices for looking at the existing process in a coarse way. They are equally suitable for looking at details of the process when the problem is to analyze the existence or nonexistence of important system elements. Systems diagrams are different from other types of flow charting techniques in that they accent the use of the systems elements as the important tool in system analysis; they do not replace flow charts, which are used for other purposes. These are the things the systems module illustrates when it is used as an analytic tool in investigating the existing system:

(1) Identify the system under study (processor).

(2) Identify the purpose for which the system exists (output).

(3) Identify the ingredients (input) whose functional relationships can be arranged to produce the required end result.

(4) Show the existence or nonexistence of mechanisms whose pur-pose is to maintain reliability, accuracy and other desirable op-erational attributes (controls).

(5) Show the existence or nonexistence of mechanisms to correct malfunctioning output (feedback).

The basic diagramming technique is to assist in identifying systems elements (see Figure 2–5). The second diagramming technique is to demonstrate the inter-dependent nature of subsystems, when the output of the first system becomes the input to its next in line sub-

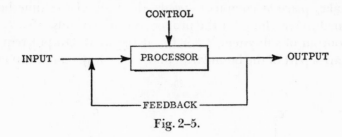

Fig. 2–5.

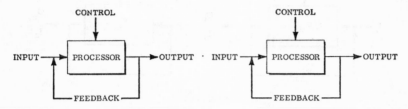

Fig. 2–6.

system without alteration (see Figure 2–6). Modules so related emphasize the integration aspect of data processing. The actual area of integration is where the output can be used as input elsewhere without alteration. A second aspect of integration is shown in the next diagram (Figure 2–7), where,

I_a = Input and output to subsystems P_{ab} and P_{ac}

P_{ab} = Processor for subsystem $_{ab}$

O_b = Output $_b$ of subsystem P_{ab}

F_{ab} = Feedback from O_b, subsystem P_{ab}

C_{ab} = Control over subsystem P_{ab}

P_{ac} = Processor for subsystem $_{ac}$

O_c = Output $_c$ of subsystem P_{ac}

F_{ac} = Feedback from O_c, subsystem P_{ac}

C_{ac} = Control over subsystem P_{ac}

Note that the initial input (I_a) is an output of subsystem P_{ab} and is reused in subsystem P_{ac} as input, without alteration. This is a typical use of systems integration where a computer is the data processing device. It is not uncommon in computer applications to have a single file of sorted input transactions update or operate against half a dozen basic files. If the computer carries the files in external storage (magnetic tape units), passing one input across the six tape units takes place at computer speeds, the bulk of the time being consumed in searching for the proper record. Note also that I_a can be an output of subsystem P_{ac} or P_{an}, if required. Output requirements are a part of the boundaries under which system design takes place.

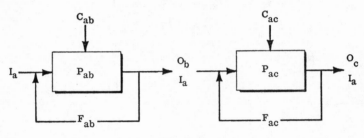

Fig. 2–7.

The third diagramming technique is of a coarser nature and intended to implement the early need to look at the major subsystems of an ongoing process, breaking the system into its component subsystems (see Figure 2–8). In this type of diagram, the need to show

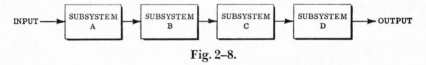

Fig. 2–8.

controls or feedbacks will be entirely optional, depending on the usefulness of the detail. The absence of intermediate inputs and outputs is intentional. In this method of analysis it is not essential to supply all details, if the purpose is to make an over-all breakdown to represent the full system. Intermediate inputs and outputs (as well as all other systems elements) are invariably implied, however, because the definition of a system is an on-going process containing all of the five systems elements.

THE STEPS IN SYSTEMS DESIGN

To state the boundaries one must make an appraisal of the problem prior to actually working on the problem. This appraisal would normally be limited by how much detail one would have to collect to make a careful statement of the problem. The extent of this preliminary appraisal of the problem would be related, as well, to the amount of material required to solve the problem. The danger in developing the boundaries is that it is possible to be carried into the back alleys of distantly related problems. The need to appraise familiar or unfamiliar problem areas in establishing boundaries and, subsequently, to investigate problems makes it desirable to explore the process by which this should be done (see Figure 2–9).

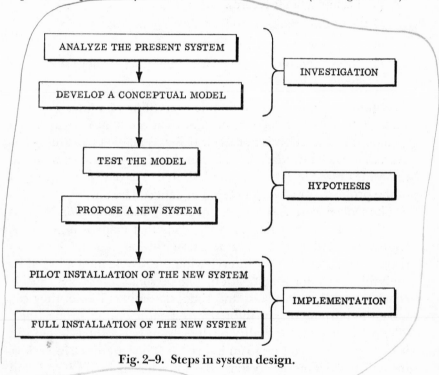

Fig. 2–9. Steps in system design.

Investigation

What is the existing system? This is the first and sometimes the most important question the systems analyst can ask; it contains the important objectivity requisite to effective investigation. It does not presuppose that there is no existing method for coping with a problem. The existing method may be malfunctioning or poorly conceived, but these are precisely the symptoms the investigator must understand in order to be able to document the problem carefully.

How does one determine the nature of the existing system? This is a period of intensive data collection and interviewing. Basically there are two types of informants: Those of the written word and those of the spoken word. Both must be used. The written materials which are pertinent might take the following forms:

(1) Examples of inputs or outputs.

(2) Examples of file records.

(3) Actual examples of system malfunction.

(4) Memoranda, letters, and notes which may be pertinent.

(5) Other reports or commentaries indicating previous study of or attention to the same problem.

The guiding principle is to sample everything of value. Take advantage of every type of existing information. Naturally, this can go too far if discretion is not used. It is reasonable to assume, however, that more raw material is better than less—it is always easy to cast aside unusable data. It is not desirable to have to hold up a part of the problem for an extra period of data collection.

The spoken word is at least as valuable. The organization imposes certain restraints that make it very likely that many things can be learned by word of mouth that will never be found on paper. Thus, there are good reasons for interviewing the people most affected by the problem under investigation. But personal interviews can become confused, redundant, and time-consuming. Worse, they can serve the purpose of putting the investigator on the wrong track. The position and personality of the person being interviewed can inject a pronounced bias to an interview. The hazards of interviewing only make it more necessary to plan each contact in advance and fit the material collected by each contact into the pattern which begins to emerge early in investigation.

Interviewing can take the form of an opinion poll when improperly handled. Generally, the investigator wants facts, not opinions. However, if opinions which may be necessary or desirable are solicited, they must be treated as such. The following gives some general rules on the conduct of an interview.

Interviewing

The role of the interviewer is to obtain specific information. He will have organization precedents to guide him in his task. He will attempt to control the interviewing process without cutting himself off from vital information by obstructing an important channel of questioning. He will be forced to make decisions as the interview proceeds as to what line of questioning is valuable, and what information is relevant—what data he can get elsewhere with higher reliability, and how much of the data being collected will require confirmation before being used.

A workable interview technique gets the problem in narrative form first, and then follows the leads that come out of the narrative to ask specific questions. The interview should start with mutual recognition of why the problem is being investigated. The material to be covered must be preplanned with the idea of keeping the interview within bounds. Sometimes it is valuable to compose a statement which will describe the purpose or object of the interview, and to use this as a guide if the problem is very complex.

Here are some valuable "don'ts" that apply in interviewing:

(1) Don't interrupt the story to insert your own ideas.

(2) Don't let the interview get diverted into paths that are obviously not pertinent.

(3) Don't let blanket statements or broad generalizations obscure the facts.

(4) Don't let half-understood problems go; leave the interview with a clear concept of the issues.

(5) Don't be overpowered by the person being interviewed; be sure you leave feeling you were the interviewer and not the interviewed.

(6) Don't become involved in operational problems or offer solutions that will distract from the prime purpose of information gathering.

(7) Don't ask questions that can be answered "yes" or "no" without recognizing that the question sometimes will call for an opinion and not a fact.

Here are some valuable things to do during the process of interviewing for data collection:

(1) Make personal contact with your subject immediately; keep the contact "human." Five minutes of warm-up before you start will pay off in good cooperation.

(2) Describe the assignment briefly so the person being questioned will see his part in the total picture; make him feel he is on the "inside"; tell him what your role is; invite him to feel the importance of his role in the program.

(3) Have an outline of the material you intend to cover and other pertinent data with you when you interview; use these as a guide to be sure you are getting all the data.

(4) Make your notes telegraphic but not unintelligible; take care in writing so you can read your notes.

(5) This is a suggested type of indenture in outlining the narrative:
   a) Roman numerals
   b) Capital letters
   c) Numbers
   d) Small letters
   e) Numbers in parentheses
   f) Small letters in parentheses.

(6) If you are making lists or enumerating data, organize the information for logical and easy understanding on separate sheets, noting where to insert or pick up the data.

(7) If you miss a point and want to insert it, use this method:
   a) Draw an arrow to the point of insertion marked by a capital letter (A); in the margin by the arrow, refer to the page where the insertion will be found:
   See Insert (A) on Page 9 ←——————————→ (A)
   b) Keep inserts on separate sheets.

(8) Be sure to note data such as the names of persons interviewed and their titles; head each interview separately for easy identification; indicate page number and date.

(9) Be sure references to flow charts are clear and unmistakable so notes and flow charts can be easily associated.

Soon after the start of the investigation the conceptual model will begin to take shape. The conceptual model is the analyst's first idea of how to attack the problems of the system and of the way in which the system should be redesigned. The conceptual model might be a reliable indicator of how the final system will be designed —or it might be very unreliable. Inadvertently, the systems engineer may become involved in solving a problem even at the investigation stage. Unfortunately, it is difficult to avoid trying to find a solution during the investigation period; this, however, must be the period during which investigation is still the primary goal and the systems analyst must make a conscious effort to be a data collector.

Hypothesis

This study area can be defined as the period which lies between investigation and implementation. It is, despite this somewhat loose identification, concerned with two important logical steps, the first of which is testing the conceptual model; the second is proposing the new system.

Although Figure 2–9 shows no feedback process, what happens during a study is something like that illustrated in Figure 2–10. Block 2 is going back to block 1; 3 is returning to 2; and, hopefully when the study moves into block 4, there will be a minimum need

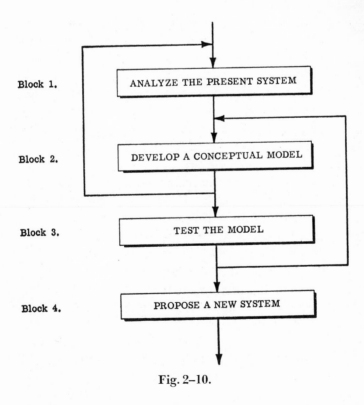

Block 1.   ANALYZE THE PRESENT SYSTEM

Block 2.   DEVELOP A CONCEPTUAL MODEL

Block 3.   TEST THE MODEL

Block 4.   PROPOSE A NEW SYSTEM

Fig. 2–10.

for more testing. The return arrows which block the proposal of a new system reflect the feedback from incomplete boundary definition in earlier phases. In other instances, feedback could be of a positive type where the system is adequate but simulated operation has shown ways in which it can be improved.

Block 4 is sometimes called postulating the system. This term has wide use among engineers doing feasibility studies, because they have the need to document and preplan an entire system on paper, far in advance of actual use. Thus, their paper plan is known not as an actual but as a postulated system, since it presupposes its workability without empirical proof.

The model of the system may be in many forms. As a mathematical expression, it might be readily tested. This is not always possible. As a business system it will meet its most severe test in use. But short of this, it can receive a real test by presenting it to its potential users for their criticism and comment. If paperwork will change hands in the operation of the system, representatives of departments affected by paper handling should be called in. Completing forms, making sample computations, and preparing resultant outputs by simulating the operation of the system, will reveal some of the inherent weaknesses. An excellent practice during the design of systems would be to bring affected departments into the picture as early as possible and to keep them there throughout the study. Systems are not designed for individuals and especially not for the credit of the systems group. Natural resistance makes it mandatory to bring those who must change into contact with those who are bringing about the change. If the model of a system is mathematical, its usefulness in testing will be restricted unless the data introduced for processing are empirical. In the absence of data scaled to the problem, extensive testing may have to wait until implementation begins, and the testing will be continuous.

In a new system, it is desirable to test the over-all operation in any way feasible. It is also desirable to test separately the subsystems that combine to form the over-all system. For instance, in a machine loading subsystem, it would be desirable to check out all the paper handling that would have to go on in the factory, in order to be certain that the handling of job cards was in keeping with the system concept. Following are some of the subsystems which it is important to test in the design of a machine loading subsystem. To the extent that they may be independent, they may be tested independently; to the extent that they are dependent serially, they must be tested both independently and serially:

(1) Check-in for new job assignment

(2) Pick-up tooling for new job assignment

(3) Check-out setup after first piece

(4) Clock-in on production

(5) In-process spot inspection

(6) Clock-out on production.

These subsystems each have a marked effect on the successful operation of the over-all system. Their proper operation will determine to some extent the success of the over-all system. Why test them separately? Because each is somewhat complicated in its own right. Also, a change in one may have no effect, or may have a marked effect on the other—the only way to know this is to understand all about each subsystem in detail. Finally, it is important to establish subsystem compatibility. This is only possible by linking the outputs of subsystems as interdependent units, to see that those which happen first in time satisfy all of the requirements of those which operate later in time. In the laboratory, the experimenter attempts to reproduce reactions a number of times to obtain statistical validation. He also does this to be certain that all of the data from his experiments are properly understood and expressed. Systems analysts agree that this is a sound technique and that business will reap a high order of effectiveness from its systems if they are designed and tested according to this method.

The problems encountered in testing systems will be complicated by the unstructured nature of the problem. Thus, in business systems statistically predictable variance will have wider limits than that acceptable to the laboratory experimenter. The unstructured nature of the problem must be considered in designing the testing format to be employed much as it must be considered in the design of the system itself.

Implementation

It is not always possible to have the opportunity to make a pilot installation. However, it invariably proves its value when one can be arranged. Pilot installations have the obvious advantage of allowing the system in miniature to operate under real-life conditions. This means that defects can be corrected before large scale commitments are made.

A good example of a pilot operation would be one which permitted the trial of a new timekeeping subsystem designed for 1000 employees working in a factory but did not involve all 1000 employees from the outset. The systems engineer in this instance might obtain Management's agreement to have one cost center of one department (a subdepartment, or the smallest factory unit) trained in the use of the new system. This group would be relieved in the test period of any responsibility for the old system which is being superseded. The group must be large enough to be significant. If this factory operates on a multi-shift basis, it would be important to determine whether or not the pilot operation should also sample second or third shift problems.

Pilot operations are good in that they concentrate attention on the new system. Systems engineers may require many months to design a large scale system. If Management becomes impatient, once in the pilot stage they will begin to see the fruit of the labor that has been expended. The pilot operation of a system thus becomes an important goal, both for Management and the systems designer. As soon as a subsystem is in pilot operation, it becomes more of a reality than it can ever be on paper (see Figure 2–11). Note again that problems can occur even at Block 6, forcing alterations in system design. It is even conceivable that problems occurring at Block 6 might go back to Block 1. In the design of physical systems, this is not uncommon. The system designer must work against the probability that Block 6 will require the feedback to Block 1. This is best done by adequately describing system boundaries and designing ample testing devices before implementation begins. If a boundary change occurs due to greater insight obtained in a pilot operation, system redesign may be mandatory. Testing the subsystems adequately is therefore only a part of the solution to efficient system

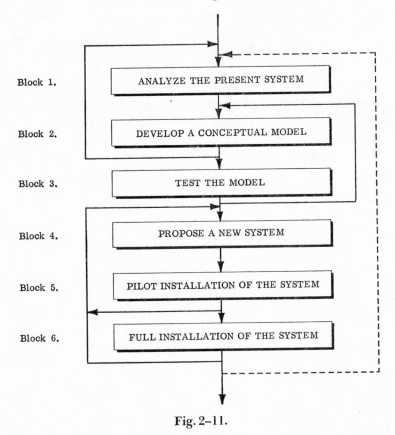

Block 1.   ANALYZE THE PRESENT SYSTEM

Block 2.   DEVELOP A CONCEPTUAL MODEL

Block 3.   TEST THE MODEL

Block 4.   PROPOSE A NEW SYSTEM

Block 5.   PILOT INSTALLATION OF THE SYSTEM

Block 6.   FULL INSTALLATION OF THE SYSTEM

Fig. 2–11.

implementation. Changes in output requirements may reflect a situation where the sum of the optimized subsystems is equal to something more or less than the desired optimum system. In this sense, the term optimum may be difficult or impossible to achieve, and something less than optimum may have to prevail. If the system designer can determine within certain limits what the optimum may be, this in itself is of considerable help. The system designer must act with the idea that his role is to *improve* the existing process. If such an improvement does not achieve the optimum, this does not mean that a measurable advantage has not been introduced.

The concentration of personnel on the problem of a pilot installation has the added advantage of newness. New systems are attention getters for systems engineers, and they provide an opportunity to ask and obtain concerted effort from the individuals involved in the test. This could have the disadvantage of obtaining exceptional performance which is not desirable. What the systems engineer needs is attention and willingness to change or follow a new set of instructions. Few systems do not affect humans. A certain amount of the systems engineer's time will be expended in making the necessary adjustments (trade-offs) to satisfy the people directly concerned in the systems design.

The final phase of the system study is that which extends the pilot operation, step by step, until it covers the full, operational scope it is intended to have. At each step of the way, the new system will have to be monitored because enlargement is in itself a test of adequacy. And finally, following complete implementation, there will be a policing period to insure that the system elements are functioning in use as they were planned. Policing, in this sense, makes the systems analyst a control element—he acts as a system monitor. In systems implementation, policing is mainly concerned with the adaptation of individuals who may have to relearn their new routines many times. This is a task requiring diplomacy as well as firmness. The systems engineer may police the system on the level of the individual operator, but more frequently works with supervision in order not to infringe on supervisory prerogatives.

The systems approach requires that there should be a plan for conducting a system study which borrows liberally from the scientific method. In addition, the systems approach dictates that a problem be analyzed functionally and operationally and that it consider suitable alternatives. To achieve a high order of effectiveness in problem solving, the systems engineer attacks the task using all available tools. He looks at problems as potential systems requiring input, processing, output, control, and feedback. Among the first tasks is the isolation of the problem area by specifying the boundaries around it. The systems approach dictates that a problem be attacked in an orderly way—first by investigation, then by establishing a reliable hypothetical model of the problem.

3

Fundamentals of
system design

Investigation of a business system means the collection of volume
and activity figures for each step of data processing and system design. If these figures were being collected for a computer application, they would include the number of characters per record, the
number of records in the file and their extension to determine the
total size of the file in characters, separating alphabetic from numeric. In addition to this, frequency of processing would be stated.
Data specifications would be included by obtaining samples of
input, output, and file forms, perhaps utilizing a common detail
specification sheet to bring all data on one subsystem together in
one place. The natural accompaniment to this data would be flow
charts describing the information transmission processes and data
on existing semi-automatic or automatic data processing techniques. Where does the systems analyst go from here?

The system design invariably reflects the philosophy of management. System design is a result of Management's policy, its knowledge of and orientation to company problems, and the excellence of
the systems staff doing the work. Some philosophies of system design are better than others under special circumstances. Since all
firms cannot order large scale computers, a philosophy gauged to
maximize the effectiveness of changing over to computers only
would not be very useful. On the other hand, a philosophy dedicated
to the *status quo* will never put the most sophisticated tools of the
modern world at the service of industry. Some appreciation of useful goals in system design would clearly be of assistance. Figure 3–1
illustrates some possible alternatives in systems design.

ALTERNATIVES IN SYSTEM DESIGN:
ONE-FOR-ONE SYSTEM CHANGEOVER

Under this philosophy, the system analyst replaces the existing processor with some other processor justified either on the basis of faster reporting, more accurate reporting, or some similar improvement; savings in cost of data processing may or may not exist. This is a fairly common philosophy, although it is frequently disguised with admirable rationalization. The shortcomings of this approach are many. First, of course, is the failure to exploit available analytic techniques in the selection of the data processing system. The one-for-one philosophy substitutes two things in place of the analytic approach:

(1) Reduction of elapsed time to install the new system. *Example:* Studies leading to the evaluation and selection of alternate equipment are eliminated. Whatever equipment advantages may exist, of one system versus another, are not explored. Equipment is thus selected on one of the following bases:
   a) Lowest in cost
   b) Outstanding (but unevaluated) performance
   c) Personal preference
   d) Integration with existing equipment (or enlargement of existing complement)

(2) Minimum study costs to implement the changeover to the new system (see Figure 3–1). *Example:* Costs of studies to analyze equipment characteristics are eliminated. Costs to study an existing *versus* a proposed system are, by and large, bypassed.

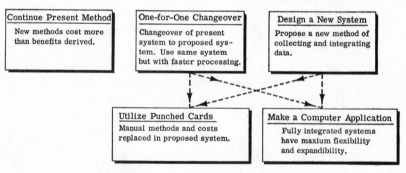

Fig. 3–1. Alternatives in designing the system.

Whatever systems problems are in existence, remain unsolved. Whatever cost advantages may be possible by and large are unrealized.

Without exception, the one-for-one changeover results in far from optimal system design and/or equipment utilization; the systems approach, on the other hand, emphasizes that the system requirements dictate the physical feature of the equipment to be utilized. An "off the shelf" philosophy has some further disadvantages. The time saved installing new systems and the consequent "savings" could be easily swept away by the need for system redesign, which in turn increases the study costs. Frequently, the one-for-one changeover fails because the increased speed of data processing cannot overcome the significantly higher costs of using more advanced data processing equipment. Sometimes this philosophy results in the selection of equipment that will be poorly utilized. The worst situation that frequently results from this "minimum science" approach is that the equipment complement is not well suited to the task. This does not say that the equipment utilized will not execute the task; the task, of course, will be executed—but awkwardly, inefficiently, slowly, and probably at a higher per unit cost of information than some other complement of equipment.

There are some cases where the one-for-one changeover will work:

(1) When the input or output is being revised to accommodate subsystem changes and the function of the input or output proves to have a limited use or impact on the system as a whole.

(2) When the changeover affects only the model or type of equipment employed, and both pieces of equipment operate in a similar or identical manner requiring no revisions elsewhere in the system.

DESIGNING A NEW SYSTEM

Diametrically opposite is the philosophy which looks upon any change as an opportunity to re-evaluate the soundness of an existing system. This may or may not result in the decision to expend funds for redesign. If the existing system is manual and existing volumes of data processing warrant investigation of equipment, almost invariably it will be necessary to study the system. One of the necessary considerations while selecting equipment is to consider not only current data processing loads but future, expanded loads as well. Thus, the redesign of a system provides an opportunity to consider more variables than would be ordinarily possible. Present and future data processing loads must, of course, be expressed quantitatively. These quantities must be reconciled, to achieve the requisite goals, with the requirements of a minimum cost system. This rationale points to the need for optimizing a series of dependent (and sometimes, independent) variables. The variety of equipment currently available indicates a recognition of more special purpose needs than five years ago. The future will bring more diverse and modular equipment to the market—even less general in purpose than some existing equipment. Each complement of equipment is characterized by physical characteristics which are well known to the manufacturers—but which must also be made well known to the purchasers. The process of determining alternative equipment complement advantages is known as equipment evaluation (see Chapter 7). Familiarity with equipment characteristics demands special training. This must then be utilized objectively in the light of data processing systems requirements, since the system requirements must always dictate the processor.

This is an imposing demand to place on personnel who carry the responsibility for systems design. As a result, some firms employ consultants specializing in data processing. The alternative route, less costly but replete with problems, is to select equipment based upon a set of rules—some of which *may* be quantifiable—almost without regard for the systems requirements. The only means by which systems requirements become known is the time consuming, costly, and orderly investigation and hypothesis of business facts. If the requisite skills do not exist within the organization, and if the move toward mechanization involves substantial outlays of capital, help from data processing specialists may prove to be the most inexpensive course of action.

If the problem is to convert to a computer, the issue becomes critical. Computers are still so new that the vast majority of potential candidates have little or no preparation for evaluating the usefulness of one system over another. The use of a computer, except in those special cases where an extremely sophisticated punched card (tabulating) installation has been in operation, will necessarily point a company toward extensive systems overhaul. For some companies, the most significant value in their impending computer program is the opportunity to reorganize departmental operations on a more modern, more economical basis. More and more experts in the data processing field agree that significant improvements are mainly in the area of systems design, under a philosophy that recognizes the attributes of individual units of equipment.

Benchmark problems

When one or two applications dominate the total data processing requirement of an establishment, the benchmark approach is to order the equipment complement based upon the system requirements of these few applications. The key word in this rationale is *dominate*. Ordinarily, it would not be realistic to order equipment unless sixty per cent (or more) of the total known data processing work load were known and analyzed. It follows that the benchmark approach would be perfectly adequate if the systems planned for conversion were sixty per cent or more.

It is possible that the size of the problem would restrict the choice of equipment, or perhaps limit the choice to one complement of equipment. Should this be the case, the benchmark approach would eliminate other alternatives. When these special circumstances do not exist, however, the usefulness of the benchmark approach is severely restricted. Benchmark problems occur relatively seldom; thus, it is a highly specialized data processing problem.

Mechanization in system design

The move away from manual systems toward man-machine systems is a step toward mechanization. Both utility and economy demand that such a move be considered in the light of the full system requirements. The insular view considers only one problem or a limited number of problems, without looking at either the future requirements or the full system requirements. Utility becomes a factor because the limited use of equipment on a few tasks will leave it idle for long periods, which, in turn, effectively raises the cost per unit of information. Economy becomes a factor because the uncoordinated acquisition of equipment may lead to parallel data processing facilities which can be marginally justified. Parallel installations are somewhat more difficult to centralize after equipment is operating.

Figure 3–1 illustrates three possible alternatives (*A, B,* and *C*) in system design. These conclusions are *a posteriori*, i.e., after the fact. They are conclusions which grow out of alternatives 1 and 2. They are not the only possible viewpoints, since it follows that each business (system) will have its highly individual requirements. A rationale must be developed to guide the changeover from the original system to a proposed system, and this rationale must be supportable quantitatively. The move toward mechanization or automation need not take place in a specific, serial order, i.e., it is not necessary to move from all manual to all punched cards and then to a computer. Each individual case will have its own optimum solution. However, in any case, the changeover from one data processing basis to another should be seen as raising the general level of data processing. This does not necessarily imply that the use of equipment is an all or none situation.

The move toward mechanization should be made on a schedule. Individual applications with the highest payoff should be scheduled first, with other applications following as each area is converted. It is obvious that tabulating equipment and punched cards will never wholly replace humans in data processing. Thus, some combination of *A* and *B* or *C* (Figure 3–1) will always remain even in the most advanced business systems.

Raising the general level of data processing requires a careful look at all business activities and a judgment as to which parts of the business can or cannot benefit from mechanization. The intent of such a survey of data processing is to build in the following:

(1) The potential for optimizing economy and utilization
(2) The assurance of equal and full evaluation of all data processing tasks
(3) The advantages which may result from organizational adjustments
(4) The advantages which result from implementing the alternate which has the highest probability of success

This survey is what is commonly called a feasibility study (see Chapters 5 and 6), and can provide the long term plan of attack so necessary in mechanization of data processing.

Both punched card and computer equipment offer something special to the systems engineer. They are, in many ways, ideal tools, since their physical design calls for an organization of data processing along the lines of the systems module. In a punched card application such as key-punching, a transaction of some kind will act as input. The processor will be a man-machine combination. The output will be the punched card. In the instance of a computer, a deck of punched cards or a magnetic tape carrying the same data may be introduced as input. The processor will be the computer and its operators. The output will be an updated file or files and the original input. The use of mechanization in data processing enlarges many times the problem solving ability of the business world. Both the size and complexity of normally difficult problems become less critical when equipment is at hand to aid in problem solving.

The computer as processor

The computer offers some unique advantages. For speed and reliability, manual systems will never be its equal. Interestingly enough, however, it is through the computer that the human being is able to attain the position in the business organization where his real capabilities can be properly utilized. Chapter 6 traces the development of this equipment.

It is by now popularly recognized that computers make only the simplest of man-instructed decisions. The computer is the dumb beast which can do everything for which it has been especially designed—and can do it in a superior way. The individual must still be reckoned with as the ultimate decision maker. He can accept or reject the computer outputs, putting to work his judgment, experience, maturity and intuition. This is precisely what makes the systems purchaser (the person or group who must *buy* the system) so important in the design of the system. Not only must he have confidence in the system outputs, but the organization of the process must be completely useful and meaningful for the intended purpose. The systems analyst must *sell* the system, not only to gain acceptance of his idea but to assure its continued use after the installation is complete. The systems purchaser must be made to recognize that the system, though capable of revision, should not be installed until it meets the exacting requirements with which it must deal when it is in full operation.

The computer presents certain unique problems, mainly in the area of technical know-how. The central data processing facility presents other problems precisely because it is a *central* data processing facility. Data processing is no longer a function scattered through a number of different departments, and the scheduling of work loads can become a major issue, each business department placing a certain priority of importance on each automated task. Here again, the systems designer must optimize the conflicting needs of interested parties. Scheduling also imposes a restriction on users of computer systems. All needs cannot be met on demand, but must either wait for scheduled processing or an unforeseen break in computer center operations when it is practical to interrupt normal routine. Once on the machine, the speed of problem solving frequently overcomes the delay of waiting.

Computer capabilities such as simultaneous interrogation of many externally stored records places special emphasis on system integration. In the typical manual or punched card system, one operation is performed at a time; then the second operation; the third, and so on. Automatic control and other features enable the computer to do the first, second, third, and many other operations sequentially without stopping, except to report errors. Further, the computer can do more than one task at a time, relying on internal control to be the traffic monitor. The segments of integrated systems seen in Figures 4–1 and 4–2 show how a variety of inputs are planned to update several basic files. The ability to bring these diverse items of information into one processing pass is the goal of integration. The special attributes and capabilities of four electronic data processing systems are described in Chapter 7.

SIDE EFFECTS

Operations research specialists tell us that it is impossible to maximize more than one variable at a time. This is why it is essential to appraise carefully those things which happen in seemingly unrelated portions of the system when a system change is recommended. If a controlled laboratory experiment is viewed as a series of intimately related processes according to the systems concept, it is easy to understand the problem of side effects.

Assume that the first output of an experiment provides satisfactory output, and can be repeated over and over again with identical results. However, the economics are unfavorable, and other materials (inputs) must be tested to determine, (1) whether the same product (output) can be achieved, and (2) whether it can be achieved at a lower cost. When the experiment is conducted, a different product is obtained. It is lower in cost but does not behave with the stability required. A third experiment produces a third product which is usable for the intended purpose but prohibitive in cost. Perhaps the four hundredth experiment will produce the desired product and the cost balanced in an optimal fashion. The large number of experiments have been occasioned by the following:

(1) The variety of input possibilities
(2) The nature of the processor which cannot cope with all types of input with equal efficiency
(3) The resultant variation in output
(4) The need to optimize cost, product quality and performance
(5) The absence of controls to monitor all processes with equal effectiveness
(6) Lack of *a priori* knowledge to cope with all the new functional relationships established in the on-going process

In the design of the business system, side effects occur frequently. By altering input or output requirements, the system designer has introduced a new series of considerations. The redesign of a process imposes on the designer the need to test his model, first theoretically and at a later date in some practical way, to remove the hazards of side effects. The ability to recognize undesirable side effects is in part conditioned by the effectiveness with which boundaries have been drawn. They will be related also to the uniform coarseness or fineness with which the system has been designed. Side effects in a redesigned system create undesirable symptoms, most of which can be traced to inadequate collection or assembly of information prior to implementation. There is always some likelihood, in the process of consolidation and elimination of files or the development of multi-purpose reports and multiple forms from a common recording source, that side effects will occur. They should be expected and dealt with in an orderly way.

Frequently, an undesirable symptom will become chronic, and the demand for system redesign will be made. The following are generally undesirable methods of solving such a problem:

(1) Try a countermeasure, a typically short range solution which temporarily relieves the symptom.

(2) Write an instruction to clarify the process in its existing form; add more rules.

(3) Amplify an existing instruction.

(4) Increase the number of copies of a report or form.

(5) Add more equipment or personnel.

(6) Add another input or output.

(7) Borrow a system.

(8) Provide an alternate process.

(9) Add more checking, editing, or other operations.

(10) Require more signatures, processing, and so on.

(11) Increase the frequency of processing and output preparation.

OPTIMAL SYSTEM DESIGN

The weapons system is a composite of a number of electro-mechanical, electronic, hydraulic, physical and non-physical subsystems. The operational characteristics of the physical systems have been made completely compatible with interrelated subsystems and with the over-all system. In this way, the unit subsystem functions as an integral part of the end item and is said to be fully integrated. The complete design accommodation of one part of a system to another works against parts interchangeability and design standardization. Each weapons system has a special mission toward which the design effort has specialized it, although it may inadvertently contain characteristics similar to those of other weapons systems. In details, however, similarities cease to exist, and the unique requirements of each system must dominate.

Business systems are dominated by similar considerations, whether they are recognized and exploited or not. It is not enough to say that the goal of every business is to maximize profit. Profit is one of many outputs and is the measure of a multitude of interacting systems which have been combined by a processor called the factory (Chapter 1). There are other desirable goals, and few businesses can survive on a "profit-only" view in the business world.

Systems purchasers

Clearly, the "mission" as we know it from the example of the weapons system, was dictated by a purchaser, perhaps the Air Force, Navy, or Army. The requirements of the system purchaser are stated in the request for bid, to which the competitive prime contractors will respond by preparing proposals according to the rules, specifications, and boundaries which have been laid down. When a contract is awarded, one of the functions of the *prime* contractor, who may also be a system manager in individual cases, is to interpret the contractual requirements for the *sub*contractors. Thus, the prime contractor becomes the system purchaser, one level below the government purchaser. The diagram for the system just outlined resembles Figure 3–2. The diagram for the system purchaser is given

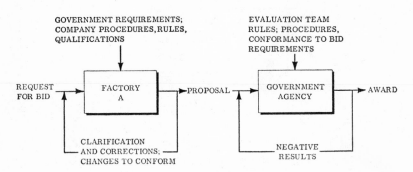

Fig. 3–2.

in Figure 3–3. Every system without exception will have a system purchaser. The function of the system purchaser is to dictate the objective, purpose, or goal for which the system exists. Hence, in the

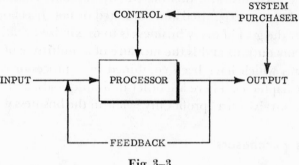

Fig. 3–3.

example above, the system purchaser is the responsible government contracting agency (see Figure 3–4). In the system which illustrates the relationship of the prime contractor to the sub-contractors, the module might look something like Figure 3–5. Here are two inde-

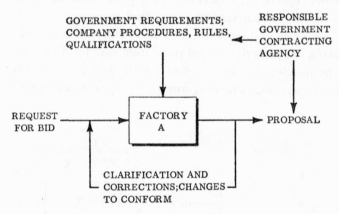

Fig. 3–4.

pendent forces acting as system purchasers. System purchasers act as a special type of control mechanism. Note that they do not operate on the processor directly but on the output and the controls. This may appear to say that the system purchaser is not interested in the means but only the end. This of course is not true; the system purchaser will monitor the *means* by evaluating the intermediate outputs of subsystems. Control is not effectively vested in the system

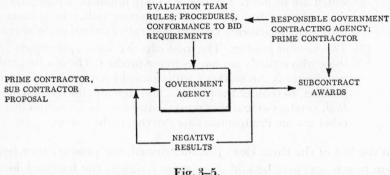

Fig. 3-5.

purchaser; its role is to provide the objective for which the system exists.

Note also the relationship of the system purchaser to the control mechanism of the system. An operational relationship must exist whereby the system purchaser's objective is consistent with controls which determine how the processor will satisfy the system requirements. An example of this relationship is in the administration of *technical orders.* An individual contract specification might incorporate a thousand technical orders into the quality requirements of a product. The responsible government agency may see fit to revamp many of the existing technical orders (as they did in the case of the ballistic missile programs) to implement the special objectives of a given program. The objectives of the ballistic missile program were made consistent with the standard control requirements (enforceable technical orders) of the contract by the action of the system purchaser.

The system purchaser is a valid concept in the business world, as well. Behind the corporate executives who set the policy of the firm, stand many system purchasers:

(1) *The board of directors:* Their function as system purchaser may be to examine current policy, relate it to profit, the market, long term objectives, and so on, and make new policies which might impose new constraints on output and control mechanisms. They are internal to the system.

(2) *The stockholders:* Their function is more distantly related to the system, but the desire to buy or sell the corporation stock reflects a willingness to accept or reject the current policies

which are in force. The desire to buy might be a reflection of the desire to alter the existing corporate policy by gaining a voice in management. They are generally external to the system.

(3) *The users of product:* The most effective system purchasers are those who actually pay money to use product. The test for product success is the market's willingness to pay the price of the product, to reorder the product, and to maintain the design of *their* product so that they must continue to use an output of another system. Product users are external to the system.

In the last of the three cases just mentioned, the product user (system purchaser) may be said to energize (trigger) the feedback loop which sets in motion the special input mechanisms. In this same case, an optimization process is taking place. The need for product on the part of the system purchaser and the need for profit as an output of the system in point, are meeting in a trade-off. The knowledge that a system purchaser is always somewhere in the background must play an important part in determining how a company will attempt to secure a market and produce a product at a profit.

There are systems purchasers for subsystems as well as systems. Some subsystems can be related directly to the product user. For instance, if the major objective of a production control subsystem is maintenance of schedule (see page 16), this would appear to satisfy the system purchaser's requirement that his order be shipped and delivered on time. Other subsystems, may relate outputs to systems purchasers within the organization, mainly the people who direct sections, departments, groups of departments, plants, or divisions. The concept of the system purchaser provides another test of the validity of system design. In addition, it relates the system to something more than an objective, *as such*. Now it is possible for us to pass on the validity of an objective, having in mind some person or some group which stipulates the need or desire for a particular system.

The users of systems may have conflicting requirements which will require the development of an optimum solution to resolve the problem. The systems analyst is the processor through which this optimization will take place. His role is to reconcile the conflicting demands and systems requirements as he sees them; he will determine what system processor will best suit the problem.

Criteria and measures of effectiveness

Another element is operating on output in some subsystems and systems. Criteria or measures of effectiveness supply a qualitative (non-numerical) or quantitative yardstick to gauge the effectiveness of output in satisfying system requirements. Measures are conceived concurrent with the design of the system. They must, like the system itself, be put into operation to determine if they are in fact measuring that which they were intended to measure. It also must be determined whether the measure in use is the most indicative or critical yardstick which is available to measure the effectiveness of system operation. Some systems or subsystems will have only one measure; others will have several. A number of easily operated measures will have the advantage of providing more than one way to look at systems outputs. Criteria are seen operating in Figure 3–6. The infer-

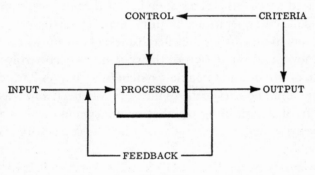

Fig. 3–6.

ence here, because of his position in the system module, is that the system purchaser dictates the criteria. This is not necessarily so. Most of the system requirements which are stated as boundaries, such as 99 per cent system reliability for a missile, are control mechanisms. The ability of a missile to meet the on-line test routines of a missile site, for which the missile would be generally prepared only in its final acceptance testing, might be considered a criteria of this system (see Figure 3–7). In this instance, the using command would be the systems purchaser. Their specification that the missile meet certain on-line requirements may be resolved far earlier than

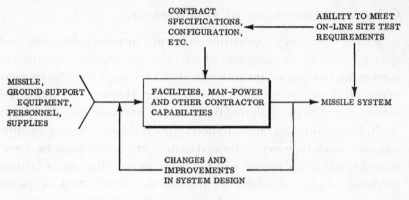

Fig. 3–7.

the actual letting of the contract and the early design activities which characterize the beginning of a project of this type.

The need for criteria for a system is, like the need of a system purchaser, mainly an operational requirement. The system analyst perceives a way of measuring the effectiveness of output when the output is known and the design of the system has been resolved. The ability to postulate and test a new system (see Chapter 2 which deals with system boundaries) utilizes measures of effectiveness as one of the means of determining whether or not system outputs are reliable, accurate, and so on, and meet the objectives which may be quantifiable.

Criteria may be qualitative. In business systems, it is likely that there will be a mixture of both qualitative and quantitative criteria. An example of the development of criteria in a business system, will illustrate this idea.

Inventory status as criteria for a scheduling system

There are three classes of inventory; raw or purchased, in-process, and finished. Most manufacturers have all types. Each is related to different parts of the scheduling system. Status of raw materials will be closely connected to the lead time of the ordering system. Raw materials inventory will tend to increase under the following conditions:

(1) Purchase requisitions or purchases are generated early or materials are received early

(2) End item requirements are overstated in the purchase requisition

(3) Lots are released late to production

(4) Engineering changes which make inventory obsolete are not incorporated promptly

(5) Requirements are not combined to achieve optimum order quantities

Thus, if the level of units and dollars invested in raw materials inventory are monitored through a reliable system, at least five major parts of the scheduling system will have been tested. There are more than five areas which can be tested by raw material inventory. The number of tests possible are related to the type of inventory record which is maintained, and the accessibility to inventory data.

Work-in-process inventory will tend to fluctuate under the following conditions:

(1) The availability of raw materials

(2) The product mix-in-process

(3) The number of lots and size of lots in-process

(4) Availability of manpower, machine time, and tooling

(5) The number of lots waiting for delayed operations

Here again the tests would be for the number of units and dollars invested. Doing this adequately requires many more inputs than the previous example. For exactly this reason, maintenance of work-in-process is very difficult. Until the advent of electronic data processing techniques, medium to large companies have found the day-to-day file maintenance of work-in-process was very costly, time consuming, and, in some cases, impossible. The five factors cited above themselves require subsystems with some dependence on the status of inventory. Late delivery of raw materials (item 1) can have an effect like a chain reaction throughout the entire factory system, although only a limited number of side effects have been noted here.

The level of the finished goods inventory will be a reflection of the following:

(1) Anticipation of customer demand

(2) Anticipation of rejections in the manufacturing process

(3) Scheduling of parts, subassemblies, and final assembly

(4) Anticipation of delays in test, rework, down time, and so on

(5) The number of units being packed and shipped to fill orders on hand

Note that the measure of effectiveness, which in this case would be the number of units or dollars of finished inventory, might show an undesirable increase. None of these five subsystems may be responsible. Perhaps the increase is due to the failure of Production Control to schedule end-item rework on finished goods which must be made to conform to new field specifications before being shipped.

Here are some additional inventory measures which would be useful to consider in the design of an inventory system:

(1) Dollar value of purchased and manufactured parts

(2) Number of dollars invested in parts

(3) Number of dollars invested in dead or slow moving inventory; number of items in dead or slow moving inventory

(4) Overtime hours and dollars related to shipments

(5) Subcontract costs or delays related to shipments

(6) Number of items on back order

Measures of effectiveness can be coarse or fine. They can measure trends such as those demonstrated above, or they can be made very precise. Both are useful for their own special purposes at the option of the system designer—based upon the systems requirements. Measures or criteria, as cited, are yardsticks because they provide a continuing index to the way in which the system is operating. They are a part of the practical testing mechanisms usable as soon as the postulated system is ready to be tested. They continue to be useful through all stages of system design and system operation.

Can completely manual systems be optimal? The answer is yes. The alternatives of each system problem must be analyzed and solved in their own frame of reference. Solving a problem on a manual level does not mean that alternatives do not exist, or that a fully integrated system cannot be achieved. There will always be limitations placed upon speed and accuracy of processing, but econ-

omy of system operation is another matter. The systems requirements will dictate the number and rates of pay of the processors,
human beings in this case. Optimal business system design means
design of the system taking full advantage of integration possibilities, excluding the unnecessary or nonproductive portion of the
system. In the design of the integrated system, the systems analyst is
seeking the optimum combination of data, redundance, and static
which enables the message to come through. In this information
theory frame of reference, the *data* are the information to be processed; the *redundance* is its format, display, and mode of transmission; *static* becomes the variances or unanticipated special cases that
arise and demand individual attention.

A fully integrated system contains the most economic combination of men, machines, and data that can be devised to execute a
business routine. This is achieved only by linking individual data
processing tasks intimately, so that they cease to function of and
for themselves, but exist as a part of a total functioning unit. In this
format, the outputs of the most elemental subsystems become inputs
to higher order systems. In turn, the outputs of these higher order
systems, become inputs to still higher order systems. Each level of
the system operates under one or more control mechanisms, utilizing the results of output wherever possible as a feedback to condition and modify input.

The fully integrated system provides not only the basic, requisite,
system elements, but recognizes at each system level the need to
equate the output with the satisfaction of an objective. The objective must, in turn, be a requirement of some system purchaser,
directly or indirectly concerned with the operation of the system.
Likewise, each subsystem must meet the quantitative or qualitative
test of criteria or measures of effectiveness which function as yardsticks to gauge the reliability, accuracy, or performance of the
output.

4
Postulating data processing systems

Symbols may be used to represent any value, idea, or object, providing only that the symbol has been carefully defined. Note that symbols do not necessarily have to represent quantities, but may also represent qualities. This is important, because the ability to work with symbols means quicker, more facile manipulation than is possible by extensive description of a condition, over and over again. The use of symbols in analysis of problems is, in some ways, similar to shorthand because it precisely and quickly records otherwise lengthy expressions. Symbols are used to represent quantitative values. It is also possible to set up symbols whose quantitative values will temporarily be unknown, and for the present may only be expressed as qualitative ideas.

The system modules are symbols of qualitative ideas. When they are interlinked to describe an on-going process, they become a model or miniature of the process itself. Model building shows the cause and effect relationships that exist between inputs and outputs. The processor acts as the place where the functional relationships are expressed in the form of arithmetic or logical operations. The control mechanisms may be implied; but, in actual systems analysis, the controls must either be found or, if nonexistent, created. This is also true of feedback mechanisms. They frequently are expressed; but, when they are only implied, they must be found or created. The feedback property is essential since the modification of input as the result of actual experience (output), is highly desirable. To the extent that feedback may cause input modification, it

operates like a control mechanism. Unlike the control which operates over the processor as the result of predetermined knowledge
about how the system should operate, feedback is an *after-the-fact*
control. Other controls on input, e.g., editing (filtering) of raw data,
machine verification, and so on are possible. Analysis of the subsystems where editing and machine verification occur would reveal
that the actual control mechanism is a part of the process.

On page 62, Figure 4–1 shows another type of abstraction. This
chart illustrates the way in which a segment of a data processing
system operates. This is a shorthand way of describing a series of
individual operations that may number into the hundreds. Although all of the details are not here, adequate information has
been abstracted to make it possible to understand what this system
is intended to accomplish.

At the outset of model formulation, the only knowledge of the
problem may be the methodology to be employed in solving it. This
is not bad. The predisposition to provide solutions before adequate
facts are gathered and tested under a set of assumptions is all too
common in the business world. The prime rule is to let the systems
requirements dictate the system design. This, of course, puts the
burden on investigating the facts and carefully interpreting their
relative importance. Primary evidence in problem investigation
will be copies of existing documents which energize the system (inputs) and intermediate or final reports (outputs) which contain the
results of the completed process.

In Chapter 6 on page 108, you will find a Data Specification Sheet
which is a suitable form on which to gather all of the data concerning a document, its use, its design, necessity, and character count.
Some or all of the spaces provided may be relevant; the size or
number of form copies may be adequate, or may not. The process of
collecting data becomes extremely precise when carried to the level
of individual processes. For instance, it is essential to look in detail
at the circumstances under which the system is triggered into action.

If a required form does not exist, then the system designer must
postulate its introduction into the conceptual model of the system.
He is saying, in effect, that this system cannot work unless there
is some orderly way in which it can be energized. It will be up to

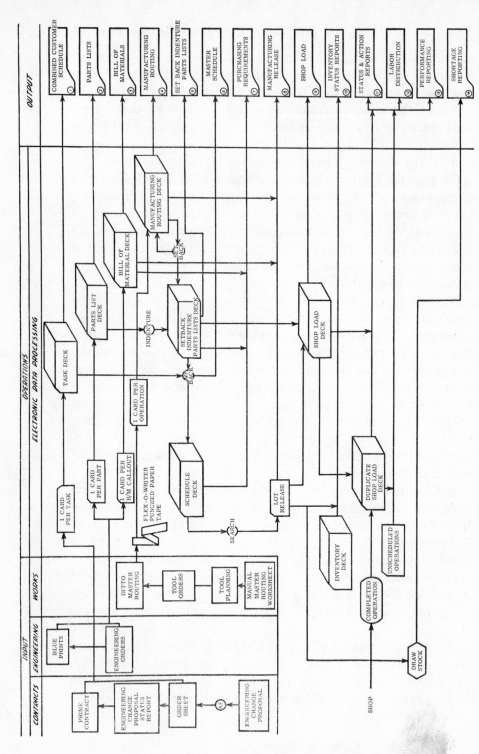

Fig. 4–1. Segment of an integrated data processing system for Production Control.

the system designer to provide adequate controls over the introduction of this new subsystem, so that it will function as anticipated in the system design.

DESIGN OF FEEDBACK LOOPS

The identification of the feedback loop will follow the same general pattern. Feedback, which in business systems is a device for modification of input, must be considered by looking at the way in which the output is used. It is conceivable that systems can function properly without limiting in any way the effectiveness of the individual subsystem operation, but this is a rare situation. This *does not mean* that, in the ideal system, the processor should be called upon to do the same job twice—once, the way in which the input dictates, and, a second time, the way in which the modified input dictates.

Feedback loops are variable in character. Figure 5–4 on page 87, indicates how the feedback loop takes an intermediate output which is transmitted to a planner; the act of providing him with intermediate output which can be modified prior to its use elsewhere, is feedback at its best. But there are other types. In Figure 4–2, a number of feedbacks are itemized:

(1) The invoice from Shipping which will be compared with the purchase order

(2) The stock ticket from Stores which will modify the work-in-process inventory

(3) The scrap ticket, resulting from a rejection, which will also modify inventory

(4) The cancellation or order reinstatement which will modify requirements as they may be expressed in work-in-process, raw materials, or finished goods

(5) The job card (direct labor time ticket) which will adjust upwards the cost expended in work-in-process, as each operation is completed

(6) Shipping orders which will relieve inventory (in this case the item is shipped as soon as it leaves the work-in-process stage, there being no finished goods stage), as items are consigned to customers

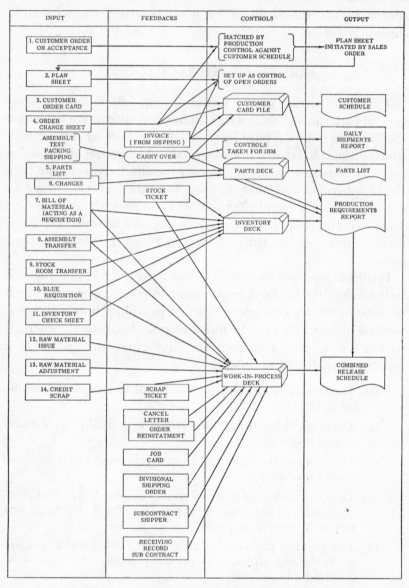

Fig. 4–2. Segment of an integrated data processing system using punched cards or computer as the processor.

(7) Receiving records which will likewise modify requirements and stock status and will be compared to quantities on order.

Note that feedbacks as just described have all been generated as a result of the output of some other subsystem. From the system designer's standpoint, the problem is to be certain that feedback actions are sustained and become as important a part of the system as any other. A company, convinced of this need, might originate an *Action Notice* to supplement the feedback; its purpose would be to record in the form of a report the serial numbers of transactions and a coded reference to the type of action that was required in order to close an information loop. This seems like placing undue emphasis on one part of the system module; one way in which it can be justified is by examining the consequences of improper implementation of feedback.

Other feedbacks may originate from outputs—but, nevertheless, be outside the system. For instance, an employee receiving a paycheck for four days of work in a week where he worked five will soon correct a system error; few systems can be designed with as much feedback as payroll. The use of reliably interpreted data having no connection with system operation but maintaining a steady relationship (correlation) with it may provide effective feedback in a corporate planning system. At the top business level, the profit and loss statement or the sales figures for an operational period provide great opportunities to use the feedback principle. If profits are lower in this period than any other, the cause may be traceable to higher costs of materials; following this hypothesis, the material values can be inserted in the cost equations and sales projections of coming periods to determine the future probable profits from operations.

An example of the use of sales data as feedback might be the firm that projects its price on an anticipated retail volume that does not materialize. If the price of the product is based on an annual volume, the firm must wait for reorders to determine the rate of production. Reorders, of course, will depend upon the sale of initial deliveries; if they do not turn over at the retail level, feedback will illustrate the reduced level of sale by smaller than anticipated orders—or none at all. The manufacturer will then have to move quickly to redesign styles and assist retail outlets in moving merchandise, or else his business life may be threatened.

Competition creates a number of feedback opportunities. If a manufacturer receives his orders to introduce a new line at a semi-annual market, one of his indications of success would be how well he fares in terms of new orders, first, compared to his pre-market estimate; second, compared to the intelligence he may be able to get about the status of his competition. Perhaps a more meaningful example would be two sets of dining room furniture in the same price range and otherwise suited to the same use within the home. One sells at rate x; the second sells at rate $3x$. Each feedback must be interpreted by each manufacturer in the light of his own sales program. If, however, the rates of sale are different when each dining set is competing with a third model, or if sales rates are strikingly different in other outlets in the same or different cities, the manufacturer will have data on which to create a new or, perhaps, more effective strategy. Most important, the sales strategy is going to be extremely difficult to design unless the manufacturer has provided the feedback loop to give him the desired data as a part of his sales program.

DESIGN OF CONTROL MECHANISMS

As a result of using the feedback loop, there may be additional action or there may be none. Action will be determined by the control mechanisms (rules or procedures) which have been established. If a clerk is posting a manually operated inventory file, it is easy to see that feedback is dependent upon explicit rules such as the following:

(1) Sort transactions according to stock number: first, additions to stock; subtractions from stock following.

(2) Enter all transactions affecting each stock number and strike a new inventory balance.

(3) Recheck operation 2 for accuracy.

(4) After posting, compare the new balance with the last withdrawal, inventory in-transit, replenishment cycle, and inventory minimum:

a) If inventory in-transit or stock on hand is adequate for current withdrawal rate, go to the next transaction.

b) If inventory rate, level, or in-transit will not satisfy current requirements, generate a stock replenishment notice indicating inventory status, stock description, and so on.

This control mechanism is working if the operator follows all rules explicitly, especially rule 3. These mechanisms are in the process part of the systems module. They are integral to the operation of the system. If this process has no external control, it is possible with twice the number of rules to incorporate and perpetuate errors in the system with far-reaching effects, as outputs become inputs to other systems. Ideally then, some external control to the system would be desirable, if it could be achieved at a cost compatible with the need. Control could be achieved in this way:

> Have a different clerk go through operation 3 above, making inventory adjustments if errors are detected. However this raises two points:
>
> *a)* What assurance is there that she will detect errors, if they exist?
>
> *b)* What assurance is there that the second clerk will not make errors as she makes adjustments to the stock records?

If this sounds like an argument against using humans wherever and whenever possible, it is of course only partly true. Humans do make errors; about 2 per cent is the rate in efficient operators. But the fact is humans are the requisite to the processor in most systems. The cost of machine equipment to do the work of humans must be less than the costs generated by the humans operating the system. Systems must be fairly large in size, complex, or heavily burdened with transactions before they become candidates for advancing to some level of automation. Thus, if we are to be dependent upon humans in a system design, we must attain control not by duplicating original operations which may double the cost of that operation, but by some summary operation done by the same or a second clerk. Here is a suggested control which will achieve the desired result:

(1) Separate stock numbers against which postings have been made into lots, no lot to be larger than thirty transactions.

(2) Sum all stock numbers added to or removed from stock to strike a total.

(3) Separate inventory cards against which postings have been made, into lots, comparable to operation 1.
(4) Using inventory cards, go through operation 2.
(5) If the sums of stock numbers in 2 and 4 do not agree, check the following:
    a) the sums of transactions and cards for errors in addition;
    b) postings to inventory cards.

This is not the ideal way to control the accuracy of a system; it is only one way; there are many others besides this *nonsense sum method*. Although there is always the chance of compensating errors, some control has been achieved at a fairly low cost. It has nothing to do with the way in which the original process was done, and is thus not subject to the same kind of error. An interesting exercise would be to create several such alternate control mechanisms for this operation.

Control may be achieved, with a little less fuss, in a punched card or computer system. In Chapters 6 and 7 which deal with computers, the logical and automatic control features take on special importance. You can see that it is possible to present to the computer a large number of very detailed rules, at many stages of the operation, in the form of coded instructions. At tremendous speed and 99.99 per cent plus reliability, the computer will post and report any errors or inconsistencies in input through exception outputs. Sometimes exceptions will be automatically generated in the form of cards; other times, from the computer operator's console typewriter. When a problem is dependent for its successful completion on early computations, the computer may be programmed to stop if an error of some type occurs.

Control over the process can be achieved in a computer system in many ways:

(1) Integral with hardware
    a) Bit or parity checks
    b) Logical checks
    c) Duplicate operations
(2) Integral with system (external to hardware)
    a) Comparison of values with value limits
    b) High speed number checks (check digits, control sums, and so on)
    c) Decision rules and logical rules

Interpretation of results will of course return the burden of control to the human, where it must ultimately reside. It is possible that the computer would go through a complex routine without stopping, providing an apparently perfect output. Once results are printed, they must be edited and reviewed for consistency and reasonableness.[1]

A fundamental premise under which the systems approach is utilized in business is its ability to bring the techniques of other disciplines to bear on qualitative problems. It is proposed that these techniques can become a framework in which large or small scale systems can be viewed. In addition, it is proposed that objects not customarily analyzed as systems can be looked at in this new framework, whether the object is a city, a war problem, a traffic problem, or the operation of a manufacturing business.

The first requirement during the investigation will be to establish a model of the system under study. In every case, the ingredients of the system, its inputs, must be isolated and carefully enumerated. Then the goals or purposes for which the system is supposed to exist, which we call outputs, must likewise be isolated and carefully enumerated. The ways in which the inputs are manipulated to obtain the outputs are the operations we have confined to the processor. It is the processor which combines the inputs so that they fulfil the functions expected of each. These functional relationships may or may not be arranged to optimize the outputs; in some cases, they merely perform the steps necessary to obtain the outputs. A diagram of this much of the system module would look like Figure 4–3.

The foregoing examples describe the procedure for dealing with both qualitative and quantitative problems. Industrial problems

1 Dr. H. I. Ansoff, in his paper "State of the Art in Making Plans—Some Comments on the Ill-Structured System," distinguishes between two types of conceptual models. The outcome-oriented method would start with the development of a model to simulate the behavior of the part of the business under study. The modes of behavior which would result from the selection of different strategies would be determined, and evaluated. The alternate method is to devise a model which compares the salient characteristics of the strategies which contribute to the formulation of the system. Since the characteristics contribute to the realization of system objectives with varying force when they are evaluated in their several possible modes, the one that gets the highest rating is chosen. In the latter method, the outcomes are computed and only characteristics which induce favorable outcomes are used. This method called process-oriented, relies on the assumption that the more force which can be developed in a strategy, the greater is the likelihood of its success. Both methods are useful, although outcome oriented solutions may be easier to deal with.

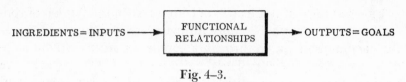

Fig. 4–3.

are generally qualitative and complex, and thus present a chore to the systems analyst. The systems model proceeds from top flow diagrams through several stages until it reaches the machine instruction flow chart stage (see Chapter 5) and is in actual operation. In addition to flow charts, the model may be supported by mathematical or other symbolic data, which in themselves become models of some part of the total system.

Only recently has it become possible to think of optimizing industrial systems. This does not mean it has been successfully achieved on an organization-wide basis. But some industrial operations lend themselves to mathematical-statistical models which have, as a part of their usefulness, the end goal of attaining an optimum combination of the following:

(1) Fixed assets (plant and equipment) to end products

(2) Inventory (of all types) to end products

(3) Employment to manufacturing schedule

(4) Financial requirements to short range and long range planning

There are many possible optimums that may be stated. In this text, however, we are directing ourselves at the analytical tools by which it is possible to see processes as systems. Selection of factors to be optimized will be the job of the operations analyst (see Chapter 9).

5

Preparing for the systems study

THE ASSIGNMENT

The very first steps in the systems study can have an important impact on its success. The experienced analyst looks hard at two things:

(1) *Is there adequate time to prepare for the study?* The time requirement can vary from a few hours to several weeks, and must be incorporated as a part of the over-all schedule, since complex tasks generally require more time than simple ones.

(2) *Is the assignment clear and precise?* Understanding the assignment is the first order of business. Verbal assignments are most unreliable in interpretation. Written confirmation of a verbal assignment may sometimes prove that the same words can have more than one meaning to different people. Once the assignment is in written form, careful analysis of the premises and conclusions under which the assignment was made is essential. Examination of the written assignment may reveal that unfounded assumptions have been made. It is sometimes also true that, in giving assignments, the conclusion has already been built-in, and that, in effect, the assignment is to support an unwarranted or intuitive conclusion.

In a department or section where a large number of investigations may be handled, it becomes necessary to set up a form to document individual tasks. Such a form is shown as Figure 5–1. This form provides a means of shuffling assignments and looking at the total work load in a variety of ways. It also provides a simple way of examining an individual problem from time to time to determine if the objectives, the means of achieving them, and the schedule for achieving them are still valid.

WORK ASSIGNMENT		Serial #	Date Entered	Requestor Date Due
Department , Section or Group Requesting			Name of Requestor	☐ Manual ☐ E D P
Task Title			Task Order	Authorized Hours
Requestor Approval	Acceptance Date		Primary Responsibility	Date Assigned

Objective of Task

Plan of Attack	Step	Manpower	
		Type	Hours
	Total		

Schedule of Acoomplishment

Fig. 5–1. Work Assignment Form.

The time to conduct a study must be proportionate to its complexity; the problem may sometimes be so stated, during the process of determining an assignment, that it becomes clear it cannot be solved within the time available. The need to scale the problem to the time or the time to the problem becomes a factor in successful analysis, if the engineer does not have adequate opportunity to do research.

The Work Assignment Form suggests a way of examining the problem. It will clarify how much time to allow—or how to define the assignment so it can be done within requisite time constraints. The systems concept outlines six broad steps (Chapter 2) in the typical problem solving approach. Although all problems may not be adaptable to each step, the outline indicates a way of getting into the problem area. From this outline and from some knowledge of a problem, it is possible to begin testing the declared objective. A second step might be to assemble the criteria and list the assumptions by which the objectives may be tested. A third step would be to determine if the requirements of the systems purchaser will be met by the assumptions implicit in the statement of the objective.

Once these elements have been isolated and stated, it will then be possible to begin an outline of the way in which the study will be conducted. A so-called *plan of attack* will state not only how to go about the analysis operationally, but will state the minimum number of activities that will require investigation in order to analyze the problem. This outline of the problem is a preliminary statement of the boundaries under which the problem will be studied.

The method suggested for appraising the assignment can be developed to a great degree of precision when it is the input to a preliminary proposal or estimate. The following activities are typical of an engineering department in the early phases of describing a research project: They must identify the skills, time, and costs to complete the task—and provide a schedule of completion. The systems analyst likewise must look on his assignment in an objective way. The systems analyst might suggest a review of the assignment, irrespective of the talent he brings to the task, if he cannot see the assignment output as the problem which should be under investigation.

Scaling the assignment to the time or manpower availability determines, in part, the coarseness or fineness with which a problem will be studied. It is conceivable that very complex problems can be subjected to very coarse analysis with acceptable results. This would only be true, however, if the problem was stated coarsely, and the solution supplied was uniformly coarse. Uniformity of depth in analysis is critical and must be related to the needs of the problem. The statement of the assignment must be determined by the intrinsic complexity of the problem carefully related to the depth of analysis required to supply an adequate solution.

A simple simulation of the problem may be utilized to test the desirability of the chosen level of coarseness. The analyst may try the problem under the assumptions and criteria which support the objective of the task. Loose and undefined though the system may be in its assignment stages, such tests are desirable. In the absence of a completely conceived assignment, a half-conceived assignment with appropriate criteria and assumptions is clearly more desirable.

Reviewing an assignment with other staff members as a part of the procedure of accepting tasks is also desirable. If the task to be analyzed can be logically explained to someone else without detection of major unexplored or unanticipated problem areas, there is a good likelihood that the assignment has been adequately conceived. It may be desirable as a part of accepting an assignment, to present the problem as an assignment to a group of personnel with an objective orientation, under more or less formal circumstances. Making a formal statement out of a problem, and supporting the plan of attack as it is conceived under a given set of circumstances may bring to light any buried, unresolved areas of conflict.

DEFINING THE PROBLEM AREA AND BOUNDARIES

Adequate analysis of the problem will provide a careful statement of objectives and a plan of attack. The objectives must be closely related to the assignment, whereas the plan of attack is integral with the problem area to be explored. In this way we are establishing the rules under which the analysis will proceed. The rules may be loosely defined as the boundaries beyond which it is not necessary or desirable to advance in order to solve the problem.

There is a certain cost to be associated with every problem analysis. The cost boundaries should define how much money, time, and manpower can be allocated to a problem. The schedule of accomplishment of a systems study is the time dimension under which the goals will be achieved. The budget is the dollar dimension; the staff is the manpower dimension. In a project of large scope the costs can be stated as minimums and maximums. If the problem area cannot be adequately defined, a statement of the most optimistic or the most pessimistic complex of facilities to obtain a solution may be adequate. Cost-plus-fixed-fee contracts are in many respects like this, especially in research and development. Since the contracting government agency does not expect a precise statement of anticipated costs, renegotiation is accepted by both parties as the by-product of contract termination.

The statement of costs in terms of a set of flexible boundaries is not necessarily undesirable. Since changes in direction while a project is in process always entail some loss, an adequate statement of boundaries at the earliest possible time is necessary. Changes, when they occur, must be incorporated rapidly and efficiently, in light of objectives as they may prevail or as they may be modified.

The boundary conditions as they are known in the G. W. Templar and Company case (Chapter 10) are as follows:

(1) Farber was an administrative assistant, probably a member of the corporate staff.

(2) This task was to be executed for corporate level appraisal.

(3) He was, for Mr. Templar's purposes, considered capable of handling the assignment.

(4) Production Control, in the eyes of Templar or someone else in Management, required improvement.

(5) Farber had three weeks in which to execute the assignment by himself.

With these limitations, it would be desirable next to amplify on the various aspects of the problem in order to determine something about its size. With this need to define the location of boundaries around the problem, Farber might have decided the following:

(1) What areas were dependent on Production Control.

(2) Some maximum number of areas with which he would deal in his investigation.

(3) The scope of study in each of the selected areas.

(4) The priority of studies.

(5) No area will be studied unless it contains over ten people.

(6) No area will be studied unless it is a prime input to Production Control.

(7) Production Control is a strictly data processing function; its operation depends entirely on a variety of inputs.

(8) Time to be spent in each area should be proportionate to the part of their budget which is related to some aspect of Production Control.

You may not agree to some or all of Farber's boundaries. However, as an exercise, they are quite useful because they reflect the use of an objective approach. Here are some criteria or measures of effectiveness Farber might have conceived as he began to define the boundaries of his problem:

(1) The time requirements of G. W. Templar and Company are met (are not met) by the present production control system.

(2) The accuracy and reliability requirements of G. W. Templar and Company are met (are not met) by the present system.

(3) Delays or errors related to the cost of the system versus the added costs to reduce either delays or errors.

(4) How cheaply does the existing production control system produce its outputs in terms of
   a) manpower outside Production Control
   b) manpower within Production Control
   c) Numbers of specially trained personnel; backup and training required
   d) Flexibility of system design for sharp increases or decreases in volume of data processing.

It is now clearer that the time available to analyze this problem will be a prime determinant in deciding how far to go in getting answers. And yet, Management doesn't want a poorly integrated analysis, no matter how coarse it must be. It is conceivable that in three weeks Farber could only illustrate a few significant points to Mr. Templar:

(1) Production Control is extremely complex and is performing a large number of operations which appear to be of marginal value.

(2) The cost of Production Control to Templar, according to some selected group of possible yardsticks, has risen (has decreased), and from this I draw the conclusion that further study should (should not) be made in these areas.

(3) The number of employees, number of forms used, number of reports produced, number of items controlled, time lags to generate essential shop paperwork, and so on, behave in certain ways. Compared to past experience, where we achieved these results under other (less costly—more costly) conditions, the existing situation warrants (does not warrant) further study.

Which point (there are more) shall he stress? Clearly we are doing some guessing in an attempt to understand all of the functional relationships which are represented by the processor, Production Control. Since the system compromises all of the inputs which contribute to it and forces them into a single mold, Faber must look to the purchaser of this system to make some judgment of the material to be presented after his three weeks of analysis. The purchaser in this case is Mr. Templar. However, other users of Production Control outputs, whose performance may be based in part on how well they respond to Production Control outputs (schedules, for instance) might also be considered the purchasers of the system.

A descriptive layout of the problem may be desirable. A form for this purpose is shown as Figure 5–2 on page 78. A check in the organization column might mean that the form of the organization or its place in the total organization structure is to be examined. A check in the objectives column might be a question as to the validity of objectives or their consistency, clarity, or practicability in the light of certain corporate objectives. A check in the standards column might indicate the lack of adequate work measurement or the need for an overhaul of existing standards.

A complete, descriptive layout may or may not be possible, depending on the investigator's specific experience in the problem area. In the initial phase of a study, where understanding and knowledge are certain to be at their lowest point, this task will be difficult, and yet it can be very helpful. The motivation for making the assignment must be expressed by someone in the organization, and this will provide some concept of the scope of the proposed study.

Priority of effort and schedule

In the simplest of problems, there is inevitably a choice, not only of objectives but of emphasis. Assuming that the boundary condi-

DEPARTMENTS (SECTIONS) FOR STUDY	NO. EM- PLOYEES	ANNUAL DOLLAR BUDGET	SCOPE OF STUDY									
			ORGANIZATION	OBJECTIVES	PROGRAM	PROCEDURES	STANDARDS	CONTROLS	INPUT-OUTPUT	FEEDBACK	PROCESSORS	OTHER

Fig. 5–2. Analysis of scope of study.

tions and objectives are well established, the next step is to create a step-by-step outline of how the ends will be achieved. Such an outline need not be elaborate but should pick out the salient points, weighing them to provide ample time for analysis and report preparation.

One way to prepare such an outline would be to determine the organization units affected by the problem under consideration. Existing standard practices will provide a starting point. In the absence of written procedures—and under any circumstances—the organization chart is a good place to begin. Sometimes, the analysis of functional responsibilities in the light of a specific problem may provide good leads on the study limits which must be set.

The outline itself should be carried to the point where a well organized plan is conceived. This plan should indicate if possible the types of problems, as well as problem areas where investigation is anticipated. Each major problem or problem area should then be assigned a number of days in which to be carried out, using the three major categories of investigation, hypothesis, and implementation. The Work Assignment Form is usable for this purpose. Note that any problem or problem area may contain more than one task, while, in others, the number may be indeterminate and a flat allowance based on the best educated guess must be used. These numbers can be summed with a small safety factor added, where practical.

The number of days required may be in excess of the time available. The time requirement may be overestimated; if so, this can be corrected by reexamining estimates to bring them into line. Too fine an analysis may be planned—in terms of coarseness required—and again, some of the detail must be removed or the time estimates reduced. However, the time allowed by Management may underestimate the problem scope; in which case they must accept a longer schedule of completion—or a coarser analysis not in keeping with the complexity of the problem.

Scheduling a project is important because it creates motivation. The feeling of urgency in any project is essential because this has the effect of stimulating action from the investigator and attention from those being investigated. It is desirable to break up the project into milestones, so the schedule becomes meaningful in terms of the man-days allotted to each segment of the undertaking. It is never desirable to schedule only a start date and due date, unless the elapsed time between these two is very short or the number of things to be done within the scheduled period is very specific. Overall schedules without intermediate due dates tend to be loose. Milestones act as control points and prevent a project from slowing down in one area—a slowdown in one area may jeopardize project completion on schedule.

METHOD OF OPERATION

In the case study, G. W. Templar and Company, setting up the study could be a relatively simple matter. In other projects, however, there may be a series of choices to make prior to completing the outline of the study. Consider a problem such as Marxson and Company (Chapter 12), where one of the study considerations is a choice of problems to work on first. In large scale studies, it is not uncommon to have to choose to work on some problems first and to put others in a secondary position. Adequate measures must be proposed, therefore, to describe which areas come first and why.

The establishment of priorities may rest on the purely quantitative assessment of where the most dollars are being spent or where the probability of great savings are highest. A serial problem may also present itself. The choice may be based on the necessity for certain problem investigations to precede others because the solution to problem Y is dependent upon the solution to problem X.

Blocking out a problem may serve to align the subsystems in order of their interdependency (see Chapter 2, page 30). It is useful to remember the following while using the systems module in any large scale system:

(1) There are many subsystems.

(2) The integration of subsystems is essential to proper system operation.

(3) The outputs of subsystems actually energize higher order, more complex systems.

(4) Therefore, each system must be analyzed to expose the subsystems in their proper relationship to higher order systems, with a knowledge of the input-output requirements.

Part of the master flow diagram which separates and locates the subsystems requiring analysis is shown in Figure 5–3 and is constructed from the Wesley Engineering, Inc. case study (Chapter 18). In this case, one of the requirements is to look at the task of making forecasts as a system. The analyst in examining the problem area wants to obtain a generalized picture of how the existing system operates. Each box represents a subsystem and a problem area. For instance, how is the headcount accumulated? How is it maintained?

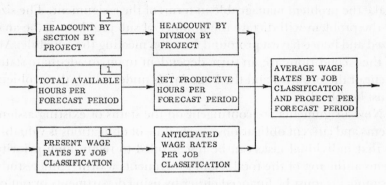

Fig. 5–3.

How are changes introduced? How is it monitored? These questions and those which can properly be directed at any of the above sub-systems reflect the existence of or need for supporting subsystems. The arrow, coming into boxes marked *1*, indicates that there are input requirements, some or all of which may depend on the pre-existence of other major systems. The headcount of a section must be predicated on these minimum factors:

(1) Existing routine work load

(2) Existing non-routine work load

(3) Personnel safety factor (numbers of employees required to operate the system—allowing for vacation, sick leave, absentee-ism, and so on)

(4) Personnel direction (supervisors, managers, project leaders, and coordinators, and so on)

(5) A system for accumulating this data

The ability to reduce personnel requirements to a format suitable for incorporation into a forecasting system, depends in part on the way in which the supporting subsystems have been organized. This interdependence works in the other direction as well. Higher order systems which will accept data must be designed so that their input requirements are compatible with lower order systems.

The analyst preparing his plan of attack will be prepared to enter the problem area if, prior to actual investigation, he has blocked out his problem and looked at the problem areas objectively. The basic requirement in investigating data processing systems is to make the problem manageable in terms of the assignment. The size of the problem will dictate the number of sub-problems to be analyzed and hence have a profound effect on meeting the schedule. All of these conditions are, in turn, dependent upon an adequate statement of the problem and the boundaries under which the problem must be solved.

New assignments are contingent on the status of existing assignments and current obligations. A schedule of obligations is valuable so that individual tasks can be rescheduled to retain high priority items at the top of the total list of assignments waiting. Since study assignments must be financed either by using departments or out of some general fund, scheduling of new tasks provides time to make funds available.

Incoming assignments should be reviewed and accepted, subject to clarification of objectives or schedule, as necessary. The Work Assignment can be utilized as the standard recording medium, filed by subject, using department, type of study, or other means. Cross referencing is desirable, especially if many assignments are being worked upon or are ready for work at the same time. Work Assignment forms should be reviewed weekly for progress against the predetermined schedule.

SUGGESTED CHECKLISTS HELPFUL IN SETTING UP
THE ASSIGNMENT

I. Systems review checklist

A. *Purpose of Operations*
1. Have conditions changed since the operation was put into effect?
2. Was the operation originally set up to correct a situation that has since been adjusted?
3. Can we change the end result and eliminate the operation?
4. Is the operation the result of habit?
5. Is the cost of the operation justified by other factors?
6. Is the operation created by an incomplete, previous or subsequent operation?
7. Is the operation performed to satisfy the requirements of all or only a few of the persons in the system?

8. How necessary is the result accomplished by the operation?
9. If it is a corrective operation, is it more costly than the difficulty it was designed to correct?
10. How else can the result be secured?
11. Are the results used as intended?
12. Are all copies of forms or reports necessary?
13. How many people or departments keep the same records?
14. Do the report costs justify the results?
15. Can the report be secured as the by-product of another operation?

B. *Machines and Equipment*
1. Does volume justify the purchase of general or special purpose equipment?
2. Would savings effected over the average life of the equipment justify capital investment?
3. Would other intangible factors, such as better customer service, valuable management reports, and so on, justify capital investment?
4. Does the operation of the equipment require specialized personnel or can existing personnel be retrained?
5. Are existing machines operating close to capacity? What is per cent utilization?
6. Is a central filing system indicated?
7. Does existing equipment need repair?
8. Does existing equipment have periodic maintenance and inspection? Is it outdated?

C. *Data Processing*
1. What collating and sorting devices can be used to advantage?
2. Would dictating equipment conserve a stenographer's time or eliminate bottlenecks?
3. Would an automatic typewriter be more economical than the use of a manual typewriter?
4. Is a duplicating process indicated?
5. Is the volume of repetitive billing, statement, or payroll addressing large enough to indicate pre-addressing from master addressing files?
6. Can the addressing or duplicating equipment economically utilize automatic feeds and ejectors?
7. Does the volume of mailing justify recommending a small or large postage meter? If a small manual one is used would volume justify a high-speed automatic postage machine?

8. Are typewriters in use suitable for the various specific jobs?
9. Would the study suggest transferring any equipment to the other points where it can be used more effectively?
10. Can office noise factors be reduced by soundproofing and the centralizing of high speed equipment in a separate room?
11. Are vital records adequately protected against loss?
12. Should permanent records be put on microfilm as fire protection and/or to conserve filing space?
13. Are circular, vertical, or horizontal filing devices the answer to some unusual reference or filing problems?
14. What time-saving advantages would an intercommunication system effect?
15. Would mechanical equipment be indicated to eliminate manual posting and recapping of columnar journals?
16. Are desks, chairs, lighting, and so on, suitable for efficiency of the task performed?

II. Internal review checklist

A. *Organization*
1. Is there an organization chart?
2. Is the organization clear-cut and definite?
3. Are there many or few layers of supervision?
4. Is the functional write-up of organization units clear and complete?
5. Are non-authorized functions being performed?
6. Is over or under organization apparent? How?
7. What numbers of people are reporting directly to each person on the chart?

B. *Procedures and Policy Manuals*
1. Have procedures been written and distributed?
2. Are procedures complete and up-to-date?
3. Are flow charts included?
4. Are the procedures presented in a manner the worker understands?
5. Do employees doing the tasks have copies?
6. Do employees refer to procedures when problems arise?
7. Are policy manuals maintained?

C. *Work Measurement and Production*
1. What work measurement standards are used?
2. Do the standards accurately reflect the work to be done?
3. What overhead functions are not covered by standards?

4. Can standards be applied to these functions?
5. Are the functions on a production basis?
6. Can a production basis be applied to functions?
7. Obtain production rates per man hour for previous periods.
8. Obtain separate figures for overtime hours.
9. Obtain overtime hours worked for these periods.
10. What justification was furnished for overtime?
11. Do the employees have production goals?
12. Are employees aware of the goals?
13. How many employees met the goals?
14. How many employees passed the goals? By what amount?
15. How many employees did not meet goals? By what amount?
16. Is non-standard work budgeted?

D. *Schedules Backlog*
1. How is the workload scheduled and controlled?
2. Is work introduced into system upon receipt? What are the factors which determine this?
3. Determine date of oldest work in process.
4. Are new batches completed before older batches?
5. Obtain backlog figures for each of last four weeks.
6. Are work priorities assigned?
7. How are the priorities determined?

E. *Personnel*
1. What job classifications are used in the system under study?
2. Obtain numbers of employees, by classification, now employed.
3. Obtain number of existing vacancies by classification.
4. Is over or under staffing apparent? What yardstick points this up?
5. Comment on employee morale, training, and supervision as they affect system operation.

F. *Facilities, Equipment, and Supplies*
1. Is the assigned area adequate?
2. Is any part of the area not utilized?
3. Does the layout lend itself to work flow?
4. Can housekeeping and orderliness be improved?
5. Are heating, lighting, ventilation, and so on adequate?
6. Are the office furniture and equipment adequate?
7. Is any equipment or furniture not being used?
8. Is equipment being used improperly?
9. What maintenance or servicing records are kept for equipment?

10. What was the cost of service and maintenance for the past three months?
11. How are stocks of supplies and forms maintained?
12. What controls are used for reordering or distribution?
13. Is there apparent, excessive stocking?

G. *Records and Files*
1. Are files and records maintained in a satisfactory manner?
2. Is the filing system adequate?
3. Have record retention or destruction dates been established?
4. Is there justification for retaining inactive or completed files?
5. Can better utilization of inactive or completed file space be obtained?
6. What records or files are microfilmed?
7. Should any additional files or records be microfilmed?

H. *Budget and Cost*
1. What cost records are maintained?
2. Are the records adequate?
3. What cost controls exist?
4. What is the basis for cost estimates?
5. What safeguards control stamps and petty cash?
6. Have costs been standardized?
7. Are cost records used in budgeting?
8. How do budget estimates compare with actual costs for past periods?

I. *General*
1. Obtain completed copies of all forms.
2. Obtain completed copies of all reports required or originated.
3. Obtain copies or examples of rubber stamps in use.

FLOW CHARTING

Some special requisites exist if problem analysis leads to the use of electro-mechanical or electronic data processing equipment. Each assignment will have inherent characteristics that make it a candidate for manual or non-manual processing, although the choice of processor may have to wait until economic analysis proves the desirability of one over the other. In most cases, the first requirement is the Master Flow Diagram, which is illustrated on page 62.

This diagram broadly defines the subsystems as elements of the higher order system, from the beginning of the process to its end. Because this chart uses rectangular blocks to show subsystems, it serves only as a generalized model of the system. Its prime usefulness is in providing the opportunity to look at the total problem early in the investigation period.

The Top Process Flow Chart (see Figure 5–4) is the second step

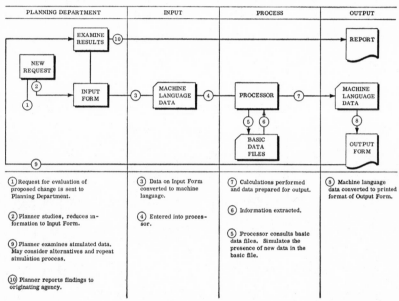

Fig. 5–4. Top process flow chart. This shows how an inquiry is introduced to a simple system.

in defining the problem under investigation. This is a gross information flow diagram, indicating the forms, processing steps, and outputs associated with a problem area. The top chart—the chart which describes the total process—must make ample reference to the Detail Process Flow Charts which contain complete data on the most minute subsystems which are under analysis. Detail flow charts and the top flow chart should form a package, together with notes, sample forms, reports, and other documentary evidence, to provide a full picture of the problem area.

If the problem is resolved into one requiring the use of electro-mechanical or electronic data processors, Top Process Flow Charts will be used as the basis for drawing a Top Computer Flow Chart, Detail Computer Flow Charts, and Detail Machine Operation Flow Charts. A set of suggested symbols for these flow charts is shown in Figure 5–5. A sample Detail Computer Flow Chart is shown as Figure 5–6.

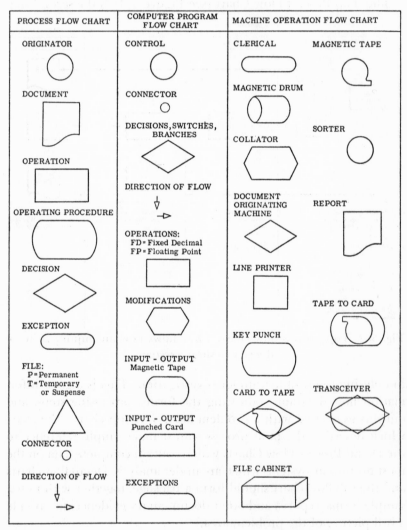

Fig. 5–5. Standard data processing symbols.

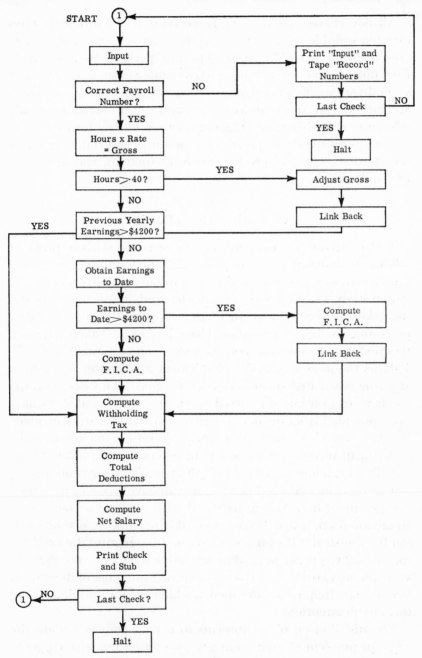

Fig. 5–6. Detail computer flow chart for payroll.

All flow charts should be prepared on standard format vellums carrying suitable reference data so they can be correlated. Ample cross reference should be provided to allow personnel to move freely from notes to flow charts, flow charts to sample forms or reports, and so on. In large scale studies, notes, flow charts, and sample materials are gathered in applications folders and paper bound for ready reference or modification. The organization of data for easy reference requires the development of procedures and codes by which card formats, applications, keypunch instructions, and so on can be standardized.

STAFFING THE PROJECT

Today's technology demands the use of varied skills in problem solving. Seldom can all the requisite skills be found in one person. Frequently, several people will make substantial contributions to a system study. On page 164, a particular study requiring three distinct skills is diagrammed. In Chapter 6, page 103, a typical data processing facility organization chart is shown. Taken together, these exhibits demonstrate how the mixed team is formed. Table 5–1 shows the steps required to implement a computer application after the postulated system has been designed. This demonstrates another organization of a mixed team: Here, technical skills have been provided from outside a department, but department members have actively participated in the project itself. In some areas the department members work alone; in others, the technical experts are, likewise, alone; in some work, their activities are combined.

The fundamental need is, of course, to have access to personnel for specialized uses. Where technical skills are unavailable within an organization, it may become desirable to employ outsiders who can furnish such skills for a short term. To recognize the need for special skill requirements and to determine whether or not they are available are two distinct activities. Both are functions of the project leader; but, frequently, the men working on the problem bring them to his attention.

The distribution of assignments to team members sets up the adjacent problem of maintaining a good fix on the selected goals. When the project leader is a working member of the team, super-

TABLE 5-1

BASIC STEPS REQUIRED TO IMPLEMENT
A COMPUTER APPLICATION AFTER
POSTULATED SYSTEM DESIGN

Departmental Activities	Combined Departmental and Technical Activities	Technical Activities
		1. Determine detailed system design.
	2. Simulate detail system design to uncover problems.	
		3. Design punched card layouts; keypunch formats.
	4. Design final input and output forms.	
5. Begin data collection.		
		6. Block diagram, program, and code; prepare for machine operation.
7. Place purchase orders for forms.		
		8. Keypunch inputs as available.
		9. Complete technical debugging and program operation.
	10. Check results of system operation as each segment is sucessfully programmed.	
	11. Complete system operation and development of machine operating instructions.	
12. Document procedures to provide permanent system capability.		
	13. Proof finished outputs.	
14. Monitor availability of new input data.		

vision and over-all project direction can become a burden. Day to day activities must be monitored and tested for conformity to ultimate objectives and schedules. Individuals tend to participate in mixed teams according to some *a priori* conception of their skill, role in the group, and understanding of the problem. The project leader's task is to mold individuals into a cohesive team working toward well defined milestones.

Selling the assignment

Too frequently, the project leader does not lead. He accepts an assignment, works at it, and delivers a result—all of this in an adequate but uninspired way. The great majority of failures in systems studies are failures in human relations. Either the project leader is not sold on what he must do, or his team members have not been sold on the importance of their individual roles. Very frequently, the primary beneficiary of the system study is not sold on the benefits to be derived or the goals which have been set up.

Inevitably, the failure to sell the study is reflected in the quality of the results and the effectiveness of the system in operation. Notable failures occur in selling the selected course of action to Management, and countless, great ideas never see the light of day because of the failure to put them across. Since recommendation to expend funds frequently accompanies the presentation of a new program to Management, the need to sell the idea becomes doubly important. Not only may personnel be displaced or reassigned with the introduction of a new system, but expenditure of dollars will occur. How then does one "sell" the assignment?

The selling must begin at the lowest level. Confidence in the assignment is primary. This has something to do with the recognition of the need and the knowledge that, if the problem is solved and implemented, good will result. Not only willingness but ability to do the work is an important factor. Personnel trained and capable to undertake the task will find it easier to accept the problems which will arise while the study is in progress.

6
Electronic data processing systems

The systems approach is best described as a way of thinking about problems. From the range of cases in the following chapters, it is clear that the systems approach is not confined to large scale problems or problems of a purely quantitative nature. There is one class of problems, however, which can be attacked using systems thinking with high quality results. These problems are in the area of electronic data processing. This section of the text deals with the use of electronic data processors in the systems design.

EARLY DATA PROCESSORS

Even though early equipment enhanced the performance of data processing tasks, there were still many drawbacks. The foremost of these was the inability to perform more than one function at a time. To overcome this disadvantage, later development emphasized equipment that could perform more than one data processing function in a sequence of operations. The first pieces of equipment produced during this stage were adding and listing machines. These machines combined the functions of computing and recording. Another well-known piece of equipment that combined the functions of computing and recording is the cash register. The latter was developed to provide automatic records of retail transactions, to issue receipts to customers, and to give detailed information to aid Management.

Another significant advance was the development of the machines of the billing, bookkeeping, and accounting types. These machines combined the functions of computing, sorting, distributing, and recording. They were designed to deal with such business problems as preparation of invoices, reports, and business documents, and were useful in that they introduced more speed, neatness, and orderliness to accounting records.

A disadvantage of the more advanced equipment was that the mechanical functions were not closely integrated. When information moved from one machine which would perform one or more functions to another machine which would perform other functions, it was necessary to have a human being do the actual transcription of the information into the second machine. It was also necessary to have a human perform the actual transcriptions from the documents generated during each step of the data processing. This introduced a source of error and was a time consuming operation.

The first attempt to overcome this lack of compatibility was punched card equipment.[1] The punched card introduced compatibility to machines of the same kind. That is, all IBM punched card machines are compatible with each other, but not with all other types of equipment. The punched card provides a method of moving from one machine which would perform one or more functions, to other machines which would perform other functions, without having a human do the actual transcription of the information punched into cards during each step, although it *is* necessary to have a human punch the information from the original source document into the original cards before the processing begins. Then the punched cards, both the originals and others generated by the processing, provide a medium for the data processing without human transcription.

Punched cards do not have unlimited compatibility. To overcome their shortcomings, a system of providing compatibility to a wide range of equipment through the medium of punched paper tape was developed. Punched paper tape carries the information from one machine which performs one or more functions, to other machines which perform other functions, thereby eliminating the need for human transcription during each step of the processing. This system makes it possible to use accounting machines, typewriters, cash registers, addressing equipment and calculators in com-

---

[1] Manufactured by International Business Machines Corporation and by Remington-Rand, a division of Sperry-Rand Corporation.

bination with each other and with punched card equipment. The technique of using the punched paper tape offers possibilities of overcoming communications problems and providing a common language for existing types of mechanical equipment.

ELECTRONIC DATA PROCESSORS

Even with punched card equipment and integrated data processing, there was still a serious drawback. Human error had not been eliminated between data processing functions. With punched card equipment, it was necessary to have an operator transport cards from one machine to another, and to initiate subsequent operations. This was also required when punched paper tape was being used. The goal was to eliminate human intervention between successive operations and to have a machine capable of performing many data processing functions. Although the automatic calculators proved highly successful, they had several disadvantages. One was that they were too slow. This slowness resulted from the fact that machines like the Mark III and Mark IV used mechanical counter wheels for arithmetic elements and for storage. The Bell machines used electro-mechanical relays for arithmetic elements and for storage. To overcome this slowness, electronic parts were used to replace the mechanical and electro-mechanical parts of automatic calculators.

The first development during this stage was the ENIAC. It was all electronic except for input, output, and certain switching functions, and had the features of automatic control and high speed. The ENIAC was the grandparent of all present-day electronic computers, and its success caused other electronic computer projects to be pushed to completion. In fact, it was originally designed for one specific type of problem, namely the computation of ballistic tables with no possible business use. ENIAC was an inflexible machine because it required a considerable amount of time and effort to change problems. The next step was to overcome these disadvantages and still maintain the features of high speed and automatic control.

The next significant development came from Eckert, Mauchley, and Von Neumann. They conceived of the idea of incorporating the instructions for the automatic control of the equipment in a digital memory device, together with the data to be processed. This indicated that existing equipment required much more storage capacity. Enlarged storage capacity greatly increased the variety and types of problems that could be handled. In addition, the incorporation of the instructions in the digital storage device also introduced a greater degree of flexibility to the equipment. With this concept, it was now possible to read the control instructions into the machine in the same manner in which the data was introduced. This facilitated the changing of problems.

Out of this advance came the design for the EDVAC, giving it the distinction of being the first piece of equipment to hold its own program of control instructions in its memory. However, the first stored-program computer to operate satisfactorily was the EDSAC at the Mathematical Laboratory of the University of Cambridge. Both of these machines incorporated the stored program feature and were the first electronic automatic digital computers of the general purpose variety.

CHARACTERISTICS OF ELECTRONIC EQUIPMENT

Electronic data processing equipment has the capability to do the following things:

(1) Perform basic arithmetic operations of addition, subtraction, multiplication, and division.

(2) Perform certain logical operations such as the selection of the larger of two numbers or the choosing of alternatives depending on previous conditions.

(3) Record, remember, and recall data in its storage facilities.

(4) Communicate the results of its operations, in intelligible form or to other machines.

(5) Accept information and instructions.

(6) Direct itself in a predetermined manner, without human intervention, through its stored program.

(7) Check the results of its operations and report when the checks are not functioning satisfactorily.

As a result of these abilities, electronic data processing equipment can simulate human beings doing many tasks. In fact, computers can do most of the clerical operations performed in manual and electro-mechanical data processing systems, including the making of routine decisions. These abilities make electronic data processing a potent tool. However, there are some things computers cannot do. These are at least as important to understand:

(1) They can perform operations only if instructions on how and when to do them have been given.

(2) They cannot construct their own sequence of control instructions, though they can modify instructions.

(3) Computers are not error free, although the frequency of errors per unit of work is much smaller than the rate of human errors, if a human were to undertake the identical job.

(4) Computers do repetitive operations more efficiently than non-repetitive operations. Therefore, the time required to prepare a problem may make it uneconomical to undertake short term tasks. New programming techniques are working against this limitation.

(5) Computers cannot sort efficiently. To sort a set of numbers into an ascending sequence requires many passes. If the set is large, this is obviously awkward and inefficient. It is still much faster than the human rate. New equipment has attacked this limitation with substantial improvements in sorting speed.

Speed

One of the inherent characteristics of electronic data processing equipment is its high speed. The high speed of electronic switching circuits makes possible a fantastic rate of data processing operations. Arithmetic operations on numbers or the comparison of two numbers are performed at the rate of thousands per second. Computer operations can be performed at rates up to 400,000 times those of manual data processing. These rates apply to the *internal* operations of electronic data processing equipment.

The speed of the *input-output* operations is not as great as that of the internal operations. However, input-output speeds become very important because data must be introduced to the computer through some input device and sent from the central computer to an output device. Thus, to some extent, they control the over-all system speed.

To overcome this limitation of the over-all speed of the entire data processing system by the input-output equipment, several things have been done. One thing is to use magnetic tape as much as possible for large volume input-output operations. Since magnetic tape is by far the fastest input-output medium, it offers a greater over-all system speed than could be obtained by other input-output mediums. The use of buffers between the input-output units and the internal processing units is now common. Buffers offer the advantage of simultaneous operation of the input-output units and the internal processing units. This also can contribute to the greater over-all speed of the data processing operation.

Even though the input-output units can cause a slow down of the over-all data processing speed, it is still possible to maintain rates up to thousands of times those of manual or mechanical methods. High speed electronic data processing may make it possible to report business activities at less cost than manual or mechanical methods. It also makes possible the solution of business problems that have not been susceptible to manual methods in the past.

Automatic operation

Another characteristic of electronic data processing equipment is its ability to perform programmed, automatic, data processing. Once the equipment has been loaded with the information to be processed and told what to do, it can process this information without further human intervention. Automatic operation is the result of a set of elemental rules of operations that have been designed and wired into the equipment. The computer uses its logical circuits and its man-given information to do a predetermined sequence of operations. Automatic operation also contributes to the high speed of electronic data processing. The computer can go from one operation to another at electronic speeds, since human intervention is not necessary between steps.

Programming is the process of preparing the procedures for processing data. The programmer breaks down a complex operation into a sequence of simple operations. He further isolates the sequence of procedures necessary to complete an operation. The coder translates the data processing procedural scheme into a detailed list of instructions that the equipment can handle.

The instruction code that is used in preparing the programs for solving the problems, determines the principle operating steps of the electronic data processing equipment. Each instruction is designed to accomplish an elementary data processing operation on one or more pieces of information selected from the storage unit, and/or to transfer the result of an operation to the storage unit.

Each instruction generates a group of control signals. These control signals select the information on which the operation is to be performed from their storage locations. In addition, the control signals can transfer the result of the operation to the appointed storage location, and they can select the next instruction from the storage unit. As a result of this, the instruction that represents the control signals has to specify the operation to be performed and the storage locations of the operands. It can also specify where the result is to be located within the storage unit and where the next instruction is located.

In machine language programming, one instruction or command generally equals one minute step in the process to be carried out. A new factor in the programming field is called English language programming. The major manufacturers of computers have developed new techniques where one instruction is equal to several—even many—detail instructions; in addition, these instructions can be written, more or less, in the English language. That is, the format of the instruction and its content can be understood, whereas in the past code letters or numbers were used. This is a major step in computer technology and has reduced the former, sizable costs associated with programming. As newer techniques are developed in association with hardware which has been designed to accommodate the new programming techniques, the cost may be reduced still further.

Flexibility

Another characteristic of electronic data processing equipment is its flexibility. Computers are designed so they can operate on a variety of problems. Flexibility arises from the ability to change the sequence of control instructions. By changing the sequence of control instructions, it is possible to change the type of problem being solved. Electronic data processing equipment can perform any operation that can be expressed in terms of sequence of control instructions belonging to the instruction code of the equipment. However, operation has to be such that it fits within the limits set by the equipment's storage capacity. If the instruction code includes the arithmetic operations of addition, subtraction, multiplication, division, and a few simple logical operations, the equipment can perform practically every data processing operation.

A piece of equipment that has this data processing capability is called a general purpose machine. Most of the recent electronic data processors are general purpose machines. General purpose machines can handle only a restricted class of problems efficiently. These limitations are a result of the equipment's instruction code, the capacity of its storage units, and the speed of its operations.

There is another class of equipment serving useful purposes in electronic data processing. This equipment is called special-purpose and is usually designed and engineered for special applications. They are not flexible since they can only perform the more limited operations for which they were designed. The instruction code is built into the equipment and cannot be changed unless an engineering change is made. ERMA, a computer, which was designed for the checking account-bookkeeping operations of banks, is a special-purpose machine.

Decision making

Another characteristic of electronic data processing equipment is its ability to make decisions. A typical decision is the comparison of two numbers to determine which is the greater. Another is the selection of one course of action from several alternatives. This decision-making ability results from the logical operations included in the instruction code.

Electronic data processing equipment can make only predetermined decisions. This means that every decision that the equipment makes must be thought of previously by a human, and that the equipment has to be directed in the method of making the decision.

Electronic data processing equipment cannot make decisions for which it has not been instructed. For example, if the equipment is to choose among alternative courses of action on the basis of a prior computation, then the equipment has to be instructed not only on how to make the selection but also what to do after the selection has been made.

ORGANIZING TO CENTRALIZE MACHINE DATA PROCESSING

Among the most fundamental problems is the premise under which systems analysis is conducted. If a computer or punched card installation is used as the system processor, it is safe to say that data processing is top management business. It is fundamental to any successful centralization of equipment that management be well informed on the importance of data processing. Thus, top management education becomes a necessary building block in centralizing data processing.

Management in one way or another sets the tone in which an organized attempt at systems analysis will be received. In addition, it is Management that will stipulate the relationship between the systems group and the departments being studied. Here are some of the possible ways in which the problem might be attacked:

    A. *Without professional aid:*
        (1) Departments will design their own systems. The rationale most frequently used is, "Who understands the problem better?" In this situation, problems are solved within a very limited frame of reference. Departments tend to see their own problems much magnified and out of perspective with the organization as a whole. The resulting systems (or more properly, methods) become data processing "islands" because they are frequently only loosely connected to their adjacent areas. Integration and economy of operation can seldom be raised as critical organization problems because everyone is playing the part of systems designer in his own area of activity.
        (2) Management will allow a certain group to document systems. In this instance, the accent is on developing procedures based upon existing practices. This is an improvement over the first alternative, since any review of a practice about to be adopted as department policy will have some benefit,

even when this review has no authority behind it. Procedures developed by departments for their own use may be
too specialized to get a critical review; a Drawing Room
Manual, for instance, would be a tremendous asset to any organization having a multi-section engineering department.
A quality control department might find a requirement for
writing a Quality Control Manual to document the rules
under which quality control engineers would reject materials or workmanship in receiving, in process, in final assembly, in testing, or in shipping. In both of these examples,
the review rendered by a documenting group may not be
satisfactory. If the practices being reviewed are technical
and mainly concerned with departmental methods, the balance of the organization may be only superficially affected.
As soon as these practices become reflected in interdepart-
ment relationships, the need for surveillance will increase.

B. *With equipment and/or professional aid:*

  (1) Management will provide equipment for data processing
and some assistance in converting business systems to machine systems, but will require using departments to provide
their own operators and system designers. This is the
method referred to as *open shop;* the equipment stays in one
location, frequently without operators or technical experts,
and is not aggressively used to provide service to staff. This
method of operation has been successfully applied in engineering departments where a small scale computer is used
to solve a narrow segment of mathematical problems and
the conversion to machine language is easily learned. This is
a costly method by comparison with the alternate possibilities of providing operators or technical assistance in problem conversion, or both. Note that this situation is like *A.2.*
(page 101) in that outputs are mainly utilized in a limited
number of organization units.

  (2) Management will create a data processing function reporting to some existing organization unit which is a prime user
of these services. This is frequently done, with varying success. In municipal government, the trend is to set up data
processing under the treasurer or controller. In industrial
organizations, the controller or chief finance officer frequently has prime responsibility. In both these instances,
the priority of work on the data processor becomes a major
issue. A second problem arises out of the anomaly that a
controller may be asked to provide many non-accounting
functions to users of equipment outside his department.

There is an organizational issue which invariably arises when a system analysis effort has been appended to the data processing group; some department managers will resist intrusion by another department in resolving their problems, since it appears that someone at their own organization level (or below), is claiming jurisdiction and diluting the manager's autonomy.

This problem can be solved by management's recognition that data processing is one of the largest, single, indirect costs of business. Management's education in data processing should stress the best organizational means of utilizing data processing. Here are some of the salient issues for top management:

A. Leadership of centralized data processing means a *closed shop* where three fundamental services must be provided (see Figure 6–1):

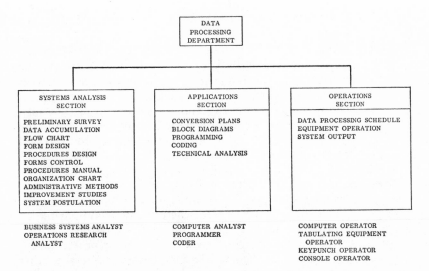

Fig. 6–1. Functional organization and job classifications associated with a typical electronic data processing department.

(1) The design of data processing systems by business or engineering-trained systems analysts.

(2) The conversion of data processing systems by specialists trained in the electro-mechanical or electronic features of equipment.

(3) The operation of equipment by personnel who are capable of obtaining maximum up-time (working time).

B. Effective working relationships demand that Centralized Data Processing be managed by a man at the executive level:
  (1) This man must be no lower organizationally than the highest using department.
  (2) The person to whom this manager would turn to obtain guidance or resolve a dispute must be at least one level higher than the disputants.
  (3) The delegation of authority to the manager of this group should come, where possible, from corporate management.

C. The organization role of Centralized Data Processing must be clearly defined by top management; the objectives must be stated when authority and responsibility are established:
  (1) The organization must be made aware of Management's backing.
  (2) The organization should be told why it must accept the closed shop and its concomitant of systems analysts who will have a voice in the internal operations of individual departments.
  (3) The central data processing group must feel it has both authority and responsibility to execute the tasks before it.

D. Centralized Data Processing is best implemented by non-users who operate under strict budget provisions:
  (1) The non-user is objective and less suspect in matters such as job priority; the non-user will respond to a conflict in the data processing schedule differently than a user who will tend to put heavier emphasis on his own problems.
  (2) The budget for Centralized Data Processing should be obtained by assessing the needs of each division (department, section, group, and so on) and burdening them accordingly. Under these circumstances, where the users are paying for service, they will insist upon the central group performing their role, and cooperation will be a minor problem. It is more likely that there will be a long list of problems waiting for the systems analyst's attention.
    a) The data processing staff members should be delegated to their assignments according to a budget. Systems analysts should work as close to the problem area as possible, and not "commute" to their assignments. A man assigned to "Department 10, Building 31," should have his desk and phone there; he must identify with the systems purchaser, without becoming involved in line responsibility of any kind. Contact with the central group should be

through frequent meetings to review work. This places a burden on the executive who leads the central data processing group to provide *esprit de corps* and group identity.

Centralization of data processing, itself, may require some justification. The economics of centralization are easy to demonstrate. It is desirable, therefore, to expose the criteria on which this judgment has been based to those who must accept the consequences of the decision.

MAKING A FEASIBILITY STUDY

The term *feasibility* has taken on the interpretation of *possible* or *probable* which, in the data processing context, is erroneous. Obviously, all of the computers analyzed in Chapter 7 could do a payroll or a mathematical problem. However, the resultant costs, time in process, and so on would vary widely. Likewise, the ability to integrate a given system into its related subsystems would vary widely, depending upon the choice of equipment.

The term *feasibility* in the possible or probable context would be used mainly by manufacturers of data processing equipment. And in this claim they are no doubt right; each major manufacturer of equipment has a system capable of handling almost any known business problem. Even an exceptionally complex military problem such as the LOGBALNET of the Air Force, was finally mastered with a special system configuration which has over fifty tape drives of which twenty-three are on-line with a 700 series IBM computer.

However, from the equipment user's standpoint, feasibility has come to mean something other than possible or probable. This enlightened view places the emphasis on the following:

(1) Analysis of equipment system alternatives in the light of data processing requirements.

(2) Relationship of current data processing loads and equipment requirements to future requirements, based upon certain growth factors and anticipated improvements in equipment design.

(3) Consideration of system utilization *versus* cost to operate, using a number of rules. One such rule might be, "No system shall be considered a candidate for this company unless its utilization is

equal to, or less than, 40 per cent of first shift capacity for all applications which have been earmarked for conversion in the opening phase of implementation."

(4) Analysis of programming costs and ease of conversion between alternate systems.

(5) Analysis of facilities requirements of alternate systems.

(6) Comparison of manufacturers' services (training, maintenance, programming, and so on) and "free" time, in a given installation.

Note that the accent here is on comparing, as nearly as possible on an equal plane, the equipment attributes. This, of course, places a burden on the user to describe his data processing requirements completely, so equipment manufacturers will be bidding on the same level.

In addition, the feasibility study places the accent on systems design. Although there is no rule, a part of the potential savings sometimes claimed for mechanical or electronic equipment, is not entirely due to equipment. Systems redesign, alone, can sometimes pick up a part of the total savings to be enjoyed by converting to equipment. So there actually are arguments for continuing the present method (see Figure 3–1, p. 42). If a company can obtain a part of its total savings by system redesign alone, the cost of equipment begins to loom very large. The truth is that, frequently, equipment becomes the catalyst and either management and/or operating personnel will accept changes in the light of a new systems processor that they would reject if only the system were being revised.

Equipment manufacturers have done a great deal to provide practical, economical, data processing systems in areas where isomorphism does not take over. Payroll is a good example. Solutions to engineering problems such as earth removals, grade computations, traverse closures, and so on have also reached a high level of efficiency because of the work of equipment manufacturers. However, in areas like production control, material control, budgeting, and so on, where the systems requirements are dictated in part by company size, the product, and the systems purchaser, equipment manufacturers can only suggest how the job has been done in certain specific instances. The burden is ultimately placed upon the user to determine if he can use a generalized system with certain minor changes. The alternative is to undertake the study and design of his own systems.

A feasibility study to determine the usefulness of a computer in data processing has become a major undertaking. From the standpoint of elapsed time, study costs, and impact on the organization, company managements have thought twice before moving ahead. And yet, there is no suitable alternative in the majority of cases, something which will become more apparent after reading the outline which follows on page 112. It will also become apparent that the properly oriented feasibility study is implemented by the systems approach.

Ostensibly, the feasibility study determines whether or not it is economically desirable to employ electronics in data processing. A study of this kind may require as little as six man-months, or take up to six man-years. Although the time dimension is very flexible, the content of such a study is generally the same.[2]

Broadly speaking, the feasibility study will undertake to examine the existing data processing operations and will determine which of these are susceptible to an electronic processor. Susceptibility will be based upon volume and frequency of processing, costs, and manpower required. Those tasks which are found susceptible in terms of some list of characteristics agreed upon by the study team will be costed to arrive at a total cost for the existing system operation. Despite the closely interwoven nature of business systems, the individual system costs must be isolated for future comparison with proposed electronic data processing costs.

The study team will generally postulate a generalized system, on the assumption that a detail system design will not be appropriate until the data processor has been selected. Such a generalized system has limited validity, since it cannot take advantage of the special characteristics of any one equipment system. This is especially important if evaluation of the proposed system results in marginal cost advantages. In this connection, intangible costs must sometimes be carefully evaluated. Although there may be no measurable dollar savings for faster or more accurate reporting, the addition of many intangible benefits sometimes serves to balance the marginal savings in the direction of an order for equipment.

2 See Marxson and Company, Chapter 12.

Using the postulated electronic system as a guide, there are two courses open to a company:

(1) Prepare general specifications (see Figure 6–2 for an example of a basic data collection form) of the data processing system

DATA SPECIFICATION SHEET						REFERENCE			

Title

Data Processing

Purpose

Physical Form   Method of Preparation

Sources

Dispositions

Quan used   Avg.   Max.   Over Period of

Quan of Records/File   Avg   Max.   Freq. of Reference

Item Group	Item Group Summary	Char/Item Group				Tot. Separate Groups			
		Average		Maximum		per Record		per File	
		Alpha	Num.	Alpha	Num.	Aver.	Max	Aver.	Max.

Internal Sequence

Item Group	Item No.	Item Description	Quantity Chars. /Item				
			Average		Maximum		
			Alpha	Num	Alpha	Num.	

Remarks

Fig. 6–2.

which has been studied. Assemble this in books together with sample forms, reports, flow charts and so forth, plus a set of rules or criteria explaining your requirements and the basis upon which the system will be selected. Turn over this data to at least three manufacturers of equipment asking for a proposal within thirty to sixty days. Equipment manufacturers are staffed to do this at no charge. After proposals are returned, the user of equipment must undertake equipment evaluation, the logical comparison of advantages and disadvantages of one system over another.

(2) Utilizing the specifications which have been prepared, assemble the manufacturers' literature, making an equipment evaluation without the benefit of manufacturers' proposals.

In either case, note that a technically oriented group must step in to do equipment evaluation (see Chapter 7). This task is becoming more and more difficult as time goes on, because of the variety and complexity of systems which are available. Each company must determine how to supply the requisite skills in this specialized field.

It is appropriate to divide the feasibility study into two parts: (1) the preliminary study to determine the coarse economics of a computer *versus* the existing method of data processing for a given company, and (2) the generalized system study (feasibility study) resulting in a system postulation which is assembled as an invitation to manufacturers of equipment to bid.

QUESTIONS TO BE ANSWERED BY A PRELIMINARY SURVEY

Prior to making heavy investments of personnel and time in extensive, detail analyses, a preliminary survey will show the economics of converting to a computer. If a preliminary survey reveals the high probability of a dollar payoff, then further study would be warranted. Following are some typical questions to be answered in a survey of this type:

(1) Does the company have computer applications?

(2) If so, what are they?

(3) Will there be a dollar payoff associated with these applications? What is the nature of the payoff? Will there be reductions in out of pocket expense?

(4) Will the dollar payoff be large enough to make it practical to sustain the costs of converting to electronics and of maintaining a computer center?

(5) What should the priority of study be in converting applications to a computer?

(6) What will be the duration of time and how much will it cost to prepare an invitation to bid?

(7) Why use electronics in preference to some other method of data processing?

Here are some typical questions one might ask of either the existing or proposed (postulated) system:

(1) Does the proposed system provide clear-cut improvements over the existing system? What are they? Are they measurable?

(2) Can the existing system be improved substantially by more intensive study? Will such improvements invalidate the bulk of the proposed savings of an electronic system?

(3) Does the proposed system call for generally acceptable organizational changes or changes in method? If some changes are unacceptable, will modification restrict the dollar benefits to be gained?

(4) Will the proposed system savings be effected by reductions in manpower? Will there be specific curtailment of expense in the proposed system? Will open requisitions for manpower be cancelled? Will personnel be transferred? Will the employee quit rate be sufficient to provide savings predicted by the proposed system? (See Chapter 8.)

(5) Does the proposed system perform more quickly, more efficiently, or more accurately than before? Is this measurable?

(6) Does the proposed system provide outputs which are permanently required? Are they currently available? Are they unavailable because of manpower, time, or communications limitations? Are they unavailable because they are beyond manual computational abilities?

(7) Is the proposed system practical and operable within the personnel limitations of the organization? Is it similar enough to other systems so its validity in operation is unquestioned?

(8) Are the training, indoctrination and orientation requirements of organization personnel within some reasonable scope? Are appropriate personnel available within the organization? Is the

labor pool for personnel sufficiently deep to insure system continuity?

(9) Do system requirements impose excessive or severe demands on personnel? Can the system operation be simulated in advance to determine its reliability, and its effect on the organization?

Here is a final checklist that might be directed at the generalized system study prior to asking equipment manufacturers to prepare proposals:

(1) Is the system requirement satisfied by the postulated system?

(2) Are the data handling steps described adequately as they are interrelated? Procedurally? In time?

(3) Are data inputs described as to source, format, method of transmission, and volume per unit of time?

(4) Have the data storage and retrieval requirements been described as to the kinds of data? The nature and size of each item? Items per record and records per file? The volume of data stored or filed? The access requirements? Interrogation and answer requirements? Methods of file storage and maintenance?

(5) Have the data processing requirements been described in terms of the kind of processing that will be required? The speed with which outputs must be made available? The volumes to be processed? On-line requirements?

(6) Are the outputs described as to format and content? Are the quantitative characteristics clear (alpha-numeric content, volume, number of copies, and so on)? Have the time requirements on output availability been described? Have peak load requirements been expressed?

(7) Has the use of outputs been clearly stated? Are they for the preparing agency control only? Are they forwarded under a priority plan? Is there some urgency factor? Are the outputs incorporated in other outputs or are they final in nature?

(8) Have the integration requirements been stated? Have the mechanics of flow charting clearly illustrated how integration is to be achieved? Have system inputs been correlated with multi-output requirements?

(9) Has the human role been defined? Do humans continue to file, sort, route, find, calculate, and copy. At what points do human judgment and interpretation enter the system? What are the control mechanisms over humans?

(10) Are the system attributes concerning feedback and control stated? Are systems fully stated as modules with all of the specific attributes?

(11) Have any special purpose requirements been stated? If so, what is the impact of the special requirement on the system as a whole from the standpoint of cost, delivery, maintenance, and so on?

The actual feasibility study may take many forms based upon the fundamental premises which have been stated. The outline which follows, is a fairly well established and successful pattern which can be utilized in most cases.

OUTLINE OF HOW TO CONDUCT A FEASIBILITY STUDY

I. Business analysis and problem statement

A. *Organization Charts*
1. By area
2. By activity
3. By operation

B. *Statements of Objectives*
1. By area
2. By activity

C. *Analysis of Present Operating Procedures*
1. Data gathering
   a. Interviewing and note-taking
   b. Organization of data
2. Data presentation
   a. Sample documentary forms
   b. Lists of files and records required
      (1) Functions
      (2) Size
      (3) Access requirements
   c. Communications requirements
      (1) Within area
      (2) Between areas
   d. Preparation of flow charts
      (1) Index
      (2) Area by activity—quantitative data
      (3) Activity by operation—quantitative data.

D. *Cost Estimates*
  1. Personnel
  2. Operating costs (direct)
  3. Overhead charges (indirect)
  4. Equipment
  5. Facilities

II. Data processing system design

A. *Analysis of Present Data Processing Procedures*
  1. Area by activity communications
     a. Inputs
     b. Outputs
     c. Processors
     d. Feedbacks
     e. Controls
  2. Activity by operation communications
     a. Inputs
     b. Outputs
     c. Processors
     d. Feedbacks
     e. Controls

B. *Description of Postulated Electronic Data Processing System*
  1. Operational flow charts
  2. Rank equipment
     a. Inputs
     b. Operations (processes)
        (1) Sequential
        (2) Decision
     c. Outputs
  3. Changes from present business systems flow charts—Consolidation and elimination of files and operations
  4. Runs to be performed
     a. List and description
     b. Block diagram
        (1) Inputs
        (2) Processors
        (3) Outputs
        (4) Feedbacks
        (5) Controls
  5. Files and records to be maintained
     a. Description

     b. Quantitative data

     c. Access requirements

  6. Recommended forms of inputs

  7. Reports to be prepared

  8. Communications considerations

     a. Integrated data processing

       (1) Within area

       (2) Between areas

     b. Facilities required

  9. Time estimates and schedule (coarse figures)

     a. Machine running time

     b. Peripheral equipment

     c. Over-all time schedules

  10. Cost estimates (coarse figures)—prorated by activity

  11. Operational features of significance in the specific application.

  12. Over-all appraisal.

C. *Determination of Specific Equipment to be Considered*

  1. Types of equipment and alternatives

  2. Manufacturers and models to be investigated

D. *Interim Feasibility Study Report*

  1. Brief description of activity

  2. Description of the data processing system (summary of Figure 6–2)

  3. Conclusions: Over-all appraisal of the suggested system

     a. Advantages and disadvantages

       (1) Economic

       (2) Operational

III. Equipment evaluation to implement a postulated data processing system

A. *Briefing on Postulated System for Specialists in Specific Equipment by the Data Processing Engineer Assigned to Each Area*

B. *Equipment Comparison Data Presentation by Each Specialist*

  1. Flow charts

  2. Specific equipment required

  3. Runs to be performed:

     a. List of runs (passes)

     b. Block diagram of each

  4. Time

  5. Cost

a. Equipment
b. Personnel

C. *Consolidated Report by Data Processing Engineer Assigned to the Area—Specific System and Equipment for Each Manufacturer Involved*

A GLOSSARY OF USEFUL TERMS USED IN ELECTRONIC DATA PROCESSING

ACCESS TIME: The time required to locate a word in storage and transfer it to the processor.

ACCUMULATOR: A register in the processor that holds sums, products, and so on; also used for comparing data.

ADDER: The component of a machine that does arithmetic; it may or may not serve simultaneously as an accumulator, and it may or may not add by "counting."

ADDRESS: The designation of a storage location.

ADDRESS PART OF AN INSTRUCTION: The portion of an instruction that tells the machine where to find the data that is to be used in an operation, or where to store a result.

ADDRESS SYSTEM: A term that designates the number of addresses contained in a single instruction.

BINARY NUMBER SYSTEM: A number system with only two digits, 0 and 1, in contrast to the decimal system which has 10 digits. All current machines are either decimal or binary. Arithmetic is done in a different manner with the binary system than with decimal.

BIT: A bit is the least amount of information that can be represented as *zero* or a *one*, as represented by a hole in a card—or no hole; or as represented by a plus or minus electrical charge. Bits are grouped in pattern to represent coded characters.

BRANCHING: Automatic selection of appropriate alternate instructions.

BUFFER: A register that can operate at (usually two) different speeds, thus permitting processing of data at high speed while simultaneously reading input and/or writing output. A temporary storage unit.

CONTROL: The section of a data processing machine that controls its operation. Most current machines are either manually controlled through a keyboard or have a wired control panel or operate by a stored program.

FEEDBACK: The technique of returning selected portions of the results produced by a processor to its own control section for the purpose of self-supervision or modification of further processing.

INPUT: Information delivered to a machine; also, the section of the machine that "reads" this information.

INSTRUCTION: A word which is sent to a register in the control section of a machine, where it causes the machine to perform a particular operation. An instruction will consist of an operation code and one or more addresses. If all instructions for a particular machine have just one address part, then the instructions and the machine are referred to as *single address*. Similarly, a three address machine will have three addresses and one operation code to each instruction (*see* Address System).

LOGICAL COMPONENTS: The sections of a processor capable of making comparisons, testing for algebraic signs, identifying zero or non-zero results, and so on.

MEMORY: The section of a machine used to store data and instructions.

MICROSECOND: One millionth of a second: .00001 seconds.

MILLISECOND: One thousandth of a second: .001 seconds.

MODIFICATION: The ability to alter the normal sequence of instructions by branching or changing the command or address portion of instructions.

OPERATION CODE: The portion of an instruction that tells the machine what operation to perform.

OUTPUT: Information delivered by the machine; also, the section of the machine that "writes" this information.

PROCESSOR: The section of a machine that performs arithmetic, makes logical decisions governing control, and processes the data in storage.

PROGRAM: A list of instructions to the processor.

READ: A command instructing the machine to accept data from a specific input unit and place it in memory.

RECORD: A group of related words.

RECORD STORAGE UNIT: An intermediate memory unit used to facilitate transmission of records between dissimilar units.

REGISTER: Any storage unit used for a specialized purpose. A register is usually designed to contain a fixed number of characters.

STORAGE: The section of a machine that stores data or instructions; the memory section.

STORAGE LOCATION: The address of any specific area of memory. In a fixed word length machine it refers to the address of a specific word. In a variable word length machine it refers to the address of a specific character.

STORED PROGRAM MACHINE: One which is controlled by having an appropriate list of instructions stored in the machine just as data is stored. The machine refers to these instructions in a specified sequence, executing each before examining the next.

WORD: A unit of information; a piece of data equivalent to a field in punched card terminology.

WORD LENGTH: The number of characters in a word.

FIXED WORD LENGTH: Storage designed to contain a specific number of characters for each addressable location.

VARIABLE WORD LENGTH: Storage designed to store words of any size in consecutive locations to make more efficient use of memory.

WRITE: A command to a machine to take information from memory and record it on some output media.

7

Evaluation of equipment systems

INTRODUCTION

New equipment and modifications of existing equipment are constantly enlarging the computer market. This section is not intended to embrace all equipment, but to provide a cross section of equipment available at this time. Direct contact with the manufacturers of electronic computers will enable the systems analyst to obtain complete information on available equipment. Manufacturers have a wide range of technical and non-technical data available, a large part of which is distributed free of cost to potential customers.

Data on each computer are arranged under the following headings for easy comparison:

General characteristics and information
Number system
Instruction system
Storage (drum, core, magnetic tape)
Input methods
Output methods

These equipment characteristics—and the more detailed technical facts of these systems—would normally be explored in the evaluation of computers for use in a given installation. Equipment evaluation is the means by which these equipment characteristics are tested through the performance of specific data processing problems. This requires not only the general type of knowledge which is contained in this chapter, but a detailed knowledge of equipment characteristics, construction (circuitry), codes, program routines, and so on. Equipment evaluation is the final test of the desirability of one computer over another, and it can only be undertaken by technically competent personnel. Competent selection of a computer will reveal the cross section of equipment most likely to produce the proper input, output, and processing capabilities which the company's data processing system requires. Differences in machine speeds and modes of operation will make the costs of data processing vary, since some computers will operate more efficiently, on a given problem than others. Not the least of the problems to be surveyed in equipment evaluation will be the ease of programming, a subject which will not be explored in this text. The costs and problems imposed by programming make this a major and sometimes determining factor in the choice of a computer system.

Four computers have been described in parallel in this chapter. They have been selected because they represent something of the current variety available in electronic equipment; there are many other computers available, and each has a number of special characteristics to recommend it. Even these examples have been superficially appraised because a full, technical description would be outside the mission of this text.

The objective in presenting this material is not to train technicians but to bring home the complexity of equipment evaluation and to stress that top management must take a *technical* point of view when it is dealing with electronic data processing. Machine data processing must be considered a level above manual systems, and, today, electronic data processing is at the highest level in this category. The use of computers imposes organization and system constraints not encountered in manual systems, something which will be readily seen by viewing the attributes of the four equipment systems that follow.

DATATRON 220[1]

General characteristics and information

This is a *general purpose* machine capable of handling a wide variety of business problems as well as scientific and engineering

[1] Manufactured by the Burroughs Corporation, Electrodata Division.

applications. It is normally considered a large scale computer because of its large memory capacity, high speed, and general price range.[2] It is a stored program machine, as are all of the other medium and large scale computers. This means that the individual steps of a complex process can be held internally, which allows the equipment to go from one step to the next without human interference. Because no two systems are necessarily made up of identical equipment, lease prices or purchase prices must be computed based upon the selected equipment system. Thus, the prices shown in this chapter should be accepted in a general way since they indicate only one system configuration. The "220" system leases for approximately $25,000 per month; its purchase price is approximately $1,250,000.

The "220" system requires in excess of 60 kilowatts for its operation. Temperature and humidity control are necessary. Approximate system weight is 140,000 lbs. Space requirements for a full system would approach 1,200 square feet; additional space would be required for personnel, files, storage of cards, and so on.

Analyst, programmer, operator, and maintenance training is provided by the manufacturer (usually free). Some problem analysis is provided, although emphasis is on initial programming assistance. Extensive library routines are made available to customers, generally at no charge except for materials. Data processing facilities are available on an hourly or fixed fee basis for specific problems; these facilities are also available prior to the installation of a customer's machine for the checking of programs and running of sample problems.

Number system

The machine's number system is important since it indicates the way in which its instructions will be constructed, and the way in which data will be held internally. In the "220," as in other machines, the number base is what is known as *binary coded decimal*. The number system is capable of showing decimal digits 0 through 9, plus 26 alphabetic characters and all other typewriter and special symbols. Alphabetic (alpha) data is carried internally by pairing decimal digits.

[2] Price quotations on equipment of all manufacturers are as of April, 1959.

Instruction system

The computer is operated by means of instructions, which, step-by-step, direct the operations which are to be performed. Instructions are carried by computer *words* of a special type within the machine. A picture of a computer word for the "220" would appear as in Figure 7–1. One of these words is required for each instruc-

Picture of Stored Numerical Information:

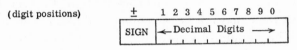

Picture of Stored Alphanumeric Information:

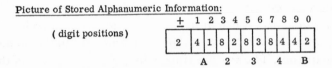

Fig. 7–1.

tion, and they are so constituted that they work sequentially. There are approximately 92 different commands (instructions) for the "220" system (Figure 7–2 is a picture of one of these instructions).

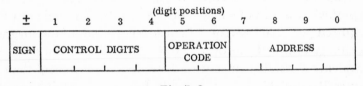

Fig. 7–2.

In this command structure, there are special instructions which allow operations to be performed on partial word fields. Other special instructions permit the transfer of 1 to 100 words of information (called a *block* of information) from one part of internal storage to another. Another special instruction tests for relative magnitude and transfers control of subsequent operation steps to one of four statuses: high, low, equal, or transfer. Through the special instruction called *magnetic tape scan,* the computer is able to locate blocks of data on magnetic tape which belong to a certain class.

Storage

This is a *magnetic core* machine. The normal system will contain from 2,000 to 10,000 words of storage (prices quoted are based on 5,000 words), in increments of 1,000 words. Memory size is of basic importance, since it will act as a restriction on either the size of files to be stored or the number of instructions that can be stored, although these may not be accommodated in the same part of the system. The amount of storage required will be a direct reflection of the types and sizes of files to be stored. Core or drum storage is referred to as *internal* storage since it is physically contained within the central processing unit of the system. The "220" system is one of the *random access* machines, since the instruction code permits direct (non-sequential) retrieval of any data stored in the memory—in any sequence. The average time to find any single piece of data in core storage is 15 microseconds (millionths of a second).

Auxiliary storage is provided in *magnetic tape units* which are external to the central processor. Ten tape carriers can be placed on-line with the "220" system. Each tape reel is 3,500 feet long and contains data at the density of 416 decimal digits per inch. Thus, any single tape reel can carry 15,000,000 digits of data. Movement of data from the carriers to core storage or other tape carriers is accomplished by means of a magnetic tape control unit, one of which is required per "220" system. The read-write heads of the magnetic tape storage unit will pass over 25,000 digits per second which is the equivalent of reading an entire 3,500 foot tape in less than six minutes. Recorded information can be found by searching in either forward or backward motion, each tape unit operating independently of others. In order to update specific pieces of information, writing heads can selectively write over recorded data.

All reading operations are done twice and compared. Imperfect tape areas are machine detected and automatically rejected for data recording. Many special error detection devices exist which are common to most computers.

The following are the average times, including time to obtain the instruction and operand from storage and time to do the operation:

Operation	Time (microseconds)[3]
Addition or subtraction	200
Multiplication	2,095
Division	3,985
Transfer	125

Input methods

The "220" employs the *Cardatron* system by which the relatively slow card handling machines are coupled to the high speed central processor via *buffers* (drums) or intermediate storage devices. There can be up to seven Cardatron Input devices per system (and seven Cardatron Output devices). One Cardatron Control Unit per "220" system is required. The Cardatron Input Unit transfers data to the Cardatron Control Unit from a card reader at the maximum rate of 480 cards per minute, without interfering with the work of the central processor. The control unit is capable of operating at the rate of 15,000 digits per second. Transfer time from the Cardatron Input Unit to the central processor is 7.2 milliseconds (thousandths of a second).

A seven channel paper tape is also used as input to the "220." Data is read by a *Photoreader* which will carry a 5½ inch (40,000 characters) or 7 inch (80,000 characters) diameter reel at a density of 10 characters per inch. Tape can be read at the rate of 1,000 characters per second (100 inches per second). The Photoreader can do automatic translation, as well as make parity checks and terminate reading by word count or control data on the tape.

The "220" system also accepts *IBM punched cards* which means that the total cost of a computer system utilizing this type of input must include key punches, key verifiers, reproducing punches, summary punches, and so on. Here again, data processing systems will dictate the combination of equipment necessary to meet the

[3] Millionths of a second. Other manufacturers express their average times in milliseconds, thousandths of a second. Times have been shown as the manufacturer customarily expresses them.

system requirements. It is not uncommon to combine the equipment of two or more manufacturers in arriving at the equipment complement.

The central computer contains a control console, one feature of which is a *Supervisory Printer*. This unit is a modified typewriter, and has a keyboard which enables the console operator to make various tests and special interrogations of the system. Likewise, it can receive data from the system, printing answers on a sheet of paper. This feature, common to most large scale systems, is valuable in error-detection, debugging and testing. This input is, of course, manual by means of a keyboard.

Output methods

The Cardatron Output Unit receives cards via the Cardatron Control Unit which controls card punching at the rate of 100 cards per minute, maximum. The Control Unit likewise monitors line printing at the rate of 150 lines per minute by means of a buffer drum which frees the central processor for its own work. Time to move from the central processor to Cardatron Output Unit is 10.0 milliseconds. Card data is independently edited under electronic format control on both input and output. Control is via a stored program.

The "220" system also utilizes a *Paper Tape Punch* which operates off an 8 inch diameter reel. This unit operates at a speed of 60 characters per second (6 inches per second feed), substantially slower than input rates previously quoted. To partly overcome this discrepancy, the "220" system can be set up to operate with Paper Tape Punches, Photoreaders and Character-at-a-Time Printers up to a maximum of 10 units per system. The Paper Tape Punch has an automatic alpha, bi-decimal translation capability (see Instruction System) as well as automatic parity generation and zero suppression.

The "220" system contains one *Character-at-a-Time Printer* (also called the Supervisory Printer). This is an off-line device. Like a typewriter, it will print alphameric data at a rate of ten characters per second. It has carriage control, tabular stops, automatic zero suppression, and can be equipped with an off-line mechanical reader. In this arrangement, it can type data direct from punched paper tape at the rate of ten characters per second with carriage control, tabular stops, and so on controlled from paper tape rather than the central processor.

The "220" system is capable of producing *IBM punched cards* as an output via reproducing punches or summary punches, at the speed of 100 cards per minute. Control is under the central processor and generally only one card output device may be operating at a time. Data pass through a card converter which acts as a buffer translating machine code into card code, and up to eight, ten-digit words can be punched in a card.

The "220" system, in addition, utilizes *IBM Tabulators* (402, 403, 407) as an output device. Format control is via the printer's control panel; sequence control is from the stored program. Data pass through a buffer as with card output, and, again only one printer may be operating at a time on line. Line speeds are normal IBM printer speeds.

Magnetic tape is an input-output device as well as being a storage device. The storage feature (external memory) is achieved when a basic file is put on line for updating. This, of course, is input to a data processing system while at the same time it is a holding device for information. After the file has been made current by deleting old data and adding new input data, it becomes output, and, as such, still retains its external storage character.

HONEYWELL 800[4]

General characteristics and information

This is a *general purpose* computer with a range of capabilities much like the Datatron 220. One significant design feature of the "800" is its all transistorized construction, which eliminates the bulk of the vacuum tubes normally used in computers. Not only is the system reliability thus improved, but, in addition, less heat is generated, less power is consumed, and less air conditioning is required. This system is in the intermediate class—between medium and large scale systems. Its approximate lease price would be $20,000

4 Manufactured by DATAmatic, a division of Minneapolis-Honeywell Regulator Company.

per month and its purchase price would be about $1,000,000, depending upon system configuration. The "800" can assume the price and memory characteristics of a medium, intermediate, or large scale system because of certain flexible design features. This has been done by providing input-output equipment which is designed on a *standard* and *high speed* basis giving two distinct operational modes. The high speed devices are more costly, and, hence, the total costs of a system with high speed devices would be substantially larger than the standard equipment. It would be logical to turn to high speed equipment if, for instance, the output requirements were such that standard printing rates (150 lines per minute) would be too slow for the requirements of the data processing system. This system shows a design relationship in many ways to the large scale DATAmatic 1000 of which there are only six in the world. The dependency which some computer manufacturers place upon IBM to supply all input-output peripheral equipment is not true in the case of this manufacturer.

The "800" system requires 25 KVA for its operation. Air cooling is built into the system and reduces the need for special facilities treatment. Room size for an intermediate scale system would be about 1,000 square feet, not including space for personnel or records storage. The system weight would be about 12,000 pounds, depending upon exact numbers and pieces of equipment.

The manufacturer offers a variety of training courses ranging from executive seminars of one day through operator's courses of six weeks, all free of cost. Complete maintenance by resident DATAmatic personnel is included in all lease contracts. Maintenance of purchased equipment may be arranged by a separate contract or by training of customer personnel at no charge. The manufacturer is establishing computing service centers at strategic points in the United States where sample problems and customer debugging can be undertaken.

Number system

This system operates on *binary* or *binary coded decimal* system internally. Externally, the "800" will operate in *octal, hexadecimal* or *decimal.* Internally, the number system is capable of 0 through 9;

externally, it can show 10 decimal digits or 16 hexadecimal digits. In addition, it can handle 26 alpha characters and 20 special symbols which are stored in a six bit binary form.

Instruction system

The "800" word is 54 binary digits, including 6 check digits; this is equivalent to an 11 decimal plus sign or 12 decimal digit word. Figure 7–3 is an example of an "800" numeric word; Figure

1101	0101	0011	0001	0010	0101	0000	1001	0110	1000	0110	1000
+	5	3	1	2	5	0	9	6	8	6	8

Fig. 7–3.

7–4 is an example of an "800" alphabetic word; Figure 7–5 is an example of an "800" mixed (alphameric) word. Note that all words

110110	011011	110010	011011	010010	110100	010011	100010
W	.	S	.	B	U	C	K

Fig. 7–4.

010010	110100	010011	100010	0010	0101	0000	1001	0110	1000
B	U	C	K	2	5	0	9	6	8

Fig. 7–5.

contain a maximum of 48 binary digits, in combinations of four and six bit blocks (check digits not shown).

This is a three-address machine (as contrasted with both the Burroughs and IBM equipment). An instruction may lead to the next instruction in normal sequence, to a temporary departure from and automatic return to normal sequence, or to a complete change to a new sequence. In addition to three addresses, every instruction specifies either of two sequencing counters as the source of the next instruction. Both automatic and programmed sequencing is possible. There are 51 basic instructions; they are structured as in Figure 7–6. The 54 bit word has great system design flexibility.

OPERATION CODE	ADDRESS 1	ADDRESS 2	ADDRESS 3	CHECK DIGITS
1----------➤12	1----------➤12	1----------➤12	1----------➤12	1----------➤6

Fig. 7–6.

The operation code specifies the instruction to be performed and (depending on the instruction category) such information as the source of the next instruction, fixed or floating point arithmetic, peripheral device involved, partial mask address, and memory location or special register option for each of the three address groups. The structure of the address groups depends on whether a memory location or a special register is addressed and whether addressing is direct, indirect, or indexed. The following paragraphs illustrate some special instructions that facilitate operation.

Multiple transfer is an instruction designed for indirect addressing. It allows the programmer to assemble or to distribute information within memory and is particularly useful in sorting or matrix computations.

Compute orthocount is an instruction which causes the automatic generation of orthotronic count information accompanying every record written upon or read from magnetic tape. This information is used to check both writing and reading and provides a means for reconstructing damaged data—in other words, it provides a virtually complete internal system to protect the files.

Shift and select is an instruction designed for use in data processing and logical computation areas. It automatically selects a course of action based on information within the item being processed, for example, in the handling of transaction codes.

Distributed read-write causes the computer to read a record into memory and distribute the items comprising the record to preassigned locations, or to assemble a record from such distributed items for writing. This ability is included in the peripheral read and write instructions.

Simulator instructions are a group of instructions, virtually unlimited in number, which can be defined in advance by the programmer, who can subsequently call for a desired subroutine, comprising a number of instructions, with a single instruction.

Whenever information is transferred within the Honeywell "800," every word is checked for accuracy. This includes transfers between peripheral devices and memory, memory and tape, and all transfers within the central processor. Similar checking verifies all arithmetic and control operations. A built-in marginal checking system permits convenient, periodic checks of component performance levels. Orthotronic control is a unique automatic data-protection technique. At the end of each record, Orthotronic check numbers are added to each information channel. Words which might become lost or garbled on magnetic tape are internally regenerated by Orthotronic procedures, which eliminates costly and time-consuming manual corrections.

Storage

The "800" is a *stored program* machine. Unlike some computers, any location can store any valid "800" word. Access to or from any memory location is in parallel. Storage is of the *magnetic core* variety in increments of 4,096 words (8,192, 12,288 or 16,284 are also available). The average access time in the standard configuration is six microseconds.

External storage is possible in from 1 to 64 magnetic tape units [5] per "800" system. Tape speed is 120 inches per second, but rewind can be done three times as fast. Tape control is via the stored program for on-line operations and manually from the console for off-line operations. Tape reels are 2,500 feet and store 1,666,666 "800" words or 20,000,000 decimal digits. Information is transferred at the rate of 96,000 decimal digits per second per magnetic tape unit. Up to eight units may be reading and up to eight other units may be writing at any time. Each group of words written or read as the result of a single instruction is called a record. Records may vary from 2 to 400 words in length and are separated by gaps of $\frac{2}{3}$ inch.

[5] Not to be confused with the DATAmatic "1000" tape units, the "800" tape units are $\frac{3}{4}$ inch mylar (plastic) like the tape units of other manufacturers. The "1000" tape units are 3 inch mylar and require their own special tape carriers which are not compatible in the "800" system.

Writing is done with the tape moving in the forward direction, but reading may be done with the tape moving in either direction.

A magnetic tape switching unit is available for selecting on-line or off-line connections. Peripheral control devices provide the necessary buffering and conversion for all input-output units. Up to 56 inquiry stations can be included for remote random interrogation of magnetic tape files. Thirty thousand three address instruction-operations per second are possible, which makes the "800" among the fastest computers. The following are average times for basic logical and arithmetic operations:

Operation	Time (milliseconds)
Addition or subtraction	.024
Multiplication	.150
Division	.312
Transfer	.018
Branch	.024
Shift	.036 (avg.)

The *Multi-Program Control Section* permits up to eight programs to function simultaneously. Each program proceeds independently of the others without the need for special programming. The *Traffic Control Section* monitors up to 16 input-output trunks and effects the necessary connections at the proper times between these trunks and the central processor. Virtually any desired combination of input devices, output devices, and magnetic tape units can be connected to these parallel trunks via appropriate control units.

Input methods

The "800" provides five flexible means of input. The first of these is the *Flexowriter* which is the console typewriter. Not only is a written record of the interrogation made at typewriter speeds, but a punched paper tape by-product is simultaneously prepared. This input device is used in debugging, error detection, and sometimes is used to insert starting or other special data directly to memory.

Punched paper tape itself can be the input device operating at typewriter speeds (ten characters per second). It fills much the same role as the typewriter and, of course, is too slow to be involved in system processing. There are two punched paper tape readers available that can be used to introduce data into the system. These operate at 200 and 1,000 characters per second, respectively, and are known as high speed readers.

There are, in addition, three *Magnetic Character Readers,* which are capable of reading documents imprinted with magnetic ink. These operate at 750, 900 or 1,500 documents per minute and add a new dimension to information processing.

The final input method is via *IBM punched cards.* Here again, great versatility is provided in card readers that operate at 240, 650 or 900 cards per minute, either on-line or off-line. Information from each card is read twice and the readings compared. Each card is converted to ten words in memory. Cards containing invalid punches may be rejected or converted with an invalid-punch signal. Card columns may be rearranged or deleted by means of a control panel. Orthotronic control information is automatically generated and attached to each record by a card reader. Note the effect on overall system cost of high speed devices.

Output methods

The "800" system provides five methods of output corresponding to input. The typewritten page is prepared by the *console typewriter* at 10 characters per second. Using this device, information about operation of stored programs, memory contents, and so on can be printed under program control or manually from the console.

Punched paper tape can also be an output device, operating at 60 characters per second. This tape can be used in conjunction with the Flexowriter for the tabulation of results of operations. It can also be introduced to the IBM tape-to-card converter to produce punched cards for storage of data or further processing.

Punched cards are, of course, a primary output of this or any system. Two card punches are available, either of which will operate on-line or off-line. Rates of operation are 100 or 250 cards per minute. In these devices, 10 computer words become the contents of one punched card. Checking devices such as double punch or blank column detection are available.

The "800" system *Printer-Punch* provides an output of punched cards and/or line printing. This device will produce 150 punched cards per minute or print at the rate of 150 lines per minute.

Printed reports can be produced by two types of printers. The first of these operates at the rate of 150 lines per minute. The second operates at high speed, 600–900 lines per minute. Either printer can be hooked up off-line or on-line. Line length is 120 characters at 10 per inch. Vertical spacing is 6 lines per inch. Available characters include 10 digits, 26 letters, and 20 special symbols. Vertical format is under program control.

IBM 305 RAMAC[6]

General characteristics and information

This is a *general purpose* computer, but is best applied to clerical and accounting applications where computation is at a minimum and file updating is the major system problem. This is a medium scale data processor which leases for $3,200 per month and sells for $189,950; these prices do not include peripheral equipment such as key punches, key verifiers, sorters, collators, and so on, if such equipment is required in the system. The "305" is a stored program machine which is generally set up to carry files in its disk storage and instructions in its drum storage. Control panels handle logical operations, format control, and input-output.

Ramac is what is called an *on-line* machine. This means it is only limited by input and output rates and is not limited to any one sequence or volume of transactions. Remote inquiry stations enable company managers directly to interrogate the computer, with a monitor, at any time. This optional feature has many advantages since it brings the decision making process right up to the next in-line subsystem without human interference. On-line equipment has the ability to provide almost instantaneous access to voluminous records at any time the central computer is in operation.

A normal "305" will require 15.1 KVA. This type of installation

6 Manufactured by International Business Machines Corporation.

will require about 600 square feet (not including peripheral equipment or personnel) and will add a floor load of 8,925 pounds. Heat generation is negligible and normal air conditioning should be supplemented by air filtration and control over relative humidity (not to exceed 80 per cent).

Programming and operator training are provided by the manufacturer free of charge. Programming assistance, education, and library facilities are made available to customers. Data processing services are furnished on a contract basis to industry, science, and government by the Service Bureau Corporation, a wholly owned but independently operated subsidiary of IBM formed on January 1, 1957. There are 82 branch office locations in principal U.S. cities, each operating punched card accounting machine systems. Seventeen of these service bureaus are also equipped with electronic data processing systems.

Number system

The "305" is a *decimal* machine using *binary code* to represent decimals internally, with a parity bit. As in the previous computer, the "305" will handle digits 0 through 9, alpha characters *A* through *Z*, and a variety of special characters.

Instruction system

Word length in the "305" is variable, although it consists of 10 digits plus sign as in the previous computer. This is what is called a *two-address* machine because two addresses can be placed in the space of 10 digits. A picture of the "305" word (Figure 7–7) shows how the two address feature is achieved. There are about 15 basic instructions. The panel exit character stops successive program steps

FROM			TO			Number of Characters		Panel Exit	Special Control
Track	Position		Track	Position					
Alpha-meric	Numeric	Numeric	Alpha-meric	Numeric	Numeric	Numeric	Numeric	Alpha-meric	Numeric
0	1	2	3	4	5	6	7	8	9

Fig. 7–7.

and activates a panel hub corresponding to that character for operation of selectors, input-output equipment, and so on. The special control digit can cause comparison of contents of *from* and *to* addresses and can setup panel connections, or it can cause the clearing of accumulators before entry. The control panel is used to perform logic operations.

Operations of the "305" are checked by reading twice and comparing results. The normal parity checks are made to and from the drum, on the program register, printer, and punch. Addressing is an important issue with the "305" since five digits is optimum and any other arrangement of digits wastes space. There are many ways in which part numbers, stock numbers, and so on can be compressed to fit this five digit requirement and it seldom creates a problem. Time sharing on the "305" will permit any or all of these operations to be going on at the same time; line printing, card punching, seeking a disk record, card reading, and performing arithmetic or logic operations. Internal checks functioning on these operations are *file write check* (reads disk record for comparison with drum track after disk write), *clock check* (autocorrelates timing pulses), *print check* (setup on stick printer compared with characters on drum track), and *double punch* and/or *blank column check* (if wired in IBM 323 punch).

Storage

The "305" is unique in that its main storage consists of fifty disks which revolve at 1,200 rpm. Each disk has 100 tracks, and in the standard configuration each track contains 10-100 character records. Thus each "juke box" will hold 5,000,000 characters, and in special configurations contains 10,000,000 characters. This is a serial machine. Average access time per record through the single arm is as follows:

	Time (milliseconds)	
	Disk-to-drum	Drum-to-Disk
Minimum	30	80
Average	55	105
Maximum	80	130

New configurations with two access arms increase the amount of data which can be retrieved by 100 per cent, through proper program control. It is thus apparent that large amounts of data can be stored and retrieved very rapidly, even though interrogation to any one file in the disk unit may have a low frequency and occur in a completely random fashion.

The instructions required to operate the "305" are carried in a separate magnetic drum which also acts as a buffer for input and output. One drum per "305" system contains 240, 10 digit words with a maximum access time of 10 ms. The drum, rotating at 6,000 rpm requires a full revolution for decoding, transfer from drum-to-core, and transfer from core-to-drum, for a total of 30 ms to execute a command. The core storage, in this case, is a buffer and is addressable; characters can be transferred *from* but not *to* the core buffer.

The "305" system is also available in a special configuration with the IBM 650 computer, with or without magnetic tape carriers. Prices quoted do not include these additional pieces of hardware; however, they deserve mention in this section since they enhance the computing capabilities of the "305" system considerably.

The basic rate of the arithmetic unit is 100 records per second. The following are average times to obtain instructions and operate from storage:

Operation	*Time (milliseconds)*
Addition or subtraction	30
Multiplication	20 plus 10 ms per multiplier digit
Division	20 plus 20 ms per quotient digit
Transfer	30
Branch	50 (via control panel)
Shift	30

Input methods

Punched cards are the principle input medium via the card reader, one of which can be connected per system. Card read rate is 125 per minute. Approximately 480 ms are required to complete input, but, through time sharing, 430 ms are available for other operations during this process.

An auxiliary method of input is provided in the *Punched Paper*

Tape Reader, IBM 382, which will move data at the rate of 20 characters per second. Input is also achieved through the *console typewriter.*

Output methods

Major output device is the *punched card.* Cards can be punched by the IBM 323 at a maximum rate of 100 cards per minute. Total time for output is 400 ms plus 20 ms per character, however, time sharing permits the use of the central processor about 350 ms plus 20 ms per character, during this operation. One unit per system.

The *console typewriter* can print 100 characters per line at the rate of 10 characters per second. One can be connected per system and is used primarily by the computer operator for debugging and error detection.

The *IBM 370 Printer* can print an 80 character line at the rate of 30 lines per minute. Because of its unique engineering features, on shorter lines of 20 characters it can print at the rate of 80 lines per minute. Printing is at the density of 10 characters per inch. Format is controlled by control panel wiring while the carriage tape controls feeding, spacing, and skipping with continuous forms. The "stick" printer can prepare up to eight good carbons. Frequently the IBM 402 or 407 printers are set up in conjunction with the "305" system to provide faster and more versatile output.

UNIVAC SOLID-STATE[7]

General characteristics and information

This machine is among the newest of the computers, and as its name *Solid-State* indicates, it is one of three all transistorized medium scale machines commercially available. In this same category are the RCA[8] 501 system variants which fall into medium, intermediate, and large scale categories. The medium scale version of the "501" is called the RCA 502; the intermediate version is

[7] Manufactured by Remington Rand Division, Sperry Rand Corporation. Carried in official bulletins as the *"New* UNIVAC Magnetic Amplifier Solid State Computer."

[8] The manufacturer of these systems is the Electronic Data Processing Division, Radio Corporation of America.

called the RCA 503; large scale is RCA 504. The IBM 1401 is similar in many of its design features to the "Solid-State," employing high speed input, output, and processing features at very low cost.

The "Solid-State" computer is a general purpose system equally suited to commercial or scientific-engineering applications. It is a stored program machine utilizing both on-line and off-line equipment. An important feature of the "Solid-State" is its ability to accept data from both IBM and UNIVAC punched cards, unlike some of the other commercial computers. The "Solid-State" system leases for $6,950 per month and sells for $350,000. To this must be added the cost of input-output devices such as key punches, key verifiers, and so on, as required by data processing systems.

The *one-run approach* to problems without tape units is a feature of this system. A typical one-run problem would be payroll or labor distribution where the introduction of all inputs would result in the completion of the run, uninterrupted by any need to divide applications into parts, utilize multi-runs or use numerous machines to complete the task. Not all tasks can be so easily handled, but one pass processing, even in limited areas, recognizes a complex data processing problem, heretofore not attacked through equipment design.

The "Solid-State" functions without control panels of any kind. Because there are only fifteen vacuum tubes in the entire system, the power requirement is only 15 KVA. The system weight is 6,000 pounds and the space requirement is about 400 square feet, not including peripheral equipment or personnel. No air conditioning is required.

Formal training courses are provided free of charge by the manufacturer. Representatives will spend several months with the customer to assist in training personnel and setting up a working organization. The manufacturer provides programming assistance and maintains a central exchange facility for distribution of library routines. A programming and coding staff is available on a contract basis for special problems. Computer facilities are available from the manufacturer on an hourly basis or on a fixed fee basis for a specific problem. These facilities are also available prior to the installation of a customer's machine for checking of preparatory coding and for running sample problems.

Number system

This computer utilizes a *four bit biquinary type of binary coded decimal system,* plus a *parity bit,* which is automatically checked moving to and from the drum. In its internal operations, the "Solid-State" handles all character bits simultaneously, which increases its operating speed.

Instruction system

The "Solid-State" word is ten digits plus sign and space. The 50,000 storage locations are arranged in groups of 200 words to make up 25 bands. Average access to normal bands is 1.7 milliseconds; access to fast bands is .425 milliseconds. Figure 7–8 is a

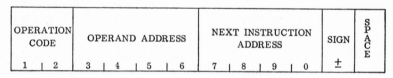

OPERATION CODE		OPERAND ADDRESS				NEXT INSTRUCTION ADDRESS				SIGN	S P A C E
1	2	3	4	5	6	7	8	9	0	±	

Fig. 7–8.

picture of a "Solid-State" word. Normally, instructions go through a four phase cycle: (1) obtain instruction, (2) prepare to operate on instruction, (3) search for the operand, and (4) execute the instruction. The previous instruction directs the machine to perform its next operation on the current instruction. This is known as a $1\frac{1}{2}$ *address system.* A cycling unit generates timing signals and, in conjunction with a timing circuit, detects any lack of drum synchronization and automatically signals this condition.

Storage

Data and instructions are stored on a magnetic drum. The "Solid-State" stores 5,000, 10 digit words on its 25 bands. Drum speed is 17,500 revolutions per minute. There are four read-write heads on fast access bands which reduces access time to a very low point. Time to extract a word from the drum under these conditions is 17 micro-seconds. Three buffers are utilized to synchronize input-output transfer with the higher speeds of the central processor. Drum buffers communicate directly with the intermediate storage buffers which are housed in input-output devices. The capacities of these buffers are in addition to the 5,000 words of the central drum. The following capacities are, thus, added to the system:

	Characters
Print buffer	130
High speed reader buffer	200
Read-Punch buffer	200
	530

Data transferred to the input-output buffer areas may be punched or printed independent of the central computer's operation. As a result, time sharing is one of the important features of this system. More complex configurations of this computer are offered in conjunction with UNIVAC magnetic tapes (UNISERVOS). Thus, external memory will be available to complement internal storage. The following are times for the basic arithmetic and logical operations:

Operation	*Time (milliseconds)*
Addition or subtraction	.085
Multiplication	.255 to 1.79
Division	.425 to 1.96
Branch (Compare)	.051
Transfer	.068

Input methods

Two basic input methods are currently available. The first is via *punched cards* into the *High Speed Reader*. This machine operates on input at 950 cards per minute, accepting 80 or 90 column cards. This reader has a selector device that allows the feed of cards from any one of three hoppers into the card reader, each hopper containing about 1,000 cards. Double reading of input data provides a check on input validity. Cards are selected for reading from stackers, and are stacked in hoppers under program control; output hoppers have a 1,200 card capacity, each. Thus, the reader has actually more than the normal input function; in addition, it can collate data in the system and also segregate input data. The cycle for this machine is 133 ms, however, time sharing makes available all but .51 ms, because of buffering.

The second method of input is through the *Read-Punch Unit.* Operating at a maximum rate of 150 cards per minute, it can function either independently or in conjunction with the High Speed Reader. Like the former device, the Read-Punch Unit has the function of entering and/or collating data into the system. It has the output function of punching cards as a result of processing. It has the ability to read a card and punch computed results into the same card. It can segregate output cards and perform the same audit as is done in the High Speed Reader. Time sharing ties up the central processor only 6.82 ms per operation, which leaves ample time for audit and checking, stacker selection, computing, simultaneous operation with High Speed Reader, sensing, and punching.

Output methods

The most important output method is the *High Speed Printer,* which operates at the rate of 600 lines per minute. Control is by means of stored program. There are 130 printing positions possible, per line, each position being capable of printing 26 alpha, 10 numeric and 15 special characters. Characters are spaced 10 to the inch; line spacing is 6 to the inch with single, double, and triple spacing optional to the programmer. Report format, zero suppression, and so on are also under program control. Paper is 4 to 21 inches wide. An original and five carbons are possible at these speeds.

SUMMARY AND CONCLUSIONS

There are a large number of additional computer systems which have not been mentioned. IBM has its well-known, medium scale 650, its new, intermediate scale, solid state 7070, and its large scale 705 (I, II and III), 709 and 7090. Remington Rand has its Series

60 and 120 small scale equipment as well as the File Computer, UNIVAC Scientific (1103, 1103A) and UNIVAC II. National Cash Register and other companies offer equipment very worthy of consideration. Each of these systems is a major contribution to the science of data processing; each possesses individual, significant characteristics which may be put to the advantage of a potential user. A technically oriented equipment evaluation would maximize the likelihood that all equipment which qualifies for the task would receive objective and adequate consideration.

The task of the systems engineer must begin to emerge in this new dimension. Who is to select the equipment complement best suited to the data processing tasks? Certainly, this can't be attempted until the data processing tasks are not only known, but organized into a data processing system. The accent here is on the use of systems analysis to design business systems compatible with each other, with clear recognition of the organization's goals.

Equipment evaluation must be done by experts. Experts may be systems engineers or they may be specialists in data processing equipment. A knowledge of machine programming is required to evaluate effectively. A knowledge of hardware is also desirable in this work. Most of all, a knowledge of systems goals must be used as the overriding criterion in determining how the attributes of each computer system can be put to best use in the company's data processing. Where the computer becomes the data processing device, the systems analyst is an essential ingredient. Efficient systems design may make the difference between a loss, break-even, or profitable system operation.

It must also be obvious that data processing is a restrictive device in that it does not permit a wide variation from rules or established patterns. Again, the role of the systems analyst becomes critical, for it is he who must define the system boundaries and then the systems, in complete detail. The job of describing system elements, system requirements, and system input-output can only fall to specialists who have the training and ability to conduct methodical analysis in a field which resists discipline and improvement.

8

Constructing
the system costs

WHAT ARE SAVINGS?

Savings is a word about which there is little semantic difficulty in everyday life. In the business world, its definition of *economical* or *not wasteful* falls far short of the need. Typically, "savings" will be claimed when a cost advantage of any kind exists, but far from being economical, such an achievement might require the expenditure of many dollars, before the economy can be realized. *Not wasteful* is an equally inadequate definition: Looking at the burn-off of a typical oil refinery which may light up the sky for miles around it, one can only conclude that it must be less expensive to waste this potentially useful commodity than to reprocess it in some marginal use.

Cost advantages equal savings. Is this true?

There are undoubtedly many, many circumstances when it is, but in the design of systems, it can frequently be untrue. First, we must determine what a cost advantage is. One definition might be *something which ultimately reduces the expenditure of funds.* There are basically four categories of expenditure: labor, material, services, and equipment or facilities. Thus, we are saying in effect that a true savings is one which will either reduce or eliminate the current costs which are being incurred in one of these four categories. Now let us test this hypothesis.

An accounts payable system is designed which will require the addition of new equipment. No personnel will be released; some forms will be scrapped; slightly larger facilities will be required. What are the advantages?

(1) Savings in time to post each account payable

(2) Reduction of errors in posting

(3) Faster reporting of accounts payable balances

(4) Analysis of accounts payable data for the benefit of Accounting and Purchasing

(5) System capability to absorb increased work load of 33 per cent

Would you approve the installation of this system on the face of these facts alone? If the new equipment and forms were budgeted at $5,000 per year, would you then accept the proposal? What if the additional costs were $20,000 per year?

This is a typical *no-relief* situation. That is, there are no real off-setting dollars to balance against the costs to be incurred by establishing a more desirable accounts payable operation. There is some possibility that item 5 might provide ultimate dollar benefits:

(1) If new activities that would require the hiring of personnel are transferred to the accounts payable group, thus eliminating the need to hire; or,

(2) If existing activities can be merged into the accounts payable group, eliminating marginal personnel, equipment or facilities

Against this no-relief situation, must be balanced the desires of Management, who as systems purchasers have their own set of rules and values. If this appears to be the only way to eliminate human error, Management might be moved to act. Likewise, if Management anticipates increasing growth, the capability represented by a man-machine system might make this an attractive proposition. Some companies might accept the increased costs of such an improved system, merely because they feel it is in their best interest to employ the most modern accounting methods which are available.

A printing establishment was approached by a consultant who studied his potential client's operation for a week, and devised this four point program:

Area to be studied	*Reason for study*
1. Redesign of incoming order data processing system.	1. Reduction in order processing time will provide a competitive advantage by enabling your firm to fill orders sooner.

2. Re-establishment of composing room and print room standards.

2. Better standards will enable Production Control to balance work flow between composing and print, which will decrease the time some orders will spend in-process. Better standards will have a tendency to increase production.

3. Re-establishment of pricing policies based upon better standards.

3. Better standards will provide a more accurate relationship between costs and selling price; more accurate cost data will give more flexibility in bidding; more accurate cost data will give the opportunity to improve competitive position in jobs where a higher number of bids are rejected.

4. Re-allocation of salesmen's time.

4. Statistical analysis will provide more data on how to use salesmen effectively.

None of the reasons given for working on the client's problems can be termed savings. A better word might be benefits. But the payoff in each case is not clearly related to dollars. If we assume that by processing orders in some unique way, two days in-house time can be saved, does this really mean the client will do more business? And if it is true, how can the dollar return to the client be identified?

Although better standards may have a tendency to pace operators, how can the increased rate be measured in a printing establishment that operates like a job shop? The mix of orders could be deceptive and cause the flow of work to move faster or slower. Balancing production is desirable, but, again, if we are going to accept or reject the consultant's proposal on the basis of dollars saved or increased earnings, we must be able to measure a very tricky, elusive value since the over-all status of each of our criteria may be affected by a number of factors simultaneously, over a long period of time. The inability of the existing accounting system to pick up the requisite detail could alone frustrate this proposal.

Item 3 is potentially an excellent project. If this portion of the presentation was backed up by actual data on completed jobs and rejected jobs, this Management might have been very enthused over the possibilities. Here it would have been important to state exactly what new tools would be used in refining the existing system —and perhaps some indication of the way in which the new system would operate and the actual dollars it might be expected to return. It is no fallacy to say that, in the consulting business, the problem must be "half-solved" before one begins to work. One might question whether this consultant could prepare for such a project and the other projects he has suggested in only a week.

The salesmen project, as stated, is very weak. Although it is possible to analyze numbers of calls and numbers of sales in various ways, the payoff to Management is not very clear. If ten calls per day provides three sales, and Management wishes to increase sales, might it not be a lot simpler just to have more salespeople? The alternative of telling a salesman to stop calling back after the second, third, or fourth call, is not a very powerful incentive in terms of the dollars Management must expend on consultant's fee.

As long as profit is the Management motive, savings or benefits will almost invariably have to be tied to the reduction or elimination of existing costs. There are a number of exceptions where Management must create a new capability, and in this case the motive may be to achieve a specific level at a minimum cost. Here, it may be necessary to make a trade-off and have slightly less capability because of the reduced out of pocket expenditures. If maximum capability is required, cost may be no factor. In many instances, time will be substituted for cost in this equation. For instance, DEW (Distant Early Warning) line radar capabilities were justified on the basis of time saved in data transmission rather than in terms of cost. Many of our current military projects represent such capabilities which have been deemed essential under current international conditions.

For the systems analyst, the systems purchaser is a primary factor to consider. Although it may be necessary ultimately to change or alter the purchaser's original view of the system (if this is possible), the objectives which are initially established will have a great bearing on the ability to demonstrate savings or benefits. The ability to demonstrate actual dollar savings is the most devastating test of a system which has been avowedly designed with this as the sole criterion.

Intangible savings, however, are equally important. They are called intangible not because they do not exist, but because it is difficult to ascribe a dollar value to the extent of the savings. How does one put a price on faster reporting? Or how would you evaluate the future expandability of a system? Of course, it is possible to place values after each of these statements and attempt to justify their tangibility. Sometimes, however, there is a high cost attached to this type of activity. Finally, Management is usually broad-minded enough to recognize the futility of trying to exhume the last dollar of accuracy in a proposal, and will look at the easily computed savings, if such exist. The proposal to Management cannot rely on these intangible factors, but they should and must be included.

ONE-TIME VERSUS RECURRING COSTS

Proposals of cost and savings require a statement of both one-time and recurring costs (see Table 8–1). One-time costs are those

TABLE 8–1

ELECTRONIC DATA PROCESSING SYSTEM
COMPARISON OF ONE-TIME AND RECURRING COSTS

	SYSTEM I		SYSTEM II*	
One-Time Costs	*Rental*	*Purchase*	*Rental*	*Purchase*
Prepare facilities	$ 13,000	$ 13,000	$ 15,600	$ 15,600
Systems studies	12,000	12,000	12,000	12,000
System conversion	8,600	8,600	8,600	8,600
Parallel operation	11,000	11,000	10,800	10,800
Miscellaneous	4,000	4,000	2,000	2,000
Total one-time costs	$ 48,600	$ 48,600	$ 49,000	$ 49,000
Recurring costs	*Rental*	*Purchase***	*Rental*	*Purchase***
Equipment:				
Electronic System	$101,100	$127,000	$ 51,800	$ 34,900
Tabulating System	80,000	80,000	72,000	72,000
Maintenance	(included)	63,000	(included)	68,300
Personnel:				
Operations	30,100	30,100	28,300	28,300
Applications	26,400	26,400	26,400	26,400
Systems Analysts	24,500	24,500	24,500	24,500
Supplies	20,000	20,000	20,000	20,000
Total recurring costs	$282,100	$371,000	$223,000	$274,400
Total annual five year costs	$330,700	$419,600	$272,000	$323,400

* Equipment cost prorated over that part of the first shift actually utilized (about 40%). System I is at 80% of first shift utilization.
** Purchase price prorated over five years.

for the establishment of the new system. Recurring costs are those which will be sustained to operate the system after it has been established. In the establishment of a proposed electronic data processing facility, the costs in Table 8–1 were evaluated for two computer systems which had approximately the same data processing capability. It is proper to prorate equipment purchase costs over a five year period if this is what Internal Revenue will permit. However, one might challenge the logic of only admitting 40 per cent of the costs of System II, which makes it appear as if this is the cheaper of the two systems.

There is no yardstick to say how much the one-time costs of a system may be, since the systems requirements of each problem will determine how long the investigation and hypothesis must be. The Work Assignment form (Figure 5–1), attempts to correlate as much of this type of data as possible. Clearly, however, the one-time costs are relatively unimportant, if there are real savings to be obtained. Eventually, the amortization (spreading of costs over some period of time) of costs will end, but the systems savings will continue, unless subsequent decisions alter the systems design.

It is important to include all relevant costs. Sometimes identical costs may be eliminated to concentrate attention on differences. Generally, this is not desirable because this has the effect of understating the present and proposed systems. Frequently, overhead is not included in such computations because of the attitude that fixed costs go on, despite systems design of one type or another. This may be true, but there are circumstances when it is not. One computer system might, for instance require no air conditioning; another might require humidity and temperature control. Sometimes, the decision to take on additional overhead will affect variable costs. If System *A* requires 40 people and System *B* requires 13, there are additional costs to be borne by System *A* to pay for the indirect costs of personnel. This was precisely the case in a timekeeping system which promised Management different levels of accuracy in direct labor reporting. It was the indirect costs of personnel that forced the selection of System *B*.

There is sometimes a tendency to misstate recurring costs, either through a desire to sell a good idea or because the system problem cannot be precisely appraised. In either case, Management is seldom sold on either side of a marginal cost or savings argument. If the margins aren't convincing, Management will tend to look more closely at the benefits and "intangibles." Precise appraisal of the load the system must carry and the allowance of adequate safety margins may make the picture less enticing, but they invariably leave the systems designer in a less vulnerable position.

DISPLACEABLE AND NON-DISPLACEABLE COSTS

If possible, the costs of the analysis should be related to the results achievable. For instance, it might actually require a minimum time of two weeks to set up a system of accounts receivable for an insurance agency. If the costs of this system design and installation are set at $4,750, it is advisable to determine immediately whether or not there are $4,750 of offsetting costs to make the project self-liquidating for the systems purchaser. Offsetting costs are either non-displaceable (they remain after the new system is in and operating) or displaceable (they are removed with the full implementation of the new system). In the example cited above, the time of 1.25 clerks was involved in accounts receivable; this was equal to $500. per month on this company's pay scale. The project was temporarily put aside because the dollars displaced were not sufficient to liquidate the cost, in a reasonable time period. Table 8–2 compares the two systems:

TABLE 8–2

Cost to design new system		$4750.00
Monthly cost to operate present system:		
Labor	$500.00	
Facilities	100.00	
Supplies	40.00	
	$640.00	
Monthly Cost to operate new system:		
Labor	$200.00	
Facilities	100.00	
Supplies	60.00	
Service Costs	60.00	
	$420.00	
Available to amortize one-time cost		$ 220.00
Months to pay off investment		21.6

This example has very complex counterparts. For example, in the proposed introduction of an electronic data processing system, the first step would be to create an accurate breakdown of existing costs. Personnel would be analyzed by job classification. Equipment would be listed in complete detail with a system of references to tie personnel to equipment (it is essential to know which clerks operate the flex-o-writer, electric typewriter, comptometer, and so on. From lists of this type, certain personnel and equipment would be eliminated (displaced) because new equipment and/or personnel would be added back. The figures which describe the net existing systems costs are the non-displaceable costs; that is, they cannot be eliminated and will be combined with certain additional costs. The non-displaceable costs plus the added cost figures are termed the new systems costs.

Table 8–4 shows a summary of costs in the displaceable and non-displaceable categories. The annualized non-displaceable costs are now ready to be added to the annualized one-time and recurring costs. The summary in Table 8–3 has been drawn from data in Tables 8–1 and 8–4. Table 8–4 is the chart, if the full costs of System

TABLE 8–3

| | SYSTEM I | | SYSTEM II | |
	Rental	*Purchase*	*Rental*	*Purchase*
Total annual five-year costs	$ 330,700	$ 419,600	$ 272,000	$ 323,400
Total non-displaceable costs	$ 969,128	$ 969,128	$ 969,128	$ 969,128
New system costs	$1,299,828	$1,388,728	$1,241,128	$1,292,528
Old system costs per year	$1,512,288	$1,512,288	$1,512,288	$1,512,288
New system savings per year	$ 212,460	$ 123,560	$ 271,160	$ 219,760

II are charged against the 40 per cent of utilization on which previous figures have been prorated.

TABLE 8–4

ELECTRONIC DATA PROCESSING SYSTEM
SCHEDULE OF DISPLACEABLE AND
NON-DISPLACEABLE COSTS ON AN ANNUAL BASIS

PRESENT SYSTEM COSTS:
Production Control

Personnel	(85)	$595,000
Equipment	(8)	100
Space	(3500)	350

Tabulating

Personnel	(40)	$280,000
Equipment	(21)	201,500
Space	(2000)	200

TABLE 8–4 (*Continued*)

PRESENT SYSTEM COSTS:

Accounting

Personnel	(28)	$196,000	
Equipment	(14)	800	
Space	(2000)	200	

Engineering

Personnel	(14)	$126,000	
Equipment	(1)	18	
Space	(1200)	120	
Other Personnel	(16)	$112,000	

TOTAL PRESENT SYSTEM COSTS		$1,512,288

POSITIONS ELIMINATED:

Production Control	(24)	$168,000	
Tabulating	(2)	14,000	
Accounting	(4)	28,000	
Engineering	(4)	36,000	
TOTAL POSITIONS ELIMINATED	(34)	$246,000	

EQUIPMENT ELIMINATED:

Production Control	(4)	$ 50	
Tabulating	(14)	184,340	
Accounting	(10)	580	
TOTAL EQUIPMENT ELIMINATED	(28)	$184,970	

SPACE REDUCTION:

Production Control	(1000)	$ 100	
Accounting	(500)	50	
Engineering	(400)	40	
TOTAL SPACE REDUCTION	(1900)	$ 190	
OTHER PERSONNEL ELIMINATED	(16)	$112,000	

TOTAL DISPLACEABLE COSTS	$ 543,160
TOTAL NON-DISPLACEABLE COSTS	$ 969,128

TABLE 8–5

	SYSTEM I		SYSTEM II	
	Rental	*Purchase*	*Rental*	*Purchase*
Total annual five-year costs	$ 330,700	$ 419,600	$ 606,500	$ 735,000
Total non-displace- able costs	$ 969,128	$ 969,128	$ 969,128	$ 969,128
New system costs per year	$1,299,828	$1,388,728	$1,575,628	$1,704,128
Old system costs per year	$1,512,288	$1,512,288	$1,512,288	$1,512,288
New system savings per year	$ 212,460	$ 123,560	$*(63,340)	$*(191,840)

* Figures in parentheses are additional costs.

Now System II costs no longer look as attractive as before, at least for the first five years. However, a decision to order System I could be shortsighted. System I is at 80 per cent of utilization, which means any additional heavy data processing burdens will push into a second shift. Second shift rentals are charged at 40 per cent of the first shift rates, for computer equipment time actually utilized. This, of course, tends to reduce the average hourly cost of equipment. Against these savings, the inconvenience of second shift operation must be weighed. If equipment is to be purchased, the second shift operation merely means that amortization will be spread over that many more hours of use, so actual operating costs will not be reduced until the system is paid out.

The amount of additional data processing hours to be connected will have an important bearing on whether the choice will be System I or System II. There are some time considerations, as well: It may be desirable to select System I on a short term basis, and reprogram (a semi-automatic operation) for System II at a later date. Thus, another variable of time of conversion has been injected, and should be evaluated for consideration. If conversion will take two years, System I savings will be enjoyed for some period before second shift operation is required. At a certain point, second shift operation may be undesirable, and then System II installation can be reconsidered.

Growth or decline of the existing system could be an important factor, as well. If the costs of the present system expand in direct proportion to the number of transactions, file size, or some other factor, it may be appropriate to inject anticipated growth into the dollar figures, to look ahead to problems which are not currently pressing. This is desirable when it can be done with some accuracy. Long term committments require this accuracy, since Management may wish to make a decision in favor of the long range policy, which extends the payoff into the future. Examples of such projections are illustrated in Tables 8–6 and 8–7 for an expanding electronic data processing center which will need to provide different levels of service over a three year period.

Side benefits may be added to the dollar pool: For instance, there may be, as a result of a new system, generally increased labor utilization. This might be expressed through the decrease in waiting time at tool cribs or reduced waiting time for new job assignment. Perhaps a system will carry along with it the benefit of reduced inven-

TABLE 8-6
ELECTRONIC DATA PROCESSING SYSTEM
PROJECTION OF HOURS, EQUIPMENT COMPLEMENT AND DOLLARS

Equipment Complement	Physical Factors	1/59-6/59	7/59-12/59	1/60-6/60	7/60-12/60	1/61-6/61	7/61-12/61	1/62-6/62	7/62-12/62
026	Total Hours	1,534	2,396	5,335	5,640	5,738	5,780	5,947	6,133
	No. of Machines	2	3	5	5	6	6	6	6
	Total Dollars	780	1,170	1,950	1,950	2,340	2,340	2,340	2,340
056	Total Hours	879	1,649	1,696	1,832	1,901	1,940	2,057	2,244
	No. of Machines	1	1	2	2	2	2	2	2
	Total Dollars	270	270	560	560	560	560	560	560
077	Total Hours	30	92	92	93	94	94	96	101
	No. of Machines	1	1	1	1	1	1	1	1
	Total Dollars	690	690	690	690	690	690	690	690
082	Total Hours	44	131	133	140	144	151	237	245
	No. of Machines	1	1	1	1	1	1	1	1
	Total Dollars	330	330	330	330	330	330	330	330
407	Total Hours	106	238	454	477	485	502	636	649
	No. of Machines	1	1	1	1	1	1	1	1
	Total Dollars	4,965	4,965	4,965	4,965	4,965	4,965	4,965	4,965
519	Total Hours	8	67	67	67	67	67	67	67
	No. of Machines	1	1	1	1	1	1	1	1
	Total Dollars	828	828	828	828	828	828	828	828
552	Total Hours	0	102	102	102	102	102	102	102
	No. of Machines	1	1	1	1	1	1	1	1
	Total Dollars	450	450	450	450	450	450	450	450
6501	Total Hours	176	270	632	671	683	712	931	954
	No. of Machines	1	1	1	1	1	1	1	1
	Total Dollars	71,748	71,748	71,748	71,748	71,748	71,748	71,748	71,748
Other	No. of Machines	7	7	7	7	7	7	7	7
	Total Dollars	1,515	1,515	1,515	1,515	1,515	1,515	1,515	1,515
Machine Total	No. of Machines	23	24	27	28	29	29	29	29
	Total Dollars	$81,576	$81,966	$83,016	$83,016	$83,406	$83,406	$83,406	$83,406
Facilities	Required Sq. Ft.	2,414	2,469	2,524	2,579	2,634	2,634	2,634	2,634
	Total Dollars	$ 1,207	$ 1,235	$ 1,262	$ 1,280	$ 1,317	$ 1,317	$ 1,317	$ 1,317
Total Costs:		$82,783	$84,201	$84,278	$84,306	$84,723	$84,723	$84,723	$84,723

1 IBM 650 Tape System with on-line 407 Printer. One shift operation.

TABLE 8-7

Electronic Data Processing System
Projection of Hours, Labor Complement and Dollars

Labor Classification	Physical Factors	1/59-6/59	7/59-12/59	1/60-6/60	7/60-12/60	1/61-6/61	7/61-12/61	1/62-6/62	7/62-12/62
Sr. Computer Operator	Total Hours	176	270	632	671	683	712	931	954
	No. of Personnel	1	1	1	1	1	1	1	1
	Total Dollars	3,328	3,328	3,328	3,328	3,328	3,328	3,328	3,328
Computer Operator	Total Hours	106	341	557	580	587	604	738	752
	No. of Personnel	0	0	1	1	1	1	1	1
	Total Dollars	0	0	2,782	2,782	2,782	2,782	2,782	2,782
Tabulating Operator	Total Hours	82	290	292	301	305	313	401	414
	No. of Personnel	0	0	0	0	0	0	0	0
	Total Dollars	0	0	0	0	0	0	0	0
Keypunch Operator	Total Hours	2,414	4,046	7,032	7,473	7,639	7,721	8,005	8,378
	No. of Personnel	3	4	7	7	8	8	8	8
	Total Dollars	5,694	7,592	13,286	13,286	15,184	15,184	15,184	15,184
Sr. Computer Analyst	Total Hours	3,654	5,655	1,044	1,218	1,131	1,044	1,305	522
	No. of Personnel	3	6	2	2	2	2	2	2
	Total Dollars	13,884	27,768	9,256	9,256	9,256	9,256	9,256	9,256
Computer Analyst	Total Hours	8,568	13,260	2,448	2,856	2,652	2,448	3,060	1,224
	No. of Personnel	9	13	1	2	2	2	2	1
	Total Dollars	34,515	49,855	3,835	7,670	7,670	7,670	7,670	3,835
Sr. Programmer	Total Hours	3,544	5,486	1,012	1,181	1,097	1,012	1,266	506
	No. of Personnel	4	5	1	1	1	1	1	1
	Total Dollars	13,312	16,640	3,328	3,328	3,328	3,328	3,328	3,328
Programmer	Total Hours	6,090	9,425	1,740	2,039	1,885	1,740	2,175	870
	No. of Personnel	6	10	2	2	2	2	2	1
	Total Dollars	14,820	24,700	4,940	4,940	4,940	4,940	4,940	2,470
Supervision and Clerical	Total Hours	5,000	5,000	5,000	5,000	5,000	5,000	5,000	5,000
	No. of Personnel	5	5	5	5	5	5	5	5
	Total Dollars	14,859	14,859	14,859	14,859	14,859	14,859	14,859	14,859
Labor Total	No. of Personnel	31	44	14	20	21	21	21	19
	Total Dollars	$100,412	$144,742	$54,821	$58,656	$60,554	$60,554	$60,554	$50,414
Facilities	Required Sq. Ft.	2,232	2,622	1,368	1,440	1,512	1,512	1,512	1,368
	Total Dollars	$ 1,116	$ 1,311	$ 684	$ 720	$ 756	$ 756	$ 756	$ 684
Total Costs:		$101,528	$146,153	$55,505	$59,476	$61,310	$61,310	$61,310	$51,098

tory; in this instance, it is perfectly correct to add to the projected annual savings the dollars required to carry that portion of the inventory that will be eliminated.

THE PRESENTATION OF SYSTEM COST DATA

The fundamental rule is simplicity. Keep in mind the audience level and gear the facts accordingly. The audience at best can only take away one or two new ideas—so organize the presentation to be certain the most important points get across. One useful guide is to (1) tell them what you're going to tell them; (2) tell them; and then (3) tell them what you've told them. Repetition is generally a good idea to assist listeners in absorbing new ideas. Length of presentations should be limited; almost any story can be told in an hour. If the time exceeds an hour, the audience's attention will begin to fall off rapidly. A question period after the presentation is generally useful because it brings the audience actively into the problem and may revive flagging interest. Color is a valuable aid in maintaining attention.

Many a good system has failed in its presentation simply because of lack of organization. A general approach in preparing presentations is to think in terms of outlines. If the story of the systems study will be presented on flip charts, the following outline suggests how to keep the package logical:

Chart   I: The Content of the Presentation
               A. Statement of the Problem
               B. Alternate Solutions to the Problem
               C. Recommended Solution to the Problem
               D. Benefits to Be Derived

Chart   II: Problem Statement
               A. Background Conditions and Method of Study
               B. The Existing System Operation
               C. Problems of the Existing System
               D. Areas Requiring Modification

Chart   III: Alternate Problem Solution *A*
               A. New System *A*
                  (1) Advantages and Disadvantages
                  (2) Dollars Saved

Chart IV: Alternate Problem Solution *B*
                A. New System *B*
                   (1) Advantages and Disadvantages
                   (2) Dollars Saved

Chart V: Selection of the Recommended System

Chart VI: Benefits of the Selected System

Note that Chart I tells the full scope of the presentation. Point *I.A* is expanded in Chart II; point *I.B* is expanded in Charts III and IV; point *I.C* is expanded in Chart V; and point *I.D,* which summarizes the presentation, is enlarged in Chart VI. Obviously, the design of the presentation must be dictated by the problem, and this sequence merely illustrates the principle of conciseness combined with a logical approach. The spoken words which accompany the display of each chart are, of course, the most important factor in a successful presentation. Careful organization of significant points in outline form will help to keep the idea which is being developed clearly before the audience. It is valuable to provide the audience with a take-away summary of the presentation which can be handed out before the question period begins. If the audience is given paper and pencils to make notes of questions that occur to them as the presentation is made, interruptions can be avoided.

Since selling the idea can be a significant factor in the success of a systems program, time spent to prepare the presentation is as important as any other phase of the program. A rule of thumb is a man-hour for every man-day; for instance, a task of ten man-days should require about ten man-hours for organization.

9

Operations research
in business

The purpose of this chapter is to provide a basic understanding of
the practical role of operations research in business. Because operations research is a relatively new field, a brief history of its special
contribution is given, followed by some examples of applications.
Its role in the study of business systems is discussed, and the place it
occupies in the search for a general systems theory is cited.

BRIEF HISTORY

Early in World War II, new devices were introduced which
created vast tactical and strategic problems for England. Radar was
among these. It had a marked effect on bombing strategy. Sonic
devices, developed around this same time, made it necessary to re-
appraise submarine warfare techniques and a host of associated
defensive and offensive tactics. The global nature of the war created
complex logistics (supply) problems, the equal of which had never
been undertaken.

England formed teams of men whose experience was in the broad
field of the physical sciences and mathematics. These men were told
to attack and solve these problems of broad scope. In their work,
they were to use the tools of the disciplines in which they were
trained, and were to bring them to bear on the new problems with
which they were confronted. It was natural that the scientific
method would be the operating framework for their work. The in-
sistence on objectivity, measurement of the observable phenomena,
and the tests of logic seemed to provide the only hope of coping
with problems for which no tools existed. History has proved the
wisdom of this step, and an extensive record is available to show how

operations analysis, or operations research, became a force in military affairs.

The United States did notable work in this field during World War II, and it is quite natural that it would carry over into civilian life in the normal course of events. Thus, since 1946, there has been an increasing quantity of material available on this subject. Many of the technically oriented professions, especially in recent years, have found ways to make use of operations research. Some industries have not as yet seen the ways in which it can be put to use. However, every month provides new literature on the applications of operations research, much of which can be located through the references at the end of this book. A large part of the operations research literature deals with the application of mathematical and statistical techniques to a wide range of problems. In much of this work, the scientific method is obvious. When these techniques are combined in the solution of real problems, the results may be many times more reliable or precise than other less disciplined methods.

Dr. Philip Morse has expressed[1] the function of operations research and its methodology:

> In the physical sciences, one starts studying a phenomenon by *observing* some part of its manifold behavior. Next one tries to form a quantitative hypothesis, a *mathematical model* of the aspect observed, that will duplicate some of its behavior. If one has been clever, or lucky, in his choice of model, its mathematical framework will go beyond the observations, will predict what will happen in other circumstances. Next comes the phase of *controlled experiment*. One compares the predictions of the mathematical model with what actually occurs; if the choice of model has been good, the experiments make possible the improvement and strengthening of the model. After continued alternation of model improvement and further experiment, the mathematical model becomes a theory, which means the beginning of *understanding* of the phenomenon. This implies an ability to *control* the phenomenon. If the phenomenon as a whole is too complex to work out quantitative relations at the beginning, one isolates pieces of the phenomenon, develops a number of detailed models, then proceeds to build more and more general theories that include the pieces as special cases.

Operations research makes its most important contribution in the application of mathematics and statistics to business. Mathematical models used by operations researchers are facsimiles or representations of real-life problems expressed in the form of equations. In effect, operations research employs mathematics to make

[1] "Statistics and Operations Research," *Operations Research*, Vol. 4, page 3 (1956).

an abstraction of a real-life problem, utilizing a series of mathematical expressions as the vehicle for stating and solving the problem. The value of the mathematical model is that it provides an easily changed representation of a real-life situation. By inserting real values into a mathematical model and solving and equation, it is possible to test the operational characteristics of a system. As a testing device, the mathematical model can express the most complex processes in an abbreviated form. The danger is, of course, that the model may easily become too abstract, unreal, and hence incorrect. To be useful, the mathematical model must represent the real world. Through the techniques of operations research, it is possible to examine the validity of basic premises under which the system may be organized prior to any physical commitment of labor, material, or capital. The areas of operations research can be summarized under the headings of *probability theory, symbolic logic, decision theory, queuing theory, linear and dynamic programming, game theory, information theory,* and *Monte Carlo techniques.*

TECHNIQUES OF OPERATIONS RESEARCH

Some of the mathematical-statistical tools of the operations research specialist, are described here. This list is far from complete, but it does indicate the wide scope of specific problem solving tools which are available.

Descriptive statistics

This is a technique of summarization and may be in chart or graphic form. Such summaries express relationships between factors, and sometimes will show mean values and measures of variability such as standard deviation or percentiles. These measures present data in different visual modes, some of which may be more revealing than others. Through analysis of data presented in this way, problem identification begins, and the researcher is able to plan his next step.

Statistical sampling and inference

This technique guides the researcher in data collection. There is always a cost associated with data collection; sometimes it is very high. This technique prescribes the sample size required to be able to infer what the total population is like. Obviously, the larger the sample, the better; to reduce the error of an estimate about 30 per cent requires doubling the sample size. Eventually there is a trade-off between cost of data collection and required accuracy for the intended purpose. Statistical inference can tell whether or not an apparent relationship is truly significant, or the result of chance.

Correlation and regression analysis

Where statistical inference tells whether or not a relationship exists, correlation and regression analysis tell something of the extent of the relationship. A relationship or correlation may exist between two important factors; but, if the correlation is low, there may be no useful purpose that this relationship can serve. Where correlation gives the degree of relationship, regression is a statement of the equation that exists between the variables. Regression analysis is a form of curve-fitting with the added benefit that it tells something about how good the fit is. Another advantage over ordinary curve-fitting is that a many-variabled curve can be fitted in one computation, by performing a multiple regression.

Multiple regression would be useful in the study of the factors that determine which of three factories should produce a new product. There are a number of factors that may affect this: time for the shipment of product to market, volume of the individual factory, level of employment, cost of shipments, or any other of a number of measurable parameters. If a number of these variables are chosen as the most likely to influence the distance between factory and distributor or consumer, then a multiple regression analysis can be made of the sampled data. The result will be an equation which expresses the relationship between the factors. An examination of the equation will show that some of the variables have a great deal of influence on the decision of which factory should service each distributor, while others contribute relatively little. Thus, the important factors and the degree of their importance can be determined.

Multiple regression was seldom used as a business tool until recently. This is partly due to its complexity and partly to the time required if the problem is a large one with many variables. Computers have been very useful in solving problems of this type. Large scale equipment can handle a multiple regression of almost any dimension. Standard computer programs are available from equipment manufacturers to implement this technique. The availability of computer time, proper skills, and appropriate data would make it possible to add this type of analysis to the techniques of any organization.

Linear programming

There are many new applications of this technique, and many unexploited but obvious possibilities exist. Optimum locations for service facilities can be calculated by introducing this technique of mathematics. Analysis of optimum routes for deliveries or collections and the associated problems of the location of warehouse and factory sites are amenable to solution with this technique. Analysis of optimum shipping routes would also be susceptible to this type of analysis.

The large amount of data, number of computational processes, and sheer bulk of the problem make it necessary to think of a computer when there is a linear programming analysis to do. The application of linear programming results in more comprehensive understanding of the functional relationships of a complex system.

Factor analysis

The aim of this technique is to find underlying factors which affect the criteria but which may not be well defined before the study. An illustration of this would be a study of the effectiveness of different departments of an organization and the factors which affect them. Here, as in multiple regression, some decision would be made as to those variables which are considered most important. Sampled information concerning each of these variables would be obtained and the factor analysis performed. Initial variables chosen for the assessment problem might be organization assignments, average age of employee, years of experience (academic and professional), measures of proficiency, or any one of a number. The resulting factor analysis might lead to concepts such as a *proficiency factor.* This technique is useful in making broad studies. As with some of the previous techniques, factor analysis usually requires a computer to perform the calculations.

Control system analysis

This technique is very powerful when applied to physical systems. Its usefulness in business planning would be as a conceptual device to aid in developing an adequate model of the system.

The basic characteristic of a control system is the feedback loop. This concept has demonstrated its usefulness in analyzing the operations of an "automatic" warehouse. The growth and decay of a business may also be expressed conceptually as depending on feedbacks from overloaded communication channels, higher cost of services, and so on; however, if the specific relationships are not known, there can be no control system analysis in the classic sense. The availability of a computer to handle the manipulation of data would be an asset with this technique also.

Simulation

This is the technique which appears to have great promise for research.[2] Uses of simulation have grown rapidly in recent years largely because of the availability of electronic computers. Early simulation studies attacked problems such as inventory systems, production scheduling systems, waiting line problems, and so on. Recently, this technique has been used for the simulation of an entire logistics system for the Strategic Air Command. It appears entirely possible that a business can also be simulated in a manner which will lead to a new understanding of the functional relationships involved. The important characteristics of the simulation technique are as follows:

(1) Any number of variables can be handled. The only limitation is the computer's ability to handle the data.

(2) The data to be processed can be empirically derived and does not have to be smoothed or changed into equation form.

[2] See A. B. Fleet and Company, Chapter 17.

(3) The relationship between variables can be complex, i.e., linear restrictions do not have to be maintained.

(4) There is wide flexibility in the choice of procedure; empirical data can be used as input and the existing relationships would be output. However, *proposed* relationships can also be used as input and the forcasted data will be the output.

(5) The essential nature of simulation is that the model should vary in time, so that the process is a step-by-step reenactment of the physical or qualitative system.

In addition to these technical characteristics, there are some additional general advantages which should be noted. Because of the large amount of detail which can be built into a problem, simulation gives results which are useful for the particular system under study. Simulation is, thus, less valuable in discovering general laws, and would, therefore, be used to gain insight to specific systems. Simulation is easily understood and relatively easy to implement. The background of individuals performing this activity must be broad, but no graduate level mathematics are required.

Simulation is not practical without a computer, and is completely dependent upon the ultra high speed of electronic data processing. Thus, a significant characteristic of simulation lies in the computer's ability to digest many years of dynamic operation which are expressed by the model and compress them into a few minutes of actual time. This makes possible the study of a variety of alternative paths into the future. The selection of the best path or policy may become obvious. But more likely the policy to be followed will require a great deal of judgment, and the simulation results will aid in balancing one alternative against another.

SYSTEMS ANALYSIS AND OPERATIONS RESEARCH

Are systems analysis and operations research the same thing, or are they different? Systems analysis at the very least is the method of operation used by the operations analysts. As such, it is a part of almost every conceivable operations research project. Interestingly enough, both industrial engineers and business administration personnel have adopted many of the statistical techniques of operations research and as a result a larger number of problems have been exposed to solution via the "scientific method." There are also some good reasons why the systems analyst should be business oriented. The business oriented analyst in many ways has better communication with his own management. The great expectations of operations research have to some extent fallen into the gulf that exists between the scientific and business world. The complexity of problem solving tools, the vocabulary of mathematics and technology, and the inability to translate these into simple ideas has contributed to lower realization of some operations research programs. Thus, the business trained systems analyst may be called upon to bring the tools of operations research to management's attention, to bridge the gap of communication. In the process of applying the tools of mathematics and statistics to business problems, operations research has been limited. The most important limitation results from management policy. Each company has the problem of assessing the skills it wishes to employ and of finding a group in which the skills can be put to work. For the most part, this has meant putting operations analysts into staff positions with a loosely defined role. The vast majority of businesses are not only unaware of operations research, but are too small in size to require the full-time services of such a specialist. Some few companies have put emphasis on the use of operations research tools, the bulk of these in technically complex areas.

The scientists who pooled the tools of their various disciplines to attack complex war problems provide the model of the mixed team. Today it is typical that one man trained in the application of operations research tools will be used by many groups who have less than a full-time requirement for this special skill. However, other skills, like his, may only be required on a part-time basis. Table 9–1 is an example of a system study showing three skill requirements, none of which are full-time throughout the entire study, and only at one point, step 9, are all skills working simultaneously and full time on the assignment. The steps of a study are not necessarily restricted to those shown in Table 9–1 any more than the skill requirements are restricted. These represent one way in which a problem can be treated; other skills or other steps are a function of the individual problem.

TABLE 9–1

MIXED TEAM APPROACH TO COMPLEMENTARY WORK
ASSIGNMENTS ON A TYPICAL SYSTEM STUDY

Business Analysis	*Operations Research*	*Electronic Data Processing*
1. Interviewing		
2. Flow Analysis		
3. Flow Charting		
	4. Analysis of Problem	
6. Analyze System Requirements		5. Analysis of System Data
	7. Hypothesis of Conceptual Model	
	8. Test of Model	
9. Design of New System	9. Design of New System	9. Design of New System
10. Forms Design		
		11. EDPM System Design
		12. Equipment Evaluation
		13. Program and Code New System
		14. Test New System Routines

The role of the operations analyst as a member of the mixed team can be quite varied. Because of his technical background, he can work on equipment as well as non-equipment systems. In either case, his interest is primarily procedural and directed at improving system performance. His ability to measure performance has expanded the techniques of system design to a degree of precision in system performance seldom realized in the past. In this role, his work is basically conceptual and aimed at problem solving rather than implementation. The operations analyst brings an objectivity and desire for broad studies to business. This is mainly the result of his training in a scientific area and his orientation to problem solving. The industrial engineer, by contrast, has tended in the past to deal with problems in his own area of time standards, plant layout, and so on, rather than to take on the broad scale problems.

Notable successes of operations research in business have been in the petroleum industry. The use of linear programming mathematical models has made it possible to determine the optimum mix of raw materials in refinery operations. Using linear programming in the solution of distribution problems, the optimum selection of the route, and means of transport has returned substantial savings. The location of manufacturing or warehousing facilities, customarily resolved through the use of engineering economics alone (or intuition), has benefited from the use of operations research.

Operations research has been successfully applied in problems requiring the use of sampling techniques. Shop scheduling and master planning have been attacked using operations research methods, with results that have had practical usefulness for business and industry. Freight yard operations, routing of freight cars, cargo handling, airline scheduling, and a variety of transportation problems have benefited from the use of the operations analyst's tools. Queuing models have had wide use in a variety of traffic and service problems. In addition, a large number of theoretical problems have been attacked, many of which promise substantial payoff in the future. The broad scale of these problems emphasize the contribution of operations research. It has undertaken the solution of complex problems, usually with many variables, and attempted to structure the system by quantifying the system elements. Because of its tools, operations research has brought precise measurements to complex problems, and has sometimes obtained for management the last few per cents of efficiency in a system which was already operating very economically. In many of these cases, the problems have been very large in scale, involving millions of dollars in materiel, equipment, or personnel.

OPERATIONS RESEARCH AND A GENERAL SYSTEMS THEORY

Systems analysis in business may or may not be applied through the use of mathematical techniques. Systems analysis and operations research share a common methodology by defining an objective method of problem solving. However, after ten years of operations research in business, there has been no concerted effort to provide a general systems theory for the problems of industrial management.[3] This is not to say that operations researchers have

3 Again, H. I. Ansoff, *op. cit.*, writes convincingly about the role of operations research. He states that it has been directed at problems of the utilization of internal resources, not as much at the top management levels. He says it has been dealing with problems of "suboptimization"—the process of choosing among a relatively small number of alternatives by an administrative level other than the highest. Ansoff points out that operations research has made contributions where management decisions can be made by computational routines, but that no comparable progress has been made in the judgmental area. This latter point is a good argument for more activity in the general systems theory problem.

done less than they should. If anything, industry itself has limited their opportunities. The result, however, is this: Whatever science operations research has brought to industry has most frequently been in the solution of specific problems, the results of which have not been assembled to provide the basis for a general theory.

Industrial management principles do not provide the requisite general frame of reference either. In a few companies, the development of corporate policy and objectives has advanced to a high level. However, the analysis of operating problems generally suffers from the same drawbacks cited in the example of the pre-World War II electrical or hydraulic system (see page 5). A large number of decisions are reached without cognizance of the appropriate frame of reference. Operations research has gone a long way toward revealing the dependency of decisions on a large number of variables which may be inadequately considered.

A more fundamental shortcoming occurs in Management's inability to define its short and long term objectives. In the absence of objectives which are carefully interpreted for each level of organization, the uniformity and force of decision making must invariably dilute the effectiveness of Management. These shortcomings point to the need for techniques by which Management could integrate the activities of the organization in an economic, effective way. This would give the organization as a whole a unity of purpose from top to bottom.

By recognizing these inadequacies, operations research has contributed to a recognition of the problems which a general systems theory would attack. The continuing efforts of operations analysts and systems oriented personnel from all fields will someday produce the new concepts and provide the much needed frame of reference. It is conceivable that these tools will assist in implementing the changes which are required to keep American industry competitive in world markets.

PART TWO

CASE STUDIES

10
G. W. Templar and Company (demonstration case)

On September 1, 1958, George Templar, president of G. W. Templar and Company,[1] gave his administrative assistant the problem of deciding what was needed to improve their company's production control activity. Paul Farber, the administrative assistant, was unfamiliar with the problem area, but had a working knowledge of the company.

Farber interviewed the production control manager and his associates. In the course of a week, he saw men from the areas of Factory Supervision, Inventory Control, and Factory Engineering. Before undertaking his report, which was due on September 20, he planned some investigation in the fields of Sales, Engineering, and Accounting.

After his first week of effort, he listed a series of requirements for a successful production control system:

1. Must be usable and operable on a large scale digital computer
2. Must be expandable for future increases in volume
3. Must improve service to the customer by shortening manufacturing cycles
4. Must decrease inventories by timing the arrival of raw materials to arrive close to manufacturing release
5. Must decrease inventories by providing an orderly system of releasing parts into the manufacturing sequence on time
6. Must decrease unit costs by providing valid rules for scheduled factory operation
7. Must decrease unit cost by supplying a means of knowing machine utilization and labor requirements
8. Must provide a system of in-process controls and feedbacks

[1] The purpose of this chapter is to provide a pattern of investigation for subsequent cases in the text.

QUESTIONS

1. What is the problem?
2. What are some of the questions Templar wants Farber to answer?
3. What are the functions of a production control department?
4. What are the objectives of a production control system?
5. How does the systems concept work in this case?

ANALYSIS OF CHAPTER 10[2]

G. W. TEMPLAR AND COMPANY

QUESTION 1: What is the problem?

DISCUSSION: Farber has begun postulating a system before he has made an adequate investigation of the situation. His statements are vague generalizations that could have been taken from a text book, or the opinions of the people he initially interviewed. His statements of system requirements are purely qualitative, and as such can be easily challenged with careful questions.

Farber had the problem of learning and reporting about an unfamiliar area. His idea to interview personnel in the departments affected by the production control system, was a good one. There are ways in which he might have supplemented his interviews with information that would have shed more light on the problem area. Some of the things he might have done are:

(1) Prepare an outline of
   a) what general areas he could cover in the three weeks he has to write his report,
   b) what time he would allocate to developing material in each of these areas,
   c) how much time he will leave for writing the report itself.

(2) Prepare flow charts to show major operations of Production Control.

(3) Gather forms, reports and procedures to provide additional background material.

(4) Obtain organization charts to identify the positions and functions of the various members of Production Control and those personnel whose work would bring them into routine contact with the production control system.

2 See Chapter 5.

An assignment of this type is susceptible to the systems approach. Using the basic technique of (1) investigation, (2) hypothesis, and (3) implementation, Farber would have been provided with an orderly way of getting into the problem area. His choice of techniques to develop the problem area material would to some extent have been dictated by what was available for immediate study and how quickly he found the most fruitful areas.

His first undertaking would be to understand the big picture of Production Control, and how its operations affected the rest of the company. His first problem was, therefore, to establish the objectives of Production Control and the boundaries of the problem. Once the objectives were identified, Farber would have been able to evaluate whether or not the objectives were being achieved. Standards and measures of effectiveness of various types would have provided insight to the performance of Production Control. If, as a result of this analysis, there were time left to further evaluate his problem, Farber might have suggested some alternative means of improving the performance of Production Control.

Farber might have tried to look at his assignment as a system, as in Figure 10–1. Further analysis of how Farber intends to deliver the re-

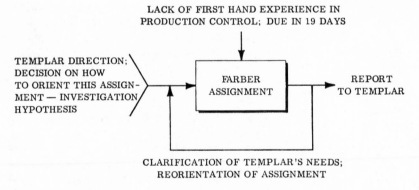

Fig. 10–1.

quired report would accent the need for the following:

(1) Clearer knowledge of the use the report will have.

(2) Assembling a report which reflects a point of view consistent with the time available.

QUESTION 2: What are some of the questions Templar wants Farber to answer?

DISCUSSION: There is no evidence to indicate how well Farber under-

stands the assignment Templar has given him. The report which
Farber must deliver in three weeks cannot contain the results of an
exhaustive search in areas with which Farber is essentially unfamiliar.
What, then, does Templar want? Here are some suggested questions
which Templar may have in his mind:

(1) Is the production control department properly organized?
- *a*) Is the staff performing properly all the functions of a production control organization?
- *b*) Is the department properly staffed? Are there some obvious
staff weaknesses? Are there surplus or marginal employees
working in any part of the department?

(2) What are the problem areas in Production Control?
- *a*) Are the relationships between Production Control and the
departments with whom it must operate satisfactory, or are
there some areas of improvement?

(3) How does the Templar production control system compare to
some other system, particularly that of some efficient competitor?

This is by no means an exclusive enumeration of all the possible questions. Many more will come to mind if this problem is pursued. It is
important to note, however, that as given, the assignment is quite
broad and indefinite. This can create many problems for the investigator. If Farber had pursued the nature of the objectives with Templar, he might have made more progress. Farber might have explored,
for instance, the use to which his report would be put. This would
have forewarned Farber about Management's objectives. Templar is
the "systems purchaser" and his needs and requirements should be
well understood.

QUESTION 3: What are the functions of a production control department?

DISCUSSION: The systems approach is typified by stepping back to take a
look at the entire system as a whole. This might have forced Farber,
who was unfamiliar with the area, to ask, "What are the functions of
a production control department?" Here are some generally acceptable functions which would have assisted him in his investigation:

(1) Translate sales department paperwork into practical production plans.

(2) Keep Management advised on the status of production.

(3) Maintain adequate records on the factors of production.

(4) Forecast anticipated labor, material, and machine usage.

(5) Control the processing of orders in factory production.

(6) Move materials to the factory floor for processing, between
operations until completion, and to the shipping department.

These functions explain how the system should operate. But they are qualitative statements and suffer the shortcomings of being non-quantitative. However, they are more helpful than the eight system requirements Farber has listed, because they are more general and provide a place to start investigating. They do not commit Farber to some idea or policy that may be outside Management's frame of reference. The analysis of the functions of Production Control might put Farber on the trail of a real problem area.

QUESTION 4: What are the objectives of a production control system?

DISCUSSION: Another way of providing an entering wedge would have been to ask the question, "What are the objectives of a production control system?" Here are some generally acceptable objectives:

(1) *Maintaining schedule*—expediting; dispatching; resorting to outside production when necessary; predicting overloads and underloads; follow-up on outside contracted operations; day-to-day contact with factory supervision; assisting in crucial decision making about priorities and split lots; interpreting the schedule and machine load, and so on.

(2) *Coordinating staff services with line operations*
  a) Providing the information bridge between the factory and the indirect departments such as Sales, Service, Purchasing, Material, and so on.
  b) Providing a part of the quantitative feedback information to guide staff in decision making, such as the following:
    1) What are the shortages and what are we doing to obtain parts or materials?
    2) What short shipments have been received today; how will this affect our manufacturing schedule; and when can we get additional parts?
    3) What parts are behind schedule, and what are the reasons?
    4) What lots have suffered unusual attrition and are below minimum quantities; shall we continue processing at higher costs, or should we release an additional lot into manufacture and hold the parts in process until the new lot catches up?

(3) *Developing and maintaining workable production plans*
  a) Providing a system capable of comparing the current and anticipated work load to the capabilities of the factory, under a variety of conditions.
  b) Providing a set of decision rules to be used under conditions which are well understood.
  c) Providing the manpower to generate and maintain information essential to reporting the status of manufacturing, and planning future operations.

Such points as 1, 2, and 3 above develop the type of data on which Farber could base criteria or measures of effectiveness for some part, or all of the system. To be effective as criteria, these points must be measurable.

Figure 10–2 illustrates one way to look at Production Control:

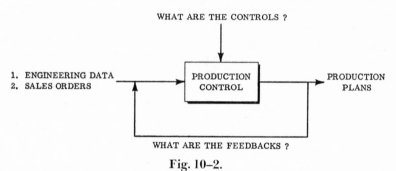

Fig. 10–2.

(1) Engineering
    a) Controls
        1) blueprint checking procedure
        2) customer approval of working drawings
        3) blueprint release procedure
        4) change incorporation procedure
        5) product standards and specifications procedure
    b) Feedback
        1) change notification and request procedure
        2) engineering order request procedure
        3) master planning notification and change procedure
        4) product standards change request

(2) Sales
    a) Controls
        1) monthly summaries of customer schedules
        2) copies of master plans
        3) notification of receipt (or absence) of engineering data
        4) sales order data transmission procedure
    b) Feedback
        1) confirmation of scheduled delivery dates
        2) confirmation of changes, cancellations, deletions, additions, or alterations in specification to existing orders
        3) reports of status of production
        4) reports of actual shipments

In fact, there are more departments whose activities are related to production control operation. The technical requirements of a customer's order involve the tooling, factory engineering, and material departments (see Figure 10–3). In each of these subsystem areas, con-

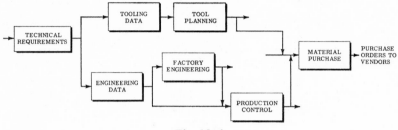

Fig. 10–3.

trols and feedbacks are required to provide for accurate and reliable transmission of information. Assign individual areas for more complete diagramming.

QUESTION 5: How does the systems concept work in this case?

DISCUSSION: Systems postulation starts in the investigation phase. It is impossible to avoid thinking of a problem area without also considering what to do about the problem. However, a requisite to systems postulation is the availability of pertinent data, particularly of an operational and quantitative character. Here are some of the typical data which would be required in each of the categories Farber has set up before systems postulation could begin:

(1) *Must be usable and operable on a large-scale digital computer.*
    a) What data is being processed?
        1) How frequently?
        2) What data must be transmitted?
        3) What subsystems are affected?
        4) What basic files and transaction files are concerned?
        5) What is the compatibility of the subsystems being processed?
        6) How many items per file are being processed?
    b) Who is processing the data now?
        1) Who originates?
        2) How many copies?
        3) Who gets them?
        4) What do they do with them?
        5) What is their ultimate destination?
        6) What equipment is currently used to accomplish the data processing in question?

7) Are the forms and procedures for this data processing application operating as they were originally designed?

8) Are the personnel originally designated for this data processing application actually doing the work?

c) What are the costs associated with this data processing application?

1) Is cost information available? Incomplete? Current?

2) How are costs allocated or assigned to this procedure?

3) Are the costs as they were assessed when the procedure was designed?

(2) *Must be expandable for future increases in volume.*

a) What were the original volume figures?

1) What are the current figures?

2) What are the projected figures?

b) How do the costs per unit transaction bear out the need for a flexible system?

1) Will an expansion in volume require changeover to more complex or costly machinery?

2) What will the effect of a shrinkage in volume be on the cost picture?

c) Can revisions in the existing system eliminate the problem of expansion or shrinkage in the volume of transactions?

(3) *Must improve service to the customer by shortening manufacturing cycles.*

a) What means are at the disposal of the company to shorten the cycle?

1) Decrease lot size?

2) Increase automation?

3) Re-engineer or re-tool for easier or more economic manufacturing?

4) Reduce quality?

5) Loosen specifications?

b) What are the side effects that may accompany the move to shorten manufacturing cycles?

(4) *Must decrease inventories by timing the arrival of new materials to arrive close to manufacturing release.*

a) Who originates the order to buy materials?

1) Who processes the requisition? The purchase order?

2) How do they know when to requisition?

3) How do they know how much to order?

b) Who gets the purchase order?

1) Is a choice among several vendors made?

2) How is the purchase order prepared?

3) Who prepares it?

        4) Is the time required to prepare a purchase order incorporated in the lead time for manufacturing?

        5) How is contact maintained with the vendor?

        6) How is the due date of a delivery determined?

        7) How does the system respond to a late, early, short, or defective delivery?

c) What is the current level of inventory compared to the volume it will support?

        1) Does quantitative data indicate inventory is too high (or too low) for anticipated deliveries?

        2) Is there competition or trade information bearing on the problem of inventory level? Turnover rate?

        3) Does management agree inventory level is satisfactory?

        4) What kinds of material costs are kept?

          a. What is the accuracy and reliability of records?

          b. How does a sampling of stock items check with

            1. quantity shown in inventory records?

            2. description shown in physical inventory records?

            3. location files?

            4. cost files maintained in accounting and physical inventory records?

(5) *Must decrease inventories by providing an orderly system of releasing parts into the manufacturing sequence on time.*

a) Will this decrease inventories? Increase inventories?

b) What measures can be devised to support the need to operate with less (or more) inventory?

c) What symptoms exist to reflect an improper level of inventory?

        1) Orders going into process late? How many? Did they catch up?

        2) How many orders are required in the pipeline? At what stages?

        3) How many releases are now in stock for some sampling of our current production schedule?

        4) How many geographically separate stocks of identical parts exist?

        5) How many lots are

          a. in process?

          b. at outside contractors being processed?

          c. in transit?

          d. on order?

        6) How do the lots in process and on order compare with the schedule requirements for some sample group of parts?

7) Is there a shortage list?
   a. How many items? Have they continuously recurred?
   b. Are the reasons for shortages known? Are they being followed by Production Control?
   c. Who issues the shortage report? How often? Who uses it? What is its reliability?

(6) *Must decrease unit costs by providing valid rules for scheduled factory operation.*
  a) is there an existing system with decision rules, control, and feedback—or is this a collection of non-integrated procedures and processes?
    1) Who designed it? Who polices it?
    2) Is it up to date, or half used and half improvised?
    3) Are the forms standard or bootlegged?
  b) Is the system followed?
    1) What are the deviations?
    2) Is there provision for changes?
    3) Has it been changed since inception?
  c) Will this decrease unit costs? Increase?
    1) What is the relationship of scheduling rules to cost?

(7) *Must decrease unit costs by supplying a means of knowing machine utilization and labor requirements.*
  a) What controls exist on the factory level?
    1) Reliable timekeeping? Who does it? How many timekeepers? What do the timekeepers do?
    2) Are department and cost center lines clear?
    3) Who moves parts? How many dispatchers?
    4) Who counts parts? Who records quantities? Where are quantities recorded? Is parts count checked?
    5) Are there rules for lot splitting? Are they applied?
      a. Who has the authority to split lots?
      b. Is lot splitting the exception? What data is available?
    6) How are employees transferred between departments?
      a. How are labor changes handled?
      b. How does a foreman know when to borrow and when to release?
      c. How are absent employees replaced?
  b) How is shop loading accomplished? Is it a "system"?
    1) What is the frequency of job changes?
    2) Are methods standardized? Are the work standards representative of the work being accomplished?
    3) How far in advance is the work load known?
    4) What is the frequency of reporting completed work?
      a. In what detail is completed work reported?

5) Are there machine classes? Machine numbers?
   a. How is a reference in the schedule tied to a particular machine in a department?
   b. How is a particular lot in the schedule tied to a lot in the factory being processed?

(8) *Must provide a system of in-process controls and feedbacks.*
   a) Where is the current system failing?
      1) Absence of accurate inputs?
         a. Standards?
         b. Factory routings?
         c. Machine assignments?
      2) Are processes too slow?
         a. Files not updated?
         b. Reports delivered too late to be useful?
         c. Performance information incomplete?
         d. High cost of making essential data available?
      3) What are the controls in the various systems?
      4) What are the feedback mechanisms?

Much more could be written under each of the above eight headings. It must now be obvious that an investigation of the size necessary to support the system requirements Farber has stated, is far outside the realm of the time available and the assignment as Templar had it in mind. It is also obvious, that qualitative, non-operational statements will not stand up unless supported by quantitative data. These questions begin to develop the line of investigation which will reveal the type of quantitative data which is desirable, if a full blown investigation is required.

SUPPLEMENTAL DISCUSSION QUESTIONS

1. Why was Farber picked to do this job? Who else might have been assigned this problem?

2. What would be suitable criteria of a production control system?

3. Has Farber's job been well defined? Who has the responsibility for stating the problem?

4. What should Farber's report contain?

5. At what point should the postulation of a system begin?

11

The Lee Company

The Lee Company has been in business in Leominster, Massachusetts, for 42 years. During this time they have built a reputation as one of the foremost manufacturers of machine shop parts in the country. Plant locations are in New England but two plants are in the deep South. Direct labor at the Leominster plant numbers 1,200. Total direct labor employees of the corporation number 3,700 at all plant locations.

The Lee Company has several competitors of equal size throughout the East. Machine shop know-how is the principal criteria of a competitor's ability to undertake manufacture. The variety of products is narrow, but the number of models produced in each category creates a long and impressive list of end products. The total number of models active at Leominster at any one time might average 300. Each model consists roughly of 25 manufactured parts and 80 purchased parts. Each manufactured part has an average of 25 operations. Customer orders at any one time might call out as many as 60,000 end products.

The facilities of the Leominster plant contain offices, shipping and receiving, stockrooms for raw materials and finished goods, machine shop areas, and assembly areas. The scope of activities at Leominster is sufficiently wide to necessitate a full organization, both direct and indirect. The direct departments are seven in number, each headed by a Foreman who has an assistant on each shift. The six machine shop departments vary in size between 50 and 200 people. The manufacturing areas in each department are divided into sub-areas called cost centers. Costs are accumulated by employee, by cost center, by department, and by division.

The Lee Company had its greatest growth from 1943 to 1955. While in no sense a "war baby," Management seized upon the opportunities offered by government financed business to expand their resources threefold over this period. The effects of this expansion not only created manifold plant problems, but personnel problems as well. The production control department was organized along the lines of what the government demanded of industry during war time. Because firm commitments were required of any major subcontractor, Management decreed that "something else" was needed between Sales and Production to coordinate the expectancies of one against the day-to-day problems of the other. Figure 11–1 is a schematic drawing of the Lee Company Production System.

Production Control personnel were recruited from Sales and Production. In addition, specialists from other companies were recruited and several people were brought in, over a period of time, from Factory Engineering and Industrial Engineering to comprise the staff. The full staff of operating and clerical personnel in Production Control eventually grew to 85 persons working on two shifts.

At the outset, Production Control carried the psychological burden of white collar personnel working and making decisions in the production area. The first efforts of Production Control to gain control over production were not effective, and yet some opinion on the staff level held they were working in the proper direction. Initial undertakings were concerned with determining what reports Management would require, what reports would be necessary as a means of achieving this end.

The end product of several years of effort were the Customer Schedule (summary of all customer orders) and the Production Requirements Report (purchased parts summary). These were the key reports in the purchasing and manufacturing process and the timeliness of each was considered extremely important. Accuracy was a major requirement. These reports were issued monthly by the Tabulating Department from punched card decks. For instance, new customer orders were key punched on acceptance, and shipments were key punched on receipt of a shipping notice. These

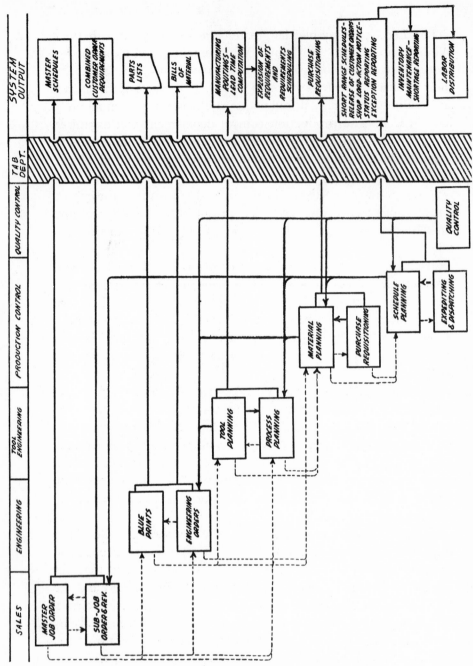

Fig. 11–1. The Lee Company production system.

inputs were merged and matched with the card decks representing the Customer Schedule.

The Customer Schedule was made available about the tenth working day of every month. The other schedules were published about the twentieth working day of every month. Although there was continuous discussion about the lateness of schedules, Production Control argued that the projection of several months on each schedule release was adequate to cover any time loss in producing paper work.

The Combined Release Schedule was the result of multiplying the Customer Schedule by the Parts List of an end product and subtracting any unallocated work in process or finished goods. Since the manufacturing cycle was four months and the procurement cycle was two or more months, it was deemed advisable to carry the requirements out to ten months. This schedule showed numbers of parts plus scrap allowances as well as indicating the status of work in process. Back Orders represented the extent to which the commodity on order was behind schedule.

From the Production Requirements Report, Production Control requisitioned the purchasing department to buy the net requirements of purchased parts and raw materials. The problems of procurement and timely delivery of raw materials were then the function of Purchasing.

Simultaneous with the release of raw materials into the production process, the Parts Production Routing was sent to the operating departments concerned. These became the processing "bible," and carried all operation numbers and information which would be required to complete each detail. Areas to be machined were indicated on each blueprint by heavy lines. Engineering changes were supposed to be incorporated in blueprints prior to production. In periods when changes were frequent, end products were serialized and changes were incorporated at irregular intervals. Changes in routing were reported to Factory Engineering, if, in the opinion of the Foreman or Dispatcher, the changes were permanent. These routings, in addition, contained pertinent information which would assist the operating department in manufacturing planning.

Although efforts to describe the release date of raw materials in

PART NAME		REL. NO.	CUSTOMER NO.	CUSTOMER PART NO.	INV.	COMM	PART NUMBER	SFX.
SHELL BRAKE ASSY		2	10891	PM 10722		4608	6720 18	10
		DIST.	CUSTOMER NAME	ISSUE DATE	SUPERSEDES DATE	CHANGE	PAGE	
		4	47801	2/13/56	7/08/53	1	1 OF 1	

CHG. NO.	DESCRIPTION OPERATION OR MATERIAL	MAT'L REQUIRED UNIT	CODE	QUAN. /100	OPERATION S K	NO.	MATERIAL NUMBER OR CH. GRP. & SETUP HRS.	SETUP HRS.	LABOR CODE	COST CTR. DIV	DEPT	GRP	SET BACK CODE	SEQ. NO.	MAN HOURS	MCH. HOURS	CODE
1	SIMILAR TO						5200 70118	01						2			
1	SIMILAR TO						5200 70818	00						2			
1	SIMILAR TO						5200 71818	00						5			
3	SHELL - COLLECTOR		P	100			5200 72153	00						10			
7	- AIR INLET		P	100			5200 72071	00									
3	ROUGH GRIND				x	10	60 2	1	7175	6304				15	37 00	37 00	
7	ANNEAL					12	7632	.5	4401	2324				20	1 96	1 96	
7	DEGREASE				x	20	8411 3	0	1115	6304				25	12 00	12 00	
7	SAND BLAST				x	22	16	1	7021	1303				30	50	50	
7						25	5926	4	7356	6304				35	50	50	
7	DEGREASE				x	27	16	1	7021	1303			1	40	50	50	
3						30	3700	3	3404	6304				45	40	40	
1	STOCK				x	40	6900 6	2	5568	1314			1	50	1 75	1 75	
	TOTAL					50		7*		1362				55	54 61	54 61	

Fig. 11–2. The Lee Company parts production routing.

The Lee Company
Customer Schedule

Customer name	Part number	Item quantity	Customer order number	Date entered	Order date	Total pieces on order	Total pieces shipped	Customer schedule	Promised schedule
Clairview, Inc.	26701		237480	6 15 4	6 5 4	180	10	170	170
St. Louis Mills Co.	40404	2870	A74601	8 28 5	7 5 4	6040	1001	5039	5039
St. Louis Mills Co.	13871	6188	A74602	8 28 5	6 5 4	12708	700	12008	12008
Seven Oceans, Inc.	71905		RM7048	12 3 4	5 5 4	621	305	316	316
Millard Corp.	51881		207418	3 14 5	3 5 5	12		12	12
Municipal Shops	14806		4128	2 14 5	8 5 4	1		1	1
ABC Machine Co.	64811		6184D	7 9 3	2 5 3	4	1	3	3
Smithview & Co.	19805		NR6478	7 20 4	1 5 4	63		63	63
U.S. Smiths Corp.	54611		23101	9 1 4	6 5 4	808	800	8	8
Brand Lock Co.	16118		L60611	10 8 4	6 8 4	1625	1420	205	205
B-T Aircraft Corp.	86788	407	81108	8 8 5	7 8 5	1271	71	1200	1200
Goodwealth Co.	98088	5100	SL78181	8 17 5	4 16 5	18678	9740	8938	8938
Tri-State Corp.	92114		34611	9 10 4	8 17 4	610	300	310	310
L & T, Inc.	87505	1000	35808	8 15 5	7 12 5	1278		1278	1278
Iron & Steel Co.	61805		6178D	12 16 4	10 10 4	61	10	51	51

The Lee Company
Combined Release Schedule

Part	Combined requirements	Requirements plus scrap	Work in Process	On Order	Back Order	Future Production Months									
						1	2	3	4	5	6	7	8	9	10
94301	12	13				13									
94718	35	39			39	12	23								
93021	2617	2745	3	3	14		97	415	987	813	40	30	28	53	140
91081	33	4541	4231	3914	3		5	25							
18008	10	84	89	82	10										
17647	31621	30778	2368	2309	4257	5744	4439	2999	4813	2574	1127	1269	916	562	2921
30771	30115	31621	847	826	6929	5744	4439	2999	3967	2314	867	843	656	302	1881
30844	2503	1327	1271	1239	25	15	723	433	460	354	129	96	134		134
90085	2	2			2										
94511	47	114	157	145	47										
22450	201	166	85	79	201										
12258	10	5	5	5	5	5									
30741	139	146	12		5		89	50							
68121	5	7	12	11	5										
10445	5238	3401	2288	2174	128	1070	1096	1003	1302	398	135	45	16	19	26
46141	9	10			9										

THE LEE COMPANY
PRODUCTION REQUIREMENTS REPORT

Part	Tot. Req. Net Req. Schd. Rec. To Order	Fin. Inv. Rec. Insp. On Order	Back Order	Future Production Months									
				1	2	3	4	5	6	7	8	9	10
20785	160 46 46	114	46	9	14	24 46	67 46						
31481	5454 4692 3115 1192	762 1923	60	621	722 641	704 704 631 68	863 863 320 400	320 320 240 400	240 240 400 324	400 400 400	400 400 400	400 400 400	724 724 324
10418	1476 975 975	501	46	160	189 88	194 88 266	266 266 80	80 80 60	60 60 100	100 100 100	100 100 100	100 100 100	181 181 81
70711	1476 305– 421– 634–	1781 213	46	160	189	194	266	80	60	100	100	100	181
61174	1476 76 76 24–	1400 100	46	160	189	194	266	80	60	100	100	100 76 76	181
80678	1476 1511– 1511– 1511–	2987	46	160	189	194	266	80	60	100	100	100	181
10401	145 162– 162–	307	39	5	10	24	67						

terms of the due date in stock of finished parts (called lead-time or set-back) had only begun, Production Control was insistent that more accurate set-backs would solve many of the problems of irregular production and long manufacturing cycles. Ganntt charts illustrating the relationship of "in dates" compared to "due dates in stock" were made for a few end products. It was noted that setup time plus machine time was about 25 per cent of the elapsed calendar time the part was in process. Man hours for machine setup and processing were produced on Machine Load Forms (Figure 11–3). Standard hours were adjusted to reflect actual anticipated hours that would be consumed.

Start and due dates were taken from the Manufacturing-Calender Day Cross Reference Chart. The use of this chart made it possible through simple addition and subtraction, to determine over a three year period, the *in* and *out* dates of any part or operation in the manufacturing schedule. There were significant problems in keeping this system up to date.

The production control department and the industrial engineers assigned to the machine shop departments met to review a tentative proposal (see Exhibit One) that would form the basis for a common understanding on scheduling in August, 1956. After some discussion, the report was set aside pending a reopening of the entire scheduling problem. The opinion expressed in this meeting confirmed the mutual agreement on the need for more system.

Mr. Albert King, Chief of Production Control, made this statement in a meeting held September of 1956 in the Division Manager's office at Leominster:

Production Control at Leo has turned from a control function to one of fire-fighting. I doubt if we have ever had control, or ever will have. The tab records and our work in process records don't tally. Our dispatchers are constantly bailing out some promise of our Sales Department; our counter-movers don't count and our rules of thumb for release of detail parts into the system are inadequate. I question the decision rules employed by the factory supervision, and Industrial Engineering gives us no practical data to support our plan for machine loading and labor utilization. We have no concept of lots, optimum lot size, or identification of lots in process. The documents that keep our system going are the scraps of paper pieced together by the Dispatcher which tell him which jobs are hottest and how high the temperature of each hot job is, compared to the others. Our shop is no longer a production shop, but a custom shop, and has been for a long time.

LOT NO. 151 | **REL. QUAN.** 1100 | **STK.QUAN.** 1000 | **REL. DATE** 51 | **STK. DATE** 90 | **CUSTOMER PART NAME** SHELL BRAKE ASSY. | **CUST. NO.** 10891 | **CUSTOMER PART NO.** PM 10722

PART NUMBER — COMM. 4608 | 672018 | SUF. 10

	MATERIAL CODE NO.		MAT. QUAN.
	GOOD	DATE	SCRAP
UNIT OF MEAS.	1000	2-57	100

START DATE	DUE DATE	R/M CODE SK	OPER.	MACH.	SET UP HOURS	MATERIAL SPEC. LABOR CODE	DEPT. NO.	SEQ. NO.	STANDARD MAN HOURS PER 100	MACH. LOAD
51	68		10	60	2.10	7175	6304	15	37.00	78.20
57	71	X	12	7632	.50	4401	2324	20	1.96	4.92
69	77		20	8411	3.00	1115	6304	25	12.00	30.00
72	79	X	22	16	.10	7021	1303	30	.50	1.20
78	82	X	25	5926	.40	7356	6304	35	.50	1.80
80	84	X	27	16	.10	7021	1303	40	.50	1.20
83	86		30	3700	.30	3404	6304	45	.40	1.40
85	89		40	6900	.20	5568	1314	50	1.75	3.90
88	90		50				1362	55		
					*6.70				*54.61	* 122.62

Fig. 11-3. The Lee Company machine load.

MANUFACTURING—CALENDAR DAY CROSS REFERENCE CHART - 1956

BOLD FACE NUMBERS = MANUFACTURING DAY

JANUARY

S	M	T	W	T	F	S
1	2	3	4	5	6	7
		1	2	3	4	
8	9	10	11	12	13	14
	5	6	7	8	9	
15	16	17	18	19	20	21
	10	11	12	13	14	
22	23	24	25	26	27	28
	15	16	17	18	19	
29	30	31				
	20	21				

FEBRUARY

S	M	T	W	T	F	S
			1	2	3	4
			22	23	24	
5	6	7	8	9	10	11
	25	26	27	28	29	
12	13	14	15	16	17	18
	30	31	32	33	34	
19	20	21	22	23	24	25
	35	36	37	38	39	
26	27	28	29			
	40	41	42			

MARCH

S	M	T	W	T	F	S
				1	2	3
				43	44	
4	5	6	7	8	9	10
	45	46	47	48	49	
11	12	13	14	15	16	17
	50	51	52	53	54	
18	19	20	21	22	23	24
	55	56	57	58	59	
25	26	27	28	29	30	31
	60	61	62	63	64	

APRIL

S	M	T	W	T	F	S
1	2	3	4	5	6	7
65	66	67	68	69	70	
8	9	10	11	12	13	14
	71	72	73	74	75	
15	16	17	18	19	20	21
	76	77	78	79	80	
22	23	24	25	26	27	28
	81	82	83	84	85	
29	30					
	86					

MAY

S	M	T	W	T	F	S
		1	2	3	4	5
		87	88	89	90	
6	7	8	9	10	11	12
	91	92	93	94	95	
13	14	15	16	17	18	19
	96	97	98	99	100	
20	21	22	23	24	25	26
	101	102	103	104	105	
27	28	29	30	31		
	106	107		108		

JUNE

S	M	T	W	T	F	S
					1	2
					109	
3	4	5	6	7	8	9
	110	111	112	113	114	
10	11	12	13	14	15	16
	115	116	117	118	119	
17	18	19	20	21	22	23
	120	121	122	123	124	
24	25	26	27	28	29	30
	125	126	127	128	129	

JULY

S	M	T	W	T	F	S
1	2	3	4	5	6	7
	130	131		132	133	
8	9	10	11	12	13	14
	134	135	136	137	138	
15	16	17	18	19	20	21
	139	140	141	142	143	
22	23	24	25	26	27	28
29	30	31				
	144	145				

AUGUST

S	M	T	W	T	F	S
			1	2	3	4
			146	147	148	
5	6	7	8	9	10	11
	149	150	151	152	153	
12	13	14	15	16	17	18
	154	155	156	157	158	
19	20	21	22	23	24	25
	159	160	161	162	163	
26	27	28	29	30	31	
	164	165	166	167	168	

SEPTEMBER

S	M	T	W	T	F	S
						1
2	3	4	5	6	7	8
		169	170	171	172	
9	10	11	12	13	14	15
	173	174	175	176	177	
16	17	18	19	20	21	22
	178	179	180	181	182	
23 30	24	25	26	27	28	29
	183	184	185	186	187	

OCTOBER

S	M	T	W	T	F	S
1	2	3	4	5	6
188	189	190	191	192	
7	8	9	10	11	12	13
	193	194	195	196	197	
14	15	16	17	18	19	20
	198	199	200	201	202	
21	22	23	24	25	26	27
	203	204	205	206	207	
28	29	30	31			
	208	209	210			

NOVEMBER

S	M	T	W	T	F	S
				1	2	3
				211	212	
4	5	6	7	8	9	10
	213	214	215	216	217	
11	12	13	14	15	16	17
	218	219	220	221	222	
18	19	20	21	22	23	24
	223	224	225		226	
25	26	27	28	29	30	
	227	228	229	230	231	

DECEMBER

S	M	T	W	T	F	S
						1
2	3	4	5	6	7	8
	232	233	234	235	236	
9	10	11	12	13	14	15
	237	238	239	240	241	
16	17	18	19	20	21	22
	242	243	244	245	246	
23 30	24 31	25	26	27	28	29
		247	248	249	

Fig. 11-4.

EXHIBIT ONE

NOTE ON SCHEDULING

I. The ideal flow situation occurring in mass production:
   A. Automation: Material handling and labor minimized.

B. Progressive Assembly: Material handling and labor optimized on another level.

    1. In a job shop, the ideal is the closest approach to progressive assembly as can be obtained without sacrificing flexibility.

        a. One way to do this is to standardize on the actual hours per lot. To do this, a mean time would be derived which combines setup cycle, production, and lot size in one value. Very little variability above the mean time would be allowed, since this would delay other lots.

II. The delay that results from unbalanced production:

    A. Unbalanced production results when mutually dependent operations are delayed by waiting.

        1. The causes of delay between operations:

            a. Wide distribution of lot sizes

            b. Wide distribution of standard hours per unit of operation

            c. Wide distribution of setup time value

            d. Other causes are excluded for the purpose of this note

        2. Waiting delays are interdependent:

            a. A delay on any one part forces the same delay on all parts following—a larger cumulative delay builds up as parts get closer to final assembly.

            b. Minimization of waiting delays will reduce total make span

III. Waiting delays—a series of distributions capable of analysis:

    A. Data are available or can be made available to analyze delay.

    B. The sum of waiting elements is a time measure.

    C. The number of lots having priority over the nth lot to be processed also have a distribution.

    D. The value of the waiting time measure, times the quantity of lots to be processed before the nth lot can be put on the machine, describes the waiting time and machining time for the nth lot.

        1. Wide variations on the high side must be compressed by

            a. Better tooling (to reduce operating cycle)

            b. Better work methods (same)

            c. Duplicate or triplicate tooling (so two or more machines do the same jobs)

            d. Use of different machines

        2. Other variations may require changes such as

            a. New setup procedure

            b. Selection of different lot size

IV. The use of the waiting measure:

    A. As a unit of production.

        1. Lot sizes are conditioned by the requirement that the total

time to do any setup and operation must be a value within certain limits. This will provide an immediate return by minimizing delay.

B. When combined with other measures, it has the capability of describing a finer setback. This application has future importance and is not timely now.

   1. Other elements of the setback, such as transit time and random delays, must be added.

   2. Operations performed outside the department must be analyzed in the same way.

C. Day-to-day situations in actual operation would benefit from any plan that would tend to equalize the number of hours any machine must run on any operation.

QUESTIONS

1. What is the problem?

2. Where would you begin in this task of making Production Control an effective organization?

3. Evaluate the proposal on scheduling.

4. What are the major subsystems required for an integrated Production Control?

5. In each subsystem, find the inputs, outputs, controls, and feedbacks.

12

Marxson and Company

Bill Heilson was a member of the Accounting Department of Marxson and Company.[1] As a senior member of Management, he was regarded as the "trouble-shooter" for a wide variety of problems. This activity was much in evidence in the design of punched card systems, tabulating routines, and cost accounting procedures.

Because he had an interest in electronics and was highly regarded by the corporate management, he was invited to attend a meeting on June 12, 1957. Sales representatives of a well known electronics manufacturer were scheduled to make a presentation on electronic data processing equipment for business. Heilson was well read on this subject and had encouraged members of the accounting department to learn about this new tool. He had no direct experience, however, with an operating computer installation.

The electronic computer manufacturers were well prepared for their presentation. They had spent several days working with their local sales representatives who serviced Marxson and Company, to personalize their talk on computers. Since Marxson was a multi-division manufacturer of ladies ready-to-wear, the presentation included examples of how other firms in the same field were planning to use electronics in business data processing. There were no completed installations to which the computer manufacturers could point; however, there were many companies either investigating or studying their data processing problems. Because this was an initial meeting, costs and savings were the principle themes of the presentation.

Henry Marxson, President of Marxson and Company, was deeply

[1] See Chapter 6, page 107.

impressed by the advantages that high-speed data processing would bring to his firm. As a result, he held several corporate level meetings in the following month. Marxson gained agreement of his officers to launch a formal investigation to determine if computers would be practical for his company. On July 20th, Marxson asked Heilson to form a committee whose purpose would be to investigate this problem. On August 1st, the committee was formally announced with Heilson acting as Chairman. Other members of the Committee were the principal members of top management, including A. M. Biddle, the Treasurer.

The committee met twice monthly to discuss the problems of installing electronic data processing. Each meeting brought out questions which required Heilson to spend time making interim investigations. Some questions had to be shelved because they were either dependent on future undetermined factors or were of a technical nature. It became obvious at an early stage that expert advice on this problem would be advantageous, despite all of the training, education, and exposure it might be possible to bring to the staff who would be involved in the studies. A possible alternative they considered was to hire a top level, technically oriented expert to head the study team.

Heilson invited all of the manufacturers of medium and large-scale computers to visit him at his office in Milwaukee, Wisconsin. Over a period of two months, a substantial amount of literature was collected and surveyed. During this time, the computer manufacturers talked with Heilson. Most of these firms offered, as a part of their services, manpower to analyze some of the primary data processing systems. However, it appeared that time and cost would not permit an equipment manufacturer to make a thorough analysis of the business data processing systems, some of which were manual and others, such as payroll, on punched cards. Furthermore, it appeared logical that the computer manufacturer's role would be to sell equipment, not business systems.

All of the manufacturers stressed economy of operation. One of the arguments for computers was that electronic equipment overcame the necessity to do extensive hiring or layoff of data processing personnel, as business volume rose or fell. Companies were advised to consider equipment with sufficient capacity to take on additional

data processing burdens and flexibility to operate almost as economically, on smaller loads. Because of the complex nature of electronic
equipment and the way in which it operated on data, the need to
design business systems with the computer in mind was also a major
consideration.

Heilson suggested to the Committee, in October, that it would
be wise to investigate the use of consultants to assist in the studies
leading to the selection of equipment. Some members of the committee agreed that this might be necessary because each computer
had distinctive technical and operational characteristics. Heilson
insisted that the need to compare equipment characteristics objectively made it necessary to use consultants. He pointed out that
all data processing systems would require evaluation on each of the
computer systems they might eventually consider for Marxson. He
passed around copies of a talk given to Marxson executives by a
systems consultant. This illustrated the detailed nature of the analysis of existing business systems which was required. A copy of this
talk is included as Exhibit One.

All members of the Committee agreed that extensive investigation and systems design would not be done adequately by equipment manufacturers. They further concluded that the existing
organization structure did not contain the technical manpower to
undertake the systems design, although they had several possible
candidates to work in such a group. Heilson discussed with department managers what personnel they might make available for his
project. Out of fifteen potential employees, six candidates were
selected after interviewing. These men were immediately enrolled
in courses to supplement their existing knowledge and experience.
They were encouraged to participate in professional meetings and
university sponsored programs and courses.

Marxson customarily worked very closely with his Treasurer,
A. M. Biddle. Biddle was a member of several organizations which
had conducted seminars on electronic data processing. He had at-
tended these and been interested in this new tool because he recognized how valuable it might prove to Marxson.

Early in December, at a regular meeting of Heilson's committee,
Biddle presented data which he said represented the costs that
would be sustained if Marxson and Company proposed to restudy

their entire business data processing system. These costs had been obtained from other large industrial firms generally comparable in dollar volume and number of employees to Marxson. It appeared that it would require one and one half man-years per major area to be studied. Biddle stated there were at least five such areas in each Division of Marxson and Company. The staff costs approximated $200,000 on this basis, in addition to which there were contingent costs that might add as much as an additional $50,000 before one problem could be run on a computer.

Biddle made other points from the experience of manufacturers who had taken up the challenge of using electronics in their business data processing. He showed examples of costly systems redesign made necessary by the selection of a highly specialized computer system. When the need for such redesign became necessary, it added to the already substantial costs. Biddle was also concerned about the problem of finding the right consultant for this task and of the additional costs they would sustain if they were to use outside services.

One of Biddle's most impressive points was the competitive advantage that would accrue to the first member of their industry to use a computer. It was obvious that the ability to process large quantities of data rapidly and react quickly to market changes and demands would give Marxson a decided advantage. Biddle emphasized that a complete system study would require at the very minimum, two to three years; thus, Marxson was a full four to five years from reaping the advantages of electronics.

Biddle proposed that Marxson and Company immediately place an order for a medium scale computer from a well recognized equipment manufacturer and save a substantial period of time. Since this computer equipment had been used in a wide variety of business applications, it appeared that it would fit the needs of their firm. Biddle pointed out that studies could begin during the one year waiting period while equipment was on order, under the guidance of the selected computer manufacturer. With a medium scale computer, it was proposed that a few of the most urgent data processing problems could be prepared before the arrival of equipment; as the load increased, consideration could be given to a large or intermediate scale machine.

Biddle estimated that if payroll and other existing punched card applications were converted for the computer, only thirty per cent of its time would be taken on one shift, leaving plenty of time for the most urgent application, Inventory Control, which was being done manually.

Heilson agreed there were some advantages to this method of getting started with computers. He presented some argument in defense of using the approach he had been exploring, but felt it unwise to argue this problem before investigating thoroughly to be certain that Biddle's point of view was not desirable.

EXHIBIT ONE

THE USE OF COMPUTERS IN BUSINESS OPERATIONS

I am glad to be here today to talk to you about electronic data processing. I'm sure there is no subject you could have chosen that has more current interest or that will, eventually, have a greater effect on the operations of business. The interest of Marxson and Company in this subject is another indication of a great source of strength in our society —the willingness, even eagerness, to investigate new and better ways of doing a job.

It is interesting to note that the first, large electronic computer was completed at the University of Pennsylvania at the close of World War II. This machine, the ENIAC, was the forerunner of all the machines which are now the hearts and brains of electronic data processing systems. Today, there are over 2,000 electronic data processing machines in use by government and business. More than 200 of these are the large-scale variety, each representing an investment of more than $1,000,000. It is evident that business has been active in applying computers to business problems.

Some day your company will be using electronic data processing equipment. The only question for me is "when?" The answer to this question is, "when the benefits of an electronic data processing system offset the cost of the installation."

Do not assume I am building an unprovable or unfounded premise into this conclusion. I must be honest to tell you, however, in my objective capacity, that:

1. The operations of Marxson and Company, as I know them, indicate a good likelihood that you could be saving money by automating your data processing today.

2. The costs of business data processing are on the rise! It is only a question of time before all but the smallest companies take recourse to automation to handle their paperwork. In this regard, one of the things we sometimes overlook is that the trend in the cost of a manual or semi-automatic system is constantly increasing per unit operation. With the electronic system, an increased burden would mean simply more time on the equipment or, at some future point, more equipment. Even if this were the case, the increase in cost per unit operation would be substantially less than the corresponding increase in a manual or semi-automatic system.

3. Your competitors are already exploring electronic data processing with the view of leasing a computer.

4. Other companies have found it profitable to use computers.

5. If there is any question, it is to determine the least costly and most effective way of making the transition to electronic data processing and in what areas to begin the transition first in order to maximize dollar savings.

I would like to devote my talk today to this subject: *What can Marxson and Company do to determine how to use electronic data processing equipment in its own operations?*

The route to electronics must invariably begin with a system study, the purpose of which is to establish the economic and operational feasibility of converting existing manual or punched card methods to automation.

The system study has four major components. We will see that they represent an orderly approach to solving your problems in the same way they have been used to solve complex commercial and military problems.

1. *The present system study:* to determine the status of the existing systems, and other rules under which present business operations are organized.

2. *The present system cost study:* to determine the displaceable and nondisplaceable structure of expenses that can be properly accrued to data processing, reflecting the present methods of operation.

3. *The proposed system study:* the proposed electronic data processing system which will do all—and sometimes much more—than its existing counterpart.

4. *The proposed system cost study:* the anticipated costs of con-

verting, installing, and operating an electronic data processing system and the resulting short and long term costs and savings.

A few words about each of these four points will clarify the issue of how to make the transition to electronics.

The way to embark on a present system study in your own company is to set up an executive steering committee whose function is to supervise and steer the efforts of the men who will actually do the work. The steering committee should include members of top management and represent the major departments.

A team of workers must be selected to make the study. It should include personnel and qualified consultants who specialize in electronic data processing. The probable make-up of such a group would be men from middle management levels representing the departments where the operational changes might be expected to be the greatest. The employee members of the team should be assigned to work full time with consultant personnel, who would be mathematicians and engineers with specialties in business analysis, operations research, and electronic data processing systems.

A planned educational program should be launched immediately in a two-pronged attack. First, there should be a program for Management, designed to explore as far as practical the various aspects of electronic data processing. Such a program, tailored to those who would not require any knowledge of the technical problems, would concentrate on system engineering philosophy, cost benefits, and operational benefits of computers. This Management orientation type of approach is extremely important. It is here, that Management and computer specialists, achieve a mutual understanding of each others' aims and a tolerance for the day-to-day problems of converting to electronics.

The second facet of the planned educational program should run concurrent with activity at your company. A nucleus of personnel should begin the process of learning about computers, utilizing as many of the front rank manufacturers' training schools as possible. A planned program would stagger this type of learning without putting undue accent on any one system of equipment. Such a program might continue for a year, during which time one to two months of schooling might be in order for each member of the team. More advanced courses can wait until the selection of equipment has been made and information can be specialized to the needs of this particular installation.

The next step is an over-all survey of the company's operations. This should be a brief but critical examination of each area to be considered. As a result, you will arrive at a priority list based upon the need for mechanization and the susceptibility to mechanization. Rough measures for determining the need might be the number of personnel involved or the cost of the present system. The susceptibility to mechanization depends upon the type of operation involved. Operations that are repetitive and performed on large volumes of data are particularly susceptible to successful mechanization and frequently show the largest savings.

Another objective of the over-all survey is to delineate integration possibilities among the various applications. Even at this early stage, it is possible to visualize how the various data processing tasks may be interrelated to achieve the most economic and effective operation of the computer.

Now you are ready to begin a detailed analysis of present system operations. The reports or documents that are produced by a system are called the outputs. The source documents going into the system are called the inputs. The outputs and inputs must be ingeniously inter-related in order to design an economic, electronic system. But to try this, without examining the present methods of operation, is to risk over-simplification—or failure to include some of the essential, re-quired processing. In a detailed examination of the present operations, it is possible to detect the unnecessary duplications of operations or files that typically creep into data processing systems that have evolved without scientific control. Elimination of such duplication is one means of effecting savings in a new system. A detailed description of the present system is a good starting point because it indicates *one* method of performing the required data processing operations.

These are some of the ways to describe the present operations of your Company:

1. *Flow charts:* illustrate the relationship of procedures or activities within departments or smaller groups.

2. *Samples of input and output forms and reports:* provide a basis for examining how well or how much the information being transmitted or processed is being used or is necessary.

3. *Specification of the processing necessary to arrive at a required output from a given input:* assures that all *fundamental* steps necessary to the proper completion of a task are going to be included in the design of a new electronic system.

4. *A list of the files to be maintained:* assembles the data essential to the system such as the number and size of records, or the aver-age number of numeric and alphanumeric characters that com-prise any individual record—in electronic data processing nu-meric quantities can be stored in less space than alphanumeric quantities. Another aspect of files which must be specified, is the access requirement. That is, how many times, over what period,

is it necessary to refer to a file? In what sequences do the references take place?

5. *In addition, there must be a specification of the activity and other pertinent volume figures:* For example, how many orders are there per day, or how many receipts? Again we must specify both the average and the maximum. In many cases, it is useful to make a distribution of the activity which specifies the frequency of occurrence.

6. *Any special communication requirements must also be documented.*

7. *The problem of centralization versus decentralization must be carefully isolated:* Certain business operations may only be partially susceptible to a centralized data processing system. The need to have certain records available for interrogation twenty-four hours a day may defeat the orderly schedule of an electronic data processing center.

The analysis of present system costs will naturally flow from the work which has been performed to analyze the system operations. The pertinent elements to isolate are:

1. Actual personnel costs—by department and section—devoted to the current processing of data.

2. The associated costs of space, equipment, and other facilities necessary to implement the use of personnel.

3. The costs of existing punched card installations, including equipment rentals and facilities.

4. The costs of data processing by *common tasks* such as payroll, personnel accounting, cost accounting, production scheduling, inventory, accounts payable, receivable, and so on. These are so-called horizontal costs because they affect the operation of all or most departments.

5. Opposed to these are the vertical or strictly non-common tasks that are associated with highly specialized data processing activities, some of which may be suitable to centralized data processing.

Analysis of the present system costs will enable your data processing task force to pick the areas in which the electronic system design will begin. Three or four areas *only,* might be sufficient to prove that electronics will have a handsome payoff. At this point a priority of effort can be established, and the task force can go to work to postulate—that is, *design*—the proposed electronic system.

The same tools used to describe the existing system are re-sharpened as we go into the back stretch! The order of the day is flow charting and some additional technical work called block diagramming. The techniques describe the new way in which the data processing operations can be done, bearing in mind some *generalized* electronic system.

Frequent conferences with the steering committee assure the responsible persons in your company of the step-by-step progress of the study. The steering committee may meet once every six weeks—or more frequently, if necessary. As the new system begins to take shape, meetings generally become more frequent.

But parallel with these reporting meetings are the many contacts your task force has with the operating members of your business to develop the new systems concept. These meetings prove the value of new ideas which are being introduced—so there will be a general concurrence of opinion regarding innovations that may be forthcoming.

During this period, the philosophy of systems engineering—something your employees must learn—is stressed. What makes a system? What are the system components? What attributes does a successful system have? What is integration, and what are the boundary conditions and subsystems that must be created to implement the design of a successful electronic data processing installation?

These and many more questions become the preoccupation of the task force. The result, however, makes itself known in a superior, economic utilization of your personnel, facilities, and dollars.

Side by side, the proposed system costs and proposed system design take form. The operational advantages will be paralleled by an analysis of the economic advantages. These will be assembled in two forms:

1. A report to the steering committee containing an outline of the next step or series of steps which eventually will place a computer in operation on your problems.

2. A request for bid suitable for analysis by manufacturers of equipment. Manufacturers, in turn, will prepare bids which must be analyzed by your personnel and your consultants. Their bids will be based upon their appraisal of how well their equipment can handle the system as proposed by your employees and consultants.

By examining the equipment evaluations of each manufacturer, based upon the common postulated system, it will be possible for the consultant to perform the last step in the system study, to make conclusions and recommendations. Among these will be the economic evaluation that must show the dollar advantages or disadvantages of electronic data processing. The economic evaluation is a comparison of the displaceable cost of the present system with the cost of the proposed electronic system. There must also be careful consideration of the so-called "intangible" benefits—more rapid reporting, more accurate information, and more sophisticated statistics and reports—these will all have a tangible benefit to which a dollar value can be ascribed, even though in some cases it may be very difficult to do this.

But we are not yet on the home stretch! Once equipment is on order the task force must begin the chore of converting human language to machine language. This process may take upwards of a year—during which time additional training, instruction, and formalizing of your electronics group must take place. In short, this waiting time for the computer to arrive is not *wasted*—far from it. Your employees will no doubt have as difficult a job before them in the home stretch as they did leaving the starting line.

A word of caution—if you were to start your system study for electronics tomorrow, depending on the size of staff and the amount of standardization in procedures, you could assume it would require about a year to send bids out to manufacturers. This means that electronics for Marxson and Company is always two years away, at the very least! This is a long time to wait in the critical days of ascending costs and high budgets.

Today you have heard how a typical electronic data processing investigation might be performed. This was called a systems study. You heard about the necessity for an education program as an essential element in data processing plans. We then reviewed how the system study is performed, outlining important steps in its conduct. These steps included education, the over-all survey, a detailed description of the present operations, a postulation of a generalized electronic data processing system, a specific equipment evaluation, and, finally, the preparation of conclusions and recommendations.

I commend to you these principles and the high quality results they have achieved for others, and can achieve for you, in planning the electronic data processing system for Marxson and Company.

QUESTIONS

1. What is the problem?
2. Should this company undertake a complete business systems study preceding the choice of a computer?
3. What would you do if you were Marxson?
4. What problems are posed by the systems approach?

13

The International
Corporation

Fred Fox, the manager in charge of special projects, reported to the vice-president in charge of operations, at the national headquarters of the International Corporation, in Chicago. His staff was drawn from various departments of the home office, on semi-permanent assignment. In their regular work in outlying divisions of the corporation, these men, who were on loan, operated as consultants. Because of years of service and specialization in limited fields, they were looked upon as experts when they were sent out on special assignments.

When a project was organized in another division, it was customary to select a *project leader.* The choice of a project leader sometimes had more to do with ability to maintain good client-consultant relations, than skills. Project leaders reported to Fox, directly. It occasionally happened that a man would be assigned to more than one project, working as a leader on one assignment and a non-leader on another. Customarily, the project leader reported his progress to the Division management, as well as Fox. On most projects, especially those exceeding three months in duration, a steering committee was formed. The project leader was a member of this committee, together with representatives of division management and interested departments. Members of such a working group, called a *task force,* had no direct contact with division management and very little direct contact with Fox. Division Managers were vice presidents on the same organization level as the officer to whom Fox reported.

Three projects were in process when Fox took over this activity on March 1, 1956. One of these at the Dallas division was a reorganization of the sales department. This project was headed by a former member of the national sales staff. It had been in process for two months and its status was satisfactory, according to the Dallas division manager. The second project was at the Newark division and had just begun. This assignment was to reorganize the division's accounting activity. The project was headed by a former controller out of the Chicago office. The third project was at the Denver division and had been in progress for two years—since March of 1954. Fox began a routine investigation of the status of this project. He started by searching the files to determine the original motivation to begin this study. He then determined the exact nature of the assignment, the personnel assigned to the task, and the schedule of completion.

Fox noted that the original assignment had apparently been put aside and a somewhat different assignment begun in July, 1955. Progress reports indicated that the original assignment was to determine the data processing requirements of the Denver division. However, soon after the project was started, two of the areas under investigation commanded more and more of the efforts of the task force. By November of 1955, the full efforts of the data processing personnel were being expended in the production control area. From March 1954, when the project was launched, until March 1956 when Fox took over, there had been several project leaders and steady growth in the size of the task force, from two to six men.

Soon after Fox took over the leadership of his department, the International corporate committee called for a review and formal presentation of the data processing study under way at the Denver division. The date was set for April 15th. It was clear that a commitment of six men costing over $90,000 per year required review and evaluation. Fox was unable to determine if the Denver division manager had asked for a review of this project because of his dissatisfaction with its progress. Since he had no basis for asking for an extension, Fox decided that an immediate, first hand investigation must be made.

Fox disqualified himself for this task, because of many urgent home office commitments. Since he had no regular staff to call on, he borrowed a member of the Tabulating Department, James Bunkker, to make the trip to Denver and report the results of his investigation. Bunkker reported to Fox three days prior to his departure, and spent this time familiarizing himself with the problem. Fox called the project leader in Denver to advise him of Bunkker's forthcoming trip. He stated the purpose of the investigation by explaining his problem of preparing a presentation for the corporate committee. Bunkker was told to prepare himself to face problems of morale and leadership, as well as technical problems. Bunkker talked extensively to Fox in order to understand what Fox wanted him to do in Denver. They decided the presentation to the corporate committee would have to emphasize the outstanding features of the new production control system. They agreed to stipulate that it was necessary to finish this study before the feasibility study could proceed.

Bunkker was disturbed by the wide variety of questions which needed answering. Although essentially unfamiliar with production control except as he had come into contact with these systems in his tabulating work, he felt he could probably evaluate the problems with sufficient advance preparation. Accordingly he set about outlining what he would do during his one week of investigation at Denver. This outline is on the following pages.

OUTLINE OF ACTIVITY

FOR TRIP TO DENVER DIVISION

I. Orientation:
   A. Meet with project leader.
   B. Explain the assignment.
   C. Meet Denver operating (factory) personnel.
   D. Tour physical facilities.
   E. Meet 2nd and 3rd shift personnel.

II. Look at the present system and proposed revisions:
   A. What are the inputs and how are they used?
      1. The forms: who originates; their flow destination, usefulness, duplication?
      2. Information: any unavailable; everything required?
      3. What part does tabulating play?
   B. What controls keep the system in balance and operating?
      1. Where are they; do they work; are there enough of them?
      2. Is everyone working with the same set of ground rules?

C. Examine the outputs.
  1. What form are they in?
  2. Is all of the information in report form?
  3. Is all of the information necessary to report?
  4. Is there redundance in content?
  5. Are the right people getting the right outputs?
      a. Do they know how to act on them?
      b. Do they act on them?
      c. What is their reliability?
      d. Is there too much detail?
D. Examine the feedback plan.
  1. What is the level of accuracy?
  2. How is the system affected by the level of accuracy?
  3. What are the feedback documents?
      a. Will they be timely?
      b. How many; of what type?
      c. Who is responsible?
      d. Will the feedbacks keep the system current?
E. Make flow charts of
  1. The gross system
  2. The major sub-systems
  3. Plan to check
      a. Areas where changes have been suggested.
      b. Areas where changes are in order, but are not planned.

III. Work on the operating level:
  A. Foremen or supervisors of operating departments:
    1. What are their duties?
    2. Scope of activity?
    3. From whom do they get information, and in what form?
    4. Contacts with other personnel.
  B. Assigned indirect labor (dispatcher, parts movers, timekeepers, inspectors):
    1. Respective duties of each.
    2. Relative authority and responsibility.
    3. Are they document originators, processors, handlers, or do they "hold?"
    4. Who gives them their orders; to what extent are they under the department foremen?
    5. What is the relationship of Material Review, Quality Control and Factory Management?
  C. Watch the operations for
    1. Transit time between operations.
    2. Number of jobs in front of each machine.

    3. What are the frequency and types of upsets to normal, pre-planned operation?

    4. Is there a "shift" problem?

    5. Is the conception of how jobs start and stop accurate?

    6. Any obvious effects of variable lot size?

    7. Are count, time, and charge reasonably accurate?

      a. What does the operator do to write up his job card?

      b. Could it be done another way?

  D. Watch outside contracted operations.

    1. Do they plan; how far ahead; how?

    2. How much capacity and versatility do they have?

    3. Transportation problems in and out.

    4. Liaison problems and delays of what type?

IV. Meet with Industrial Engineering

  A. Their organizational position.

  B. What programs are they working on?

  C. How do they see the proposed system?

  D. How do they plan to contribute?

V. Meet with project leader—review the system as seen in investigation.

  A. Areas requiring more analysis.

  B. Areas of disagreement.

  C. Pursue facts to clear up problems.

  D. Determine policies in problem areas.

  E. Restate the system.

VI. Set up the system for installation:

  A. Implementation areas.

  B. Design and study areas.

VII. Write report to Fox.

QUESTIONS

    1. What is the problem?

    2. What is the organization problem at Denver?

    3. Are some pertinent pieces missing from the outline? Should some parts of the outline be deleted?

    4. How would you have put the systems concept to work in this investigation?

14

Carlysle, Inc.

On January 1st, L. James Carlysle became chairman of the board of directors of Carlysle, Inc. His successor to the active direction of the business was Henry Armstrong, former general manager of W. S. G. Manufacturing Industries, one of the country's most profitable and cost-minded organizations. Carlysle's organization chart (Figure 14–1) is shown as Exhibit One. The sales position of Carlysle was considered better than ever. Volume had grown from $350,000 a year to $2,500,000 in less than six years. The backlog stood at $680,-000, and profits were at an all time high.

Shortly after taking over, Armstrong asked for a customer-volume analysis of sales. This analysis is included as Exhibit Two. In an effort to learn something of the principal customers, Armstrong asked the sales manager, Wendell Phillips, to prepare a short sum-

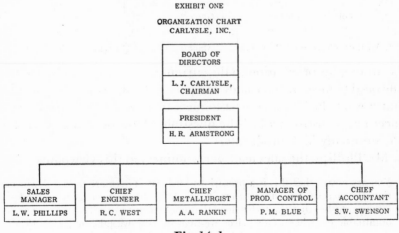

EXHIBIT ONE

ORGANIZATION CHART
CARLYSLE, INC.

Fig. 14–1.

mary of the twenty whose volume contributed most heavily to the total sales and backlog. On fifteen of these, Armstrong asked Carlysle's bank to do a thorough investigation, since accounts receivable were in five figures.

A series of meetings were initiated by Armstrong as a means of

EXHIBIT 2

CUSTOMER-VOLUME ANALYSIS OF SALES, CARLYSLE, INC.

Type of indus-try*	Cus-tomer	Accounts receivable	Receiv-ables over 30 days old	Years sold	Number of items sold	Unfilled orders on hand	Age of oldest order in months
5	A	$ 9,000	$ 6,000	2	1	$ 40,700	4
2	B	500	100	1	1	2,000	2
1	C	61,200	23,600	2	8	88,800	4
3	D	7,200	4,800	1	6	3,000	3
1	E	23,400	8,000	5	12	18,000	3
4	F	7,800	5,100	2	8	25,900	2
4	G	89,100	64,800	4	23	11,600	3
1	H	1,700	1,200	4	3	20,400	2
4	I	12,400	8,000	5	16	0	0
2	J	1,100	100	5	2	1,000	1
2	K	5,400	4,000	3	6	171,600	3
3	L	48,500	30,500	2	15	90,800	4
3	M	1,200	1,000	4	6	3,400	2
5	N	18,600	12,000	4	8	48,000	5
1	O	5,700	3,000	5	3	12,800	2
5	P	400	0	3	7	0	0
2	Q	12,100	7,000	2	3	25,600	3
1	R	3,600	2,800	3	1	4,800	3
4	S	1,100	1,000	3	3	2,100	1
5	T	350	350	5	1	800	1
	All others	100,000	65,000			108,800	7
		$410,350	$248,350			$679,300	

* 1, Military electronics; 2, Aircraft; 3, Machine tools; 4, Instrumentation; 5, Other.

beginning his orientation to the current operations. Armstrong felt the need to meet his associates on a personal basis as soon as possible, but was satisfied at the outset to meet them as a group. In the first meeting, Armstrong asked the question, "How do you account for the unusually high profit rate?"

Mr. Phillips, the sales manager, volunteered this viewpoint:

You are aware that this is a precarious business. There are only a dozen nationally successful manufacturers in this field today. As a result, we take a large profit because the technology that enables us to survive is not generally obtainable elsewhere. Our prices are high because we take on a class of jobs that our competitors won't. We ask a high price because we are in a non-competitive market where our customers normally ask for small quantities, high quality, and fast delivery. Furthermore, our customers know these prices are high and are glad to get the merchandise.

Mr. West, the chief engineer, took the position that "high prices or not, the outstanding feature of the Carlysle operation was their ingenious tooling." Subsequent discussion brought out how he and his staff had solved challenging problems that opened new markets to Carlysle. West pointed out that a sizeable part of the total volume was with companies who bought very complex, high priced castings which other manufacturers were unable to produce. Molds were procured from mold makers who specialized in this work.

Mr. Rankin, the chief metallurgist, said that in his mind the problem was only partly stated by emphasizing tooling and engineering. He pointed out how shrinkage or expansion, warpage, hardness, chemical composition, and tolerances were all dependent on a set of metallurgical factors. The selection of pouring temperatures, catalysts and introduction of control elements in the melt were also quoted as purely metallurgical contributions. Rankin said that these things might only influence profit indirectly, but this technology made the difference between successful and unsuccessful production. From his standpoint, therefore, high profit was due in many respects to advanced metallurgical technology.

Mr. Blue, the production control manager, made the comment that while "the boys are squabbling over details, they should all recognize that planning, scheduling, and meeting customers commitments on time contributed to a reputation for dependability." He cited the innovations that were responsible for increasing production and reducing lead times. Blue was unable to accept the philosophy of West and Rankin in total. He said experimenting and development—typical of processing most orders—built delays into schedules. These delays were sometimes unexplainable and created bad relations and antagonism between the customer and Carlysle's Production Control. He cited the hit or miss "genius-type" effort which was required to maintain the "Carlysle reputation."

When Armstrong asked Mr. Swenson, the chief accountant, for his opinion, he could only say that the bidding and quotation procedure administered by the sales department must be acknowledged as the fundamental reason for high profit. He said that Carlysle used a job cost system and costs were collected on each order as it went through the shop. Each worker reported his time against job order numbers that were posted in the shop. Each month he submitted a summary of total labor dollars charged to job orders. There was a great deal of unexpected fluctuation in these reports, but gross figures pretty well substantiated what the key men expected. Materials were charged in on a standard basis and showed smaller fluctuation. Swenson had nothing more to add about high profits except to note that Phillips was an outstanding salesman.

Armstrong began a series of individual meetings to explore fully the operations of each segment of the business. These first discussions were with Swenson. A review of the Monthly Operating Reports illustrated a long list of jobs in process, some of which had a mean cycle time four times as great as the average. In addition, a large number of jobs were unprofitable, while a small number were exceptionally profitable. A partial list of jobs is included as Exhibit Three. Armstrong was told the average selling price per casting was close to $6.00. Large excesses in material cost were laid to the need to cast orders more than once because the original lot would not produce minimum shipping quantities. Excesses in labor were not clearly identifiable with cause. Costs were not distributed by department, cost center, or operator.

The system of reporting was submitted to scrutiny. Labor and material dollars forecast were found to depend on original estimating and bidding procedures. Such estimates were made by sales personnel who had with long experience been able to predict accurately cost and profit, according to Swenson. Although Swenson admitted there was considerable fluctuation in individual costs, he pointed out that over-all figures were amazingly close to sales projections. Engineering was consulted, as necessary, by Sales, in the quotation process.

Armstrong had several meetings with Phillips and members of his sales staff. These meetings revealed divergent points of view regarding what kind of business was good for Carlysle. Phillips was set against large volume contracts, arguing that the Carlysle method of operation was not suitable for low priced merchandise. Some salesmen, however, contested this attitude because they felt there were big sales possibilities in repetitive, large quantity production.

EXHIBIT 3
PARTIAL MONTHLY OPERATING REPORT OF SHIPMENTS
MONTH OF OCTOBER
CARLYSLE, INC.

Job Number	Date Issued	Number Pieces Cast	Number Pieces on Order	Labor Dollars Forecast	Material Dollars Forecast	Actual Labor Dollars Reported	Actual Material Dollars Reported
16761	8/51	304	240	530	270	870	570
16804	10/51	260	180	420	180	588	290
17110	12/51	871	550	1010	460	705	421
17867	2/52	602	400	900	440	611	400
20411	4/52	104	81	190	90	421	177
26711	7/52	114	90	220	80	80	91
26713	7/52	90	60	80	20	31	21
26745	7/52	62	54	60	30	42	21
26751	7/52	145	110	120	60	401	162
26867	8/52	600	420	480	220	320	208
26868	8/52	314	220	250	120	251	124
26869	8/52	224	175	210	80	304	178
26873	8/52	187	160	180	90	120	45
26888	8/52	200	170	190	90	160	80
26891	8/52	161	125	140	60	151	63
26894	9/52	145	125	130	70	110	65
26896	9/52	40	20	45	20	30	8
26897	9/52	180	140	310	160	280	140
26901	9/52	90	40	100	45	61	20
26902	9/52	1200	675	1500	750	1810	620
26903	9/52	1000	850	1890	940	1460	800
26904	9/52	188	150	400	100	421	27
26905	9/52	221	190	480	120	321	87

They said, "Not all jobs would be so profitable that they would be able to carry high overhead rates." They further argued that diversification of jobs and higher volume jobs would be an insurance policy to Carlysle, which was, at present, entirely dependent on low volume-high profit items.

Phillips was critical of the cost system. He said it was impossible for him to know what jobs were profitable or what jobs were unhealthy for Carlysle, because reporting was so inconsistent. He said further, he would never be able to prove what kinds of jobs he should be getting because, "Engineering, Metallurgy and Production Control can't settle on a good set of ground rules for running first articles." Armstrong found out that first articles were customer samples and always had top priority.

Discussions with Blue gave Armstrong another side of the picture. Blue pointed out that the Sales Department handed out delivery ultimatums based on their promises, without consulting him first. He illustrated with data how commitments made to customers ignored his already overloaded schedule. He also pointed out that delivery dates were dictated by customers with little recognition of contingencies that always arose in the production of first articles. Blue said that changes in schedule, which were frequent, made it extremely difficult to operate economically with small quantity production. Blue asked Armstrong, "Do you think we should continue to run jobs on which we have never been able to make a profit"?

West commented to Armstrong that, somehow, parts were never really manufactured to the prescribed engineering standard and that if the shop ever started doing this, they would have a lot less trouble. West indicated that the complex technology of manufacturing would never get simpler, and that better controls on quality were necessary. Some jobs were necessarily going to be losing jobs because the role of Carlysle was to take on the tough ones. He said he was certain that this was how they had made their reputation and built the business. A description of the investment casting process is included as Exhibit Four.

Phillips asked each member of his staff to make recommendations he could incorporate into a Master Plan. Swenson submitted a report recommending an overhaul in all phases of the dollars and cents side of the business. West asked for a program of quality control. Phillips asked for better bidding, quotation, and production scheduling procedures, so he could get more business and satisfy more customers. Blue asked for a plan to revamp the organization and responsibilities of the key people in the business, making the hub of the internal operation in Production Control. Rankin submitted the shortest request, asking for an appropriation of $16,000 to set up a metallurgical lab.

EXHIBIT 4

DESCRIPTION OF THE
INVESTMENT CASTING PROCESS
AT CARLYSLE, INC.

Investment casting is a technique of casting that is many hundreds of years old. It was used successfully in the creation of art objects, but until the 1930s it had little technological development for industrial uses. In 1940, industry required high tolerance castings with finished surfaces that were difficult or impossible to machine. These parts, made from new steels, increased manufacturing costs. Some parts could not be successfully machined within required tolerances, because of hardness and other technical problems.

Investment casting processes are very complex. Each part requires a mold which may have one or more cavities. The costs of these molds are high because cavities must be machined to close tolerances. Parts to be made in low volume customarily have one cavity. Parts to be made in higher volume may have more. Cavities must be machined in negative, so impressions made of these parts can be removed in positive. The process of machining the cavities is a highly skilled project, requiring wide tooling experience and frequently requiring extensive rework or scrap due to miscalculations or corrections.

Gates are attached to the impression to facilitate pouring of metals. Gates are avenues through which metal will travel, to be removed later, after casting and cooling. Gates are machined into the mold at the same time the cavities are made. Gating must frequently be corrected as a result of poor impressions or misfills in the casting process. Molds range in size from 1″ x 1″ x 2″ for a small example, or may go up to 8″ x 16″D for a large example. They weigh up to 50 pounds and may cost as little as $200 or be as expensive as $10,000. Molds are made of aluminum or steel. The shop is operated on two procedures, one for first articles and one for production. The only difference between these is that first articles are in sample quantities of two or three pieces, while production is in larger quantities.

The first article procedure begins with mold check-out. Molds are checked out by the engineering department. Injections are tried on production equipment to do this. The injection machine forces hot wax into the mold orifice under pressure. Wax travels through the main gate into the cavity and fills all subsidiary gates. Pressures of injection may vary from 60 to 400 pounds, and take from one-half to five minutes. One injection may suffice to reject or accept the mold, although it could take more than a hundred.

After injection the molds are opened with knives or prongs, and the wax image of the part removed from the cavity with the gates. Any gates not necessary to the casting process are broken off and discarded in a scrap bucket, for reclamation. If no visual flaws are evident, waxes are taken to Quality Control for dimensional check-out. Any problems in injection or removal are noted on paperwork accompanying the mold, and selected pressure and holding time are recorded. Production quantities do not go through wax inspection on a 100 per cent basis, although all waxes require cleaning.

First article waxes are inspected for dimensional and surface condition. Out of tolerance or otherwise defective waxes are cause for rejection and molds must be sent back to moldmakers for rework. If molds are certified for production, the paper work is completed and the mold passed for payment and taken to stock. Any remarks regarding composition of wax or indications of anticipated production problems are noted for use in production. Copies of this information go to the chief metallurgist. Molds are bought by customers on acceptance of first article.

From this point forward, first articles and production have identical processing. When the production order is released, waxes are shot with an added factor to cover anticipated scrap. They are sent to the wax assembly department where they are set up prior to investing. In set-up, the wax department foreman follows the suggestion of the engineering department to insure proper gating. Despite the fact that gating is critical, it is difficult to determine for sure how many parts per flask will be possible until the first article cast is completed. This type of data is customarily incorporated in production runs. There is, however, a limitation of no more than 13 pounds of steel or 30 pounds of aluminum per flask.

Individual waxes are cleaned and partially inspected prior to set-up. Wax parts are mounted on pouring cups and specially injected gates. Parts and gates are welded into a unit called the sprue. If the set-up design is approved, set-up operators will assemble the sprue for investing. Frequently, two or more sprues will be tried because of doubt as to the outcome of the melt when first articles are being tried. Sprues are marked as to direction of pouring for identification in the casting process.

Setting up sprues is a tedious process. There are a variety of wax welding methods, and there is a tendency for sprues not to be uniform. There may be only two parts to a sprue or as many as two hundred, depending upon the size of the part and weight of metal to be poured. Wax sprues must be thoroughly cleaned and inspected prior to the next operation.

The dipping process is the core of successful investment casting. In this operation, sprues are covered with a chemical solution. After dipping, the sprue is lightly sanded and left to dry. This operation is repeated from two to five times, after which the sprue is wax welded to a steel plate. The sprue is now ready for investing.

There are two methods of investing, one for ferrous, another for nonferrous parts. In either case, a circular or square section of steel plate from 4″ to 16″ in height is sealed to the sprue. This square or circular section is called the flask. Flask sizes and heights vary widely with sprue size. Flasks are made of stainless steel and cost about $50 a unit.

Investment is a fine plaster-like material that flows easily and dries with a fine surface. Flasks are filled with this cement-like material which is shaken down to eliminate bubbles and create a solid pack. This is left to dry naturally, and harden. The base plate is removed, after which the invested sprue is set upside down on a dewaxing cart and wheeled into a dewaxing oven. The dewaxing process takes eight to twelve hours. During this process the wax melts and drips out of the investment leaving a smooth, clean negative cavity of the entire sprue. Temperature for dewaxing is 225 degrees. From forty to one hundred and twenty flasks may be in the oven at any one time.

Before the flask and its contents cool, it is transferred to one of five heating furnaces, with as few as 18 or as many as 72 flasks to an oven. Dewaxed flasks are mounted on top of each other using 1″ x 1″ x 1″ ceramic blocks to create air space between each flask. Ovens are closed and furnace programs are set to bring temperatures up as high as 1800 degrees at the rate of 100 degrees per hour, automatically. Heating cycles require up to sixteen hours and must be slowly lowered after a peak heat, to the required casting temperature. An oven load may contain flasks to be cast at several heats. When temperatures have been lowered, metal shot or bar is placed in melting pots and the metal is melted. Flasks are removed, red hot, from heating ovens and clamped on melting pots over the pouring hole. Flasks are evacuated and inverted as a unit so metal can fill the investment cavity. After pouring, the flask is removed and left to cool.

After cooling, the metal sprue is knocked out of the flask, and the parts cut off the tree with an abrasive saw. Parts are then deburred, ground and finished for inspection and shipment.

QUESTIONS

1. What is the problem?
2. If you were Armstrong, what would you do?
3. What can you learn from the description of the investment casting manufacturing process?
4. What are the systems aspects of this case?

15

The Simpson-East
Corporation

The Simpson-East Corporation devoted its full efforts to research, development, and manufacture of advanced electronic equipment. It worked exclusively on military contracts with cost-plus-fixed-fee compensation rules up to 1954. Starting in business in 1940, as the result of a merger with one of the country's oldest names in the field of communications and electronics, Simpson-East developed a reputation for high quality.

Early in its business life, Simpson-East began bidding successfully on small quantity, highly complex electronics contracts. It was on contracts of this type that the corporation built its business volume. Profits were between five and six per cent. A system of project costing was used.

In 1954, Simpson-East employed 500. There were 121 in various engineering activities. About 250 employees were direct labor. The balance were indirect, distributed over administrative and service departments. Dollar volume was $3,000,000 annually.

The corporation had a wide source of business, among which were air-frame manufacturers as well as electronics firms. In addition, they were invited to bid directly by various branches of the armed forces. Blueprints, written specifications, or samples were supplied to assist in bidding procedure. However, these contracts called out severe time schedules, since frequently a comparatively small part of a large electronics system could be holding up a sizeable, urgent project. Consequently, it was in the interest of customer relations and sometimes programs of national importance, to reduce bidding time to a minimum.

To cope with this problem, rules of thumb were conceived which made it possible to bid quickly. The motto was "get the job, and we'll figure out how to make money later." There was a uniformly low profit as a result of this method of operation. However, in renegotiation, profits were sometimes improved.

A typical order for a new commodity would begin with a contract to do research, development, and manufacturing. The first desired output of the development phase was a circuit design called a "bread-board." However, work on the bread-board started before the end of the research phase. The final engineering design followed the completion of the bread-board. When engineering design was out of the way, a prototype was built.

Production Control began its investigation of the new commodity "over-the-shoulders" of the research and development staff. The purpose of this early interest was to place on order hard-to-get items with long delivery times. This investigation period might range from 1 to 300 man-hours. During this period, Production Control was forced to accommodate its ordering procedure to the many changes in the design of the new commodity. There was a natural tendency to order as many of the parts as possible, and get them into stock. But this policy frequently led to contradictory situations. Frequently, expensive components ordered according to established rules were left unused in stock to complicate renegotiation. This occurred because changes in commodity design could take place any time prior to delivery to the customer. If new components were required, the original components were sent to stock as surplus.

An equally complex situation occasionally developed when components which should have been ordered, were not. Sometimes this problem was associated with lack of information at a sufficiently early date; other times it was laid to poor investigation or inadequate record keeping and follow-up systems in Production Control. Production Control customarily requisitioned components. Ordering and follow-up was done in the purchasing section of the materials department. Materials that were ordered on CPFF contracts became the property of the government on receipt. The urgency to maintain minimum inventories was not as great as it might have been if these inventories required the working capital of Simpson-East. Surplus inventories were carefully watched by the government and periodically reduced by direct sale to anyone who was in the market.

All materials were placed on order for production following the completion of the prototype produced by the design engineering staff. Verbal or memo sales orders were the authority to purchase. There were several members of the engineering-sales-administrative management who could authorize the "go ahead" on a project. Material requirements were taken directly from blueprints by Production Control clerks. There were no parts lists or bills of material issued separately by Research, Development, or Design Engineering. As a consequence, liaison was required whenever new commodities were placed on order. One of the big problems was whether or not to use standard parts whenever possible. Descriptions of components were not standardized, with the result that frequent changes, revisions, and clarifications were necessary to meet the manufacturer's specifications.

Production analysis was the next step in the procedure. In this period, individual parts and subassemblies were analyzed in anticipation of actual production. Parts lists were indented at this time, and lead times were estimated based upon the best information available. Analysis always revealed inconsistencies and mistakes in design, which made further changes necessary so the product would be possible to manufacture. All changes in design or parts requirements were processed through a Change Board that met once a month.

The production phase followed material order by approximately 30 to 45 days. The expected problems of tolerances not adding up and last minute revisions were accented by the embellishments to products in the process of their manufacture. There was no rule to apply to changes which were necessary versus changes which merely added to the engineering perfection of the product. The result was that production lines were continually in flux. Engineers were active in all phases of the actual manufacturing process. A bar chart (Figure 15–1) describing the phases of operations follows as Exhibit One.

In February of 1956, the accounting department, with Management, reviewed the working papers for calendar year 1955 operations. The here-to-fore acceptable profit had slipped from 5.4 per cent to less than 2 per cent. Reduced profits were associated directly with fixed price contracts which had become an increasingly important factor to provide dollar volume in early 1955. CPFF business, formerly 99 per cent of the total dollar volume of business, had slipped to 28 per cent.

Management reacted with a shakeup in personnel. Several experienced members of top management were replaced, including the general manager. New personnel were sought to fill the vacant posts. It was anticipated that some of the new personnel would come from the electronics industry; others would have diversified backgrounds. Joe Waddell, the new general manager, was among the latter.

When Waddell took this position in May, 1956, he did so with the understanding that he had six months to begin to show some acceptable signs of progress. Waddell was not impressed with the

EXHIBIT ONE

TIME SCALE OF A TYPICAL ORDER
SIMPSON-EAST CORP.

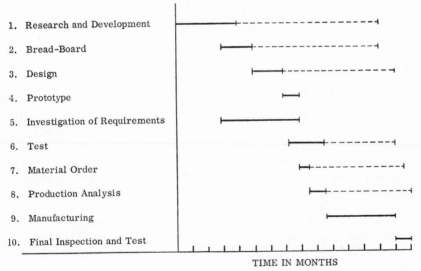

1. Research and Development
2. Bread-Board
3. Design
4. Prototype
5. Investigation of Requirements
6. Test
7. Material Order
8. Production Analysis
9. Manufacturing
10. Final Inspection and Test

TIME IN MONTHS

Solid lines are periods of initial activity.
Dotted lines are periods of liaison to incorporate changes, etc.

Fig. 15–1.

Simpson-East management, and he knew they were in trouble. But they had given him a free hand to do what he thought necessary in order to provide an acceptable level of profits.

By June, Waddell was obtaining daily information on all phases of the Corporation's operations. In addition, he had accumulated a notebook of data, outlining the functions of various departments, and brief flow charts showing the interrelationships of the various groups within each department. A staff of two men assisted in the development of data, and pursued the leads and suggestions he made in order to obtain a clear picture of the existing mode of operation.

Waddell's attention was called to a report submitted by a plant committee four months before he was installed as plant manager. Since many of the members of Management were impressed by this report, he gave its contents his careful attention. (This report follows as Exhibit Two.)

On July 10th, Waddell advised Management he was ready to meet with them and submit his findings.

EXHIBIT TWO

COST REDUCTION:
A PLANT COMMITTEE STUDY

This report outlines what our committee considers to be the most fruitful areas of overhead cost reduction.

The approach utilized is best described as The Group Process in Administration. In our earlier meetings, the problem was outlined in terms of what has happened in overhead cost and what we expect to happen, dollar-wise, during the remainder of 1955. Keying our investigations to the major cost factors, the indicated group members attacked the problem from two points of view: (1) on a departmental basis; (2) on an integrated or "across-organizational lines" basis.

What follows is a series of pointed "cost-cutting" recommendations which emerged from our integrated group discussions. These suggestions, if implemented, will result in significant reductions in operating costs.

> (1) Divisional planning of new business and project activities as they develop must give consideration to realistic lead times. Major economies can be realized by "building in" sufficient

lead times to provide for known, fixed time requirements. Among these are:

a) Reduced material procurement costs
    1) Greater productivity realized by individual buyers through systematization of material procurement.
    2) Cost reduction on air freight expenditures.
    3) A lowering of clerical personnel requirements resulting from lesser complexity in incorporation change orders in purchase orders; special follow-up systems.
    4) A lowering of telephone costs in placing "crash" orders.
b) Reduced overtime compensation in R & D and production activities.
c) Reduced personnel recruiting costs in terms of "crash" advertising program, recruiting trips, and so on.
d) Reduced labor costs by planning staff requirements rather than staffing to meet crash situations.

(2) Establish a clear definition of project and manufacturing requirements and dissemination of these requirements on a need-to-know basis. Significant overhead cost reduction results in terms of a reduction in duplication of effort in production planning and in material procurement.

(3) Accomplish a transferral of labor costs of significant numbers of employees from indirect to direct where industrial precedents in government contract activities have been established.

(4) Initiate a training program which will result in significant "upgrading" of current employees, decreased costs of recruiting experienced people, and reduced turnover ratio. Suggested programs for current implementation include

a) A formal "offhours" technician training program given by several members of the technical staff and professors from local colleges and universities. College credit should be given where possible.
b) A similar program for junior engineers.
c) An assembler training program.
d) An apprentice machinist training program.
e) A supervisory training program.

(5) Install a central laboratory equipment control to project equipment requirements and utilize currently available equipment to an optimum level. This comprehensive control would result in major cost reduction in terms of capital equipment investment, overhead servicing, and depreciation. Suggested implementation is the installation of the function in the technical section.

(6) Standardize the nomenclature of components. All components ordered on purchase requisitions or specified on designs should be defined in a predetermined format providing for their complete description. The areas of economy would be as follows:

   a) Reduced cut in man-hours in both production and publications groups by making possible a straight-forward, nearly "one-time" material analysis, minimizing the number of check and correct operations.

   b) Reduced costs in terms of purchasing man-hours spent in checking, correcting, and modifying information given to vendors.

(7) Define a standard range of continuously used components. A significant result of standard nomenclature would be a set of standard parts composed primarily of hardware and inexpensive electronic components. Initiation of this program depends upon acceptance by project and design engineering. Resultant economies would be:

   a) Inventories can be reduced by elimination of duplications with resulting savings of space and personnel requirements.

   b) Large-quantity purchases, from prime sources rather than jobbers, could be made to cover all needs. Jobbers premiums in many cases are as high as 50 per cent of the purchase price. It is suggested that production stores act as supplier to the various stores, to capitalize on large quantity purchases and reduce inventories.

   c) A reduction of numbers of purchase orders with resultant reductions in overhead clerical activity.

   d) Paper work economies by use of "Buy Cards" in Production replacing purchase requisitions.

(8) Establish a stock committee. This committee would meet once a month to consider anticipated component requirements, adjust stock levels for parts which have not moved during the month, and act as a sounding board for functional problems related to stock and its issuance. Economies would be

   a) Reduction of dollars tied up in obsolete and slow-moving stock.

   b) Minimization of the necessity of expensive rush procurement of parts.

   c) Less clerical time spent routing complaints concerning the stock room to Management.

(9) Eliminate duplication of material follow-up by Production and Purchasing. These operations presently follow a parallel course. Major economies would result from combining these

operations either as part of Purchasing located with Production or as part of Publication.

   a) Staff required could be reduced.

   b) Files could be combined and clerical personnel requirements reduced.

(10) Coordinate the cost accounting system between the operating section and the accounting section. A cost system developed in this manner will enable Production and R & D to reduce the amount of clerical effort currently required.

(11) Install mechanical tabulating and record keeping equipment. The estimated cost of a tabulating section indicates that it can be operated at a lower cost than if our full tabulating services are provided from outside. An advantage of operating our own equipment is long-term costs reduction, not now being realized, which will accrue as a result of accounting data and reports being generated on time with less clerical effort.

(12) Institute a change in material procurement procedures which will provide for charging more than one job per purchase order or purchase requisition to the same vendor. Cost reductions will be in terms of reduced numbers of purchase requisitions, and consequent lessening of clerical effort.

(13) Increase present personnel staff by the addition of two experienced men. Reduced costs will result in two major areas:

   a) Employment effort can fully exploit the personal contact approach to recruiting, resulting in significant cost reductions in terms of local advertising and extended recruiting trips. Contacts include present employees, educational institutions, employment agencies, and other companies. One local company reports that 60 per cent of new hires result from personal contacts.

   b) Employee turnover ratio can be reduced by closer screening of new hires and an increase in the informal education program for supervisors in selection techniques. A reduced turnover ratio will result in significant savings in advertising and recruiting costs.

(14) Install procedures to insure more effective control of sick leave. Enlightened administration of the sick leave policy by supervisors will result in minimizing cost by abuses of this policy.

(15) Use short form employment applications for initial screening purposes. This results in a lesser expenditure for the formal employment questionnaires.

(16) Provide a less expensive recruiting brochure to be utilized in

non-professional recruiting. Significant savings can be realized by utilizing a more concise, less heavily illustrated booklet for non-professionals.

(17) Adhere to the Temporary Added Compensation Policy for reimbursement of exempt personnel overtime. A significant reduction in premium time payments can be realized.

Evaluation

The committee feels that there have been several fruitful results of its group activity:

First of these are the concrete recommendations for cost reductions which the committee believes to be sound.

Second, a major value has been the free discussion of the operation of other sectors of the administrative activity in our plant. The resultant learning has been rapid and of permanent value.

QUESTIONS

1. What are the systems aspects of this case?
2. If you were Waddell, what would you submit as your findings?
3. What is the basic problem to which Waddell must address himself?
4. How do you evaluate the Plant Committee Report?

16

Beaver Alliance Aircraft Corporation

Beaver Aircraft Corporation, was one of the nation's small scale manufacturers of airplanes prior to 1940. Working on a job shop basis, Beaver had three models, all of which were considered highly reliable. Contracts with the Army were so small that there was no opportunity to enlarge the Corporation's activity, with the result that a small lot method of manufacture had been undertaken.

In a monthly schedule of deliveries which might vary between eight and twelve planes, it was customary to make structural changes effective in odd months in order to minimize manufacturing problems. Since the backlog of orders was relatively small, job lots were seldom over one hundred pieces. The frequency of engineering changes was high, and, since airplanes were not identical in material or labor input, the need for accurate charging of direct labor costs had been recognized as a significant problem.

Airplanes were assembled in large hangars. Crews were rotated across these locations, 19 in number, called *work stations*. Each station had a tool crib, parts crib, and a few fixtures to provide for access to the external parts of the plane. Mating operations as well as minor modifications took place in these stations. Station 20 was left vacant when the airplane was towed outside the hangar for checkout, engine run, and testing prior to its initial flight. As soon as station 20 was open, aircraft would be manually moved forward into the next position.

With the advent of war in Europe, Beaver Aircraft foresaw that demands on their ability to produce would be so far in excess of their past capabilities that they began negotiations with Alliance Aircraft Producers, Inc., to effect a merger. Alliance had facilities and good production techniques, whereas Beaver felt they could supply the designs. The merger was endorsed by the government because of the need for large capacity. A method of operation was developed, and, in 1941, the Beaver Alliance Aircraft Corporation was formed. After physical consolidation in 1943, large scale production was begun, with schedules rising sharply month by month for several years. The plant with which we are concerned employed 2,200 direct labor.

Because of the nature of cost-plus contracts, the philosophy of *laissez-faire* was easy to come by. But alert management pointed out that contracts were subject to renegotiation and every detail of their cost structure would be subject to intensive scrutiny, especially direct labor. It was obvious that over-staffing the labor force would not operate to the disadvantage of the company, since there would theoretically be a return on every dollar expended, irrespective of the efficiency with which the end product was produced. The problems of direct labor were classified as dual in nature. The first had to do with efficiency in production, the utilization of labor, and the minimization of cost to the government. The second area was that of accounting for the labor expended, whether efficiently or not, and seeing to it that work was properly charged, the time accurately stated, and the count of production consistent with lot releases. Methods of collecting costs varied between feeder shop operations and line assembly operations.

The problem of efficiency of operations was in the province of Industrial Engineering. It fell on this department to set time standards for each operation and compute the total standard labor hours required to complete each end product by division, department, and cost center. As a result of the activity of any period, usually a week, reports were issued comparing the actual performance with anticipated (standard) performance. Cost centers were said to be fifty per cent efficient if they produced fifty standard hours in a period when one hundred actual hours were consumed. The notation to measure efficiency was

$$\frac{\text{Standard Hours}}{\text{Actual Hours}} = \% \text{ Realization (Efficiency)} \tag{1}$$

Or conversely, the standards could be adjusted by the efficiency factor to change them into actuals. If the industrial engineers predicted that a new or revised job would take a certain number of standard hours, the anticipated actual hours could be set up and labor requisitioned accordingly. The notation to show this adjustment was:

$$\frac{\text{Standard Hours}}{\%\ \text{Realization}} = \text{Actual Hours} \tag{2}$$

These relationships were expressed for purposes of labor loading in terms of hours. For accounting purposes, they were expressed as dollars. Sometimes learning curves were fitted to jobs where training was an essential ingredient of efficiency. This type of system was extended into the field of direct labor forecasting in order to predict what levels of employment should be anticipated for various volumes. The shop average for efficiency was 60 per cent.

The problem of sorting increments of time so that they would be charged to the proper job was the function of the Labor Distribution Report. The operator recorded his time on daily Production Tickets indicating the airplane number, if the worker was on the production line. A job number that covered a certain series of airplanes was used if the operator was working in one of the feeder shops. The accuracy of labor distribution was considered of prime importance, although inconsistencies were apparent when charges to one series of airplanes fluctuated as opposed to the charges on a prior similar series. Occasionally a situation would arise where charges would accumulate for work that was not scheduled to take place on a certain series. The conclusion in this case was that the operator had made an incorrect charge.

The feeder shops encountered a different type of situation. The count of production frequently varied from one machine operation to the next. Sometimes it was necessary to pull parts out of the productive sequence for purposes of scrap or material review. The subsequent rework to make bad parts reusable with the special one-time customer deviation, created a vast complex of paperwork. This made it difficult to associate a particular group of parts with their proper effectivity series. The vastness of the shops and the variety of changes to complete a part prior to installation or subassembly created the necessity of lot identification.

Lot identification in the manufacturing process was accomplished by using a Travel Card, sometimes called a Traveler, or Factory Routing. These cards called out each operation, the department in which it would be performed, outside contracting operations, and the standard hours per unit. This card was designed to stay with the parts throughout their processing life until they were sent to stock or until they lost their unique identity as a detail and went into a subassembly. At this time a new Traveler would be issued with the order to withdraw parts from stock, to start the process of assembly.

The Production Ticket carried time data on each job. In the feeder shops, the operator wrote in his start time on a job when it was ready for setup. Setup time included everything from checking out tools to making the machine ready to operate, as well as producing the first few pieces. The supervision in each department was charged with checking out the operator's setup and the good parts before calling for a first article inspection. The floor inspector would sign off the good parts or send bad parts to material review if they did not meet the minimum engineering requirements. If the parts were satisfactory, the operator would mark his ticket to indicate the setup had ended and the production sequence had begun. All setups were charged as indirect. Direct charges were classified by the controller of the corporation as "any operation or work that changes the size, shape, weight, appearance or usability of detail part, subassembly, or assembly."

Indirect charges were—by the process of elimination—anything not direct, anything done by a nonproducing department, or anything not a part of the factory routing such as rework, repair, or overtime. Producing departments were those classified as using direct labor to accomplish a given amount of work. Indirect departments were looked upon as service departments, since it was argued that the service departments kept the direct or producing departments operating. Among the service departments were Maintenance, Inspection, Production Control, and Transportation.

When an operator in a feeder shop began a productive sequence, he did not have to complete his Production Ticket (Figure 16–1);

this was done at the conclusion of the operation. The Traveler served to supply the needed information as to part number, job number, operation number. The operator might work on an operation for only an hour or for several days, however the basic requirement was no less than one card a day, since payroll was computed from the Production Ticket. Operators were responsible for the accuracy of Production Tickets.

The clocking-out process on a job sometimes preceded the teardown of the machine and sometimes followed it. No particular accent was placed upon the timeliness of this function since it was supposed to reflect only a very small increment of time. At the end of the day, the operator punched his ticket at a clock and put it in the "out" side of the rack under his employee number.

Certain nonproductive time was not charged but assumed. Management policy endorsed such activities as bond drives, Red Cross Blood Donation campaigns, and various other employee activities, as well as proper union activity during working hours. In addition, the Management policy allowed two five minute clean-up periods prior to lunch and quitting time and two ten minute rest periods, on each half of the shift. There was also a policy of allowing six minutes per hour fatigue and personal allowance for each employee. Other factors that might keep machines from being operated, such as absenteeism, power failure, machine breakdown, loan to other departments, or random delays had no place in preplanning and were likewise assumed.

CLOCK RINGS	REG. HRS.	O.T. HRS.	PART NUMBER		OP. NO.	LOT NO.	CLOCK NUMBER	PART NUMBER
			MACH. CLASS	MACH. NO.		SPLIT LTR.		
			CLOCK NUMBER	SHIFT	HOME DEPT.	DEPT. CHGD.		
			BEAVER ALLIANCE AIRCRAFT CORP.				LOT NUMBER	OPERATION NUMBER
			PRODUCTION TICKET					
			GOOD PARTS FINISHED	JOB NUMBER		TOT. ACT. HRS.		
			START QUANTITY	STD. HRS./C		TOT. STD. HRS.		
Total Actual Hrs.								

Fig. 16-1.

Fourteen timekeepers working out of the accounting department had the function of totaling and extending a day's Production Tickets. They were stationed in the factory near the departments whose tickets they handled and were available if needed during the day. As a part of their routine, they checked the tickets of employees not reporting for work and reported these personnel to the personnel department. The personnel department tried to determine the reasons why an employee did not report for work.

In October of 1944, the controller's office placed a request before Division Management regarding the conflict of interest in the end of the Production Ticket as an input to both Payroll Accounting and Cost Accounting. Mr. James L. King, chief of Cost Accounting, commented as follows:

> Our system of accounting control must be improved in several ways, although changes cannot and should not be accomplished too hurriedly. The accounting department feels that the information on the Production Ticket is inaccurate. The quantity and quality of information both contribute to a variance of 30 to 40 per cent that we are unable to explain to the Government. The functions of the timekeeper must be changed. Some reconciliation between total hours of work and hours spent on each job must be installed. Greater accuracy in counting parts must be obtained. Inspection count must be integrated into this system as a control factor. We should consider the use of pre-punched tabulating machine cards to be distributed to each job in order to minimize the amount of information necessary to be manually inserted on the card. The control of labor in process at the present time is impossible, since the information being accumulated is not reliable. We need a system that will deliver cost data within 5 per cent accuracy.

A committee was formed to study the problem. In the memo which directed the formation of this committee, Mr. Roland Welch, division manager, made this statement:

> Of the two principal inputs to the cost or value of our commodity, direct labor is more important since it is such a large percentage of the selling price. For this reason, accurate control over the distribution of time and proper notation of the facts concerning the expenditure of direct labor are essential in our system. The committee set up to overhaul the methods for accruing direct labor is charged with creating an integrated system that will serve all parts of the operating business and fill all of its requirements.

The first output of the new committee headed by Mr. King was a proposed timekeeping procedure.

PROPOSED FEEDER SHOP TIMEKEEPING PROCEDURE*

1.0 Purpose: Establish uniform methods of
    a. Recording set-up, production, off-production, and tear-down worked on each operation on lots scheduled.
    b. Recording scrap and good pieces completed in each operation on each lot.
    c. Controlling work on lots according to schedule.
    d. Coordinating the supervisory, record-keeping, and expediting functions.
    e. Increasing accuracy of data on which effective machine loading and scheduling is based.

2.0 All direct labor departments are affected

3.0 Responsibilities
    3.1 Production Control
        a. Scheduling lot releases.
        b. Computation and release of raw material and castings.
        c. Preparing Manufacturing Releases, scheduling work each week.
        d. Keeping records of work-in-process.
    3.2 Dispatcher and Counter-Trucker
        a. Following and expediting work in all departments.
        b. Keeping current on status with timekeeper.
        c. Lot identification.
        d. Reviewing priority of jobs ahead with foreman.
    3.3 Foreman
        a. Review of lot schedules and job cards. Determines priority to each job. Assigns men and machine.
        b. Supervision of operators, checking their set-ups and parts counts.
        c. Arranging for inspection.
    3.4 Timekeeper (one per eighty direct labor employees)
        a. Assigning jobs to the operator on the machine or machines designated by the foreman.
        b. Recording all time reported by operators:
            1) On set-up and/or tear-down.
            2) On production.
            3) Off production.
        c. Maintaining up-to-the-minute recording of operations completed on each lot, including quantities of good and scrap parts.

* Payroll accounting to be done separately through a weekly time card under this system.

d. Computation and reconciliation of times and quantities and balancing with time on weekly payroll cards.

4.0 Shop Scheduling, Planning and Release of Lots

4.1 Each Thursday, Production Control prepares raw material releases for lots to start running during the next week.

4.2 The dispatcher and trucker arrange delivery of material by Monday.

4.3 The timekeeper receives a Manufacturing Release showing the quantity of parts in each lot to be started during the current week from the dispatcher, after review by the foreman.

5.0 Preparation of Job Cards (3 types)

The Manufacturing Release shows all operations in sequence to be done on the part, the quantity to start, and the minimum quantity of good pieces needed in stock from the last operation (prime quantity). It shows the dates (Friday, week-ending date) each operation must be completed. From this, job priority is decided by the foreman and dispatcher. The timekeeper is interested, first, in those operations to be done in the cutoff department. For each operation, he must prepare one Setup Ticket. He does this as soon as he receives releases each week and always in advance of the first shift Monday.

5.1 Set-up Ticket (Red printing)

a. Timekeeper enters in two places on the Setup Ticket: part number; operation number; lot number (this is the same number for all parts released the same week), and clock number.

b. Timekeeper enters in one place on the form: home department; the department to be charged; shift; machine class; machine number; standard hours per hundred; start quantity; job number, and split letter (if any).

5.2 Production Ticket (Black printing) Enter same information as set-up Ticket.

6.0 Shop Schedule Board

A series of job card racks will be arranged side by side on a vertical board in the timekeeper's enclosure. Each row of pockets across the board is for one of the production machines in the department. In the first pocket, cards will be placed for the job being set up or running on the machine. In the next pocket, the next job scheduled to run; in the last, other jobs ahead, in order as they should run.

When the cards for each new lot have been completed, the timekeeper will review them with the foreman and dispatcher, if available at the time. The foreman will assign each job, indicating the operator and a specific machine (or may omit this if any one of the machines of the machine class will do). Cards will be placed in the proper pockets, in line with the machine or group of machines assigned; or, arranged with other jobs ahead in the order requested by the foreman. The Set-up Ticket will always be on top.

7.0 Timing the Tooling Tear-down and Set-up of New Jobs

The foreman will follow each operator's progress on jobs and will determine with the timekeeper well in advance (two hours) the next job assignment, and will go to the tool crib and arrange for tooling to be ready. When an operator is ready for job assignment, he will come to the timekeeper, who finds the next job set-up card in the board, and tells the operator the part number, machine, and the number of pieces to start.

The timekeeper will clock-in the set-up card and place it in the rack in the first pocket (Jobs Running) next to its machine number, with the Production Card behind it. He will record the date started on his copy of the Manufacturing Release.

The operator will obtain tooling from the tool crib, tear down his last job, set up the new job, and run pieces for Inspection and foreman's OK. He will then report completion of set-up to the timekeeper who will clock out his Set-up Ticket.

8.0 Timing Production

The operator will notify the timekeeper when he is ready to start production. The Production Ticket will be clocked-in. Operator's clock number will be entered at two places on the card which is then filed in rack. It will be visible at all times while production is running.

When the operation is finished, or at the end of the shift, the operator will count and report good pieces completed and scrap. Timekeeper will clock out and record pieces on the Production Ticket and if operation is completed for the entire lot, will record date completed, total pieces good and scrap on the Manufacturing Release.

9.0 Timing Interrupted Set-ups or Production (Off-Production Ticket —Green printing)

An Off-Production Ticket will be filled-in, in the same way as Set-Up or Production Tickets and clocked-in whenever an operator reports work stoppage either on Set-Up or Production. In the Job Order box, enter the account number that explains the reason for the interruption. Also write the reason in the log column of the Manufacturing Release.

When production or set-up begins again, the operator should

be clocked out on Off-Production and clocked in on Set-Up or Production. The Off-Production Ticket will be filed behind the other tickets and may be used for other interruptions if they occur on the same lot operation.

During down-time, if the operator is assigned to another job, the Off-Production Ticket will be clocked out, but will remain in the visible position in the rack.

10.0 End of Shift

Operators will count and report pieces completed to the time-keeper. All tickets will be removed from the board and clocked out. For each incomplete set-up or production run, prepare a new ticket and place it in the rack for use on the next shift.

10.1 Computing Hours and Pieces

a. Subtract clocked-in from clocked-out times on each card and enter difference in hours to nearest tenth in columns provided.

b. Add each column.

c. Enter total of both columns in *Total Actual Hours*.

d. On Production Cards, extend Good Parts Produced and Standard Hours per Hundred and enter Total Standard Hours.

10.2 Up-Dating Manufacturing Release

Compare the Manufacturing Releases with the Production Ticket which show operations completed. Post the date completed, good pieces and scrap. If this is the last operation on this release, forward the copy by way of the Dispatcher to Production Control files.

10.3 Reconciliation with Payroll Cards

Compare daily payroll card and job card time totals and reconcile. Report major discrepancies to the foreman. Forward Job Cards to Tabulating at end of shift, for key punching and preparation of reports.

11.0 Exceptions and Special Cases

11.1 Split Lots

Production Control will occasionally authorize split lots. In these cases the letter for the split *(A, B, C)* will appear in the log of the Manufacturing Release. Timekeepers must add this split letter below the lot number on all cards affected.

11.2 Special Order Numbers

When a change in processing or routing results in assignment of a special order number to a lot in production, the foreman will inform the timekeeper. He will enter this number in the Job Order box on each card affected. This number should also be entered in the log of the Manufacturing Release.

QUESTIONS

1. What are the systems aspects of this case?

2. What is the basic problem?

3. What should Beaver Alliance do to deal with its problem of direct labor costing?

4. How do you evaluate the proposed feeder shop timekeeping procedure? In what ways is it superior to the existing procedure?

17
A. B. Fleet and Company

Bonopolis, an eastern city, was forced by expanding population and industrial growth, to re-examine their rapid transit system. Population had grown from 800,000 to 1,690,000 in ten years. Located in the industrial bowl of the United States, this city had over 3,000 factories and was located on one of the Great Lakes. It was developing as a terminal point for shipping by boat, rail, and air. Growth had created a strain on existing transit facilities and serious transit problems existed for the bulk of the population who were wage earners.

The Traffic Commission, Planning Commission, and Public Utilities Commission shared responsibility for future planning of highways and roads and the privately owned transit facilities. Equipment was old and demands for better service frequently created bitter debates in the City Council.

Typical of their problems were the new developments in outlying areas which demanded service. However, the lack of equipment and of a plan for operating a system in sparsely populated areas, forced transit owners to procrastinate. This created more bitterness and public debate.

In 1954, the matter of providing cheap, effective, mass rapid transit became the critical political issue in the city's mayoral elections. Since it was no longer possible to delay the adoption of a plan, the incumbent mayor and the City Council determined on a course of action consisting of the following steps:

(1) Increase bonded indebtedness of the city by $20,000,000 to purchase privately owned facilities and provide modern equipment and street facilities for mass rapid transit.

(2) Create feeder systems into new areas to increase the effectiveness of rapid transit coverage in the metropolitan area.

(3) Create a commission of citizens, businessmen, and council representatives to study local transit problems.

(4) Demand a program of the Traffic Commission, Planning Commission, and Public Utilities Commission which would guarantee continued study of the metropolitan transit issue.

(5) Merge and extend existing service where possible to reduce cost of operation.

(6) Study fare structures to distribute, fairly and equitably, the costs of city-wide operation of the rapid transit system.

The opposing candidate attacked this plan vigorously. His point of view, based upon the activities of other major cities and advice from the local experts in this field, indicated some problems in the incumbent's point of view. A memorandum prepared by A. B. Fleet and Company, experts in the design of mass rapid transit systems, is shown as Exhibit One.

EXHIBIT ONE

MEMORANDUM FROM: A. B. FLEET AND COMPANY

Introduction

There are a number of issues which must be met to begin the development of mass rapid transit for this city. This memorandum describes how A. B. Fleet and Company could be of assistance in this program.

One of the prominent issues requiring early decision is how best to combine the major surface lines now in operation. This is today's task. But tomorrow's decisions are infinitely more complex. How is this city to prepare for decisions that will affect the community ten years hence? The design of a mass rapid transit system will be influenced by population growth, industrial development, and changes in land use. There is a need for a sound method to assist in the selection of both today's and tomorrow's rapid transit routes.

A. B. Fleet proposes to attack these problems using tools of science and electronics. Problems of this type are so complex they defy solution by any other means. An example will assist in demonstrating how science and electronics can be of help.

Statement of Problem One

We would eliminate uncertainty in selecting rapid transit routes, if we could see into the future. A glimpse into the future would tell us where communities would spring up or where industrial development might thrive. So let us postulate a power that can make changes in population, land use, and economic growth. Our large area now becomes a constantly changing panorama. People, their homes, their places of work, and industrial firms respond to new conditions. The face of our city in 1954 and 1980 appear considerably different.

If we had the power to see our city as it will be in 1980, we would incorporate many changes in our existing plan. The more visibility we can obtain in 1954, the more certain we can be that we have provided for the future, and minimized the possibility of mistakes. The question is, *Are there in existence technical tools that will assist us in solving the route selection problem?*

The answer is yes!

The Use of Computers and Simulation

A. B. Fleet has actually solved similar problems which required the ability to predict far in the future. This has been done using a technique known as simulation. Simulation is done on a computer which has the ability to process data at lightning speeds. Because of these electronic speeds, it is possible to compress many years of experience in a few seconds of time. Simulation utilizes the high speed of the computer to reproduce in a small fraction of time the experiences of many years. In a recent simulation problem, A. B. Fleet squeezed two hundred years of inventory experience into less than two hours!

Simulation can assist in determining the capacities of rapid transit routes under different conditions. This tool has already been used to assist in solving traffic and transportation problems. In a freeway problem, traffic was represented by electrical impulses moving at very high speeds within the computer. Given the distances between entrances and exits, a variety of speeds for each car on the freeway, and various load conditions depending on the time of day, it was possible to reproduce the traffic flow the freeway was able to carry, *before the freeway was built!*

Simulation can be used to study variables that effect the design of rapid transit systems. In the process of doing this, the important variables are isolated and their effect on the system reproduced. Therefore, the first step is to identify as many variables as possible. Statistical tests must then be made to determine which variables are important and which are unimportant. Because we are using a computer, we can deal with complex, real-life situations containing many variables. Problems with a large number of variables which require an analytical solution, might require years—perhaps are impossible—to solve without a computer.

Simulation allows us to deal with minute pieces of data. Without the computer, it might be necessary merely to approximate the solution to a problem, because the analyst would be unable to cope with a large volume of data. The solution would have to be constructed from gross measures as opposed to fine measures. With the help of a computer, it is possible to solve origin and destination problems using very small zonal areas. By analyzing data in detail, the possibility of errors in route selection is considerably reduced.

Simulation allows us to study rapid transit in competition with other modes of travel. The number of rapid transit commuters will be determined by many variables, such as cost, speed, accessibility, and convenience. Given a set of facts on a proposed route, a computer can reproduce the conditions under which any segment of the system would operate. In addition, it could also simulate the competitive modes of travel. This would be invaluable in solving problems, such as how to attract more users to mass rapid transit.

Simulation would make it possible to consider many alternate routes and rapid transit systems. Given a set of data representing a tentative route, the computer can examine several alternate means of traveling from an origin to a destination. In this way, many alternate rapid transit systems could be tried and the best routes selected. The ability to examine many rapid transit routes at frequent intervals makes it possible to do better transitional planning.

Summary

Simulation is a scientific tool which can be put to use in the solution of rapid transit problems. A. B. Fleet has made successful use of simulation as a tool in the solution of nonscientific problems. Simulation on a high speed computer can determine route capacities under different conditions of load. The many variables affecting the design of rapid transit systems can best be studied using computer simulation. The high speed of simulation makes it possible to deal with large quantities of data. The competitive problems of rapid transit versus other modes of travel lend themselves to analysis through the simulation technique. Simulation makes it possible to select at frequent intervals the best route or best system out of many alternate routes or systems, and thus provide adequate transitional planning.

Statement of Problem Two

The design of a rapid transit system for this metropolitan area requires a variety of special skills. There are many technical problems associated with each phase of the program which must be solved to

bring about a successful system. Not only must these problems be anticipated, but it is essential that the entire program be expertly guided
through the many difficult decisions that will require action.

A wide range of costly decisions will be required to activate an up to
date rapid transit system. There will be a requirement for data supporting these decisions that will minimize the possibility of errors in judgment. There is an associated problem of determining what part of the
available data is valid, and what additional data are required to complete the evidence.

The design of pilot systems and the selection and development of
data and technical advice are required to coordinate and integrate
this complex program. This is a method of operation and project
organization familiar to A. B. Fleet and Co. As technical advisor to
the many industries, A. B. Fleet coordinates and oversees the activities
of many large corporations. Our efforts have been directed at solving
some of the most complex scientific and engineering problems ever encountered. In order to outline how such a technical advisor might operate for the City's Transit Authority, a tentative plan of action can be
suggested.

Plan of Action for the Technical Advisor

Phase One: Organization

Phase One is a preliminary study which has the goal of assembling
available information on the local rapid transit problem.

The unique aspects of the city's problem would be isolated and examined. The many agencies that have an interest in advancing this
program would be consulted, and liaison established on a regular basis.
The data available on studies conducted in other cities would be assembled and sifted to cull information that is of local interest. The
priority of effort would be established.

A method of operation and liaison would be established with the
Transit Authority, so organization of this project would be responsive
to their needs.

Phase Two: Preliminary Systems Design

Phase Two is the systematic study of data relating to the problems
of merging existing rapid transit lines and preparing for future systems.

Men experienced in traffic and transportation problems would study
available data to develop the system limits. They would develop criteria
which would hold for short range and long range planning. They
would develop the initial concepts to assist in the design of the rapid
transit plan, and would test these concepts by the proper statistical tech-

niques. They would draw a plan for conducting the scientific portion of this study so their work would be finished when needed.

Parallel with this effort, other personnel would begin the collection and integration of field data. The following are typical questions which would be answered in this phase:

Land use and population: How does land use affect the design of the system? Where are populations currently concentrated? Where are populations moving? What residential areas are becoming commercial or industrial? How are land use, population, and circulation interdependent?

Origin and destination: Where do people live and work? How do they travel now? What will be the influence of a completed freeway or rapid transit system? What are the other "competitive" modes of travel and how do they affect the systems design?

Route sections: What should the dimensions of key thoroughfares be? What are the possible rapid transit routes? What plans exist for widening or otherwise altering present street systems and how will they affect systems design?

Measures of actual flow: What are the capacities of present key thoroughfares? How will these change as population or land use shifts? What are desirable routes based on actual flow and how well do they correlate with other data? What can be predicted about future route locations based on anticipated changes in flow?

Rapid transit facilities: What are the present and planned facilities? What new facilities are required to fill the needs of the community? What are the present and future economic requirements of the system? What are the alternate modes of mass rapid transit and the costs inherent in each? Who are the proposed contractors for new transit systems and what are their recommendations?

Geographical and geological factors: What are the physical characteristics of the area and how do they dictate the type of rapid transit systems? What are the possible modes of mass rapid transit?

Sociological and psychological factors: How can we be certain new facilities will be used as planned? Will new transit systems be accepted by the population? Why are some routes or facilities better used than others? How can the economic success of a proposed system be tested prior to installation?

Simultaneous with the collection of field data and the initial scientific studies, a financial and legal survey would be conducted. Real estate data would be collected and studied to determine its influence on the design of a new system. Federal, state, county, and municipal legislative requirements would be studied to assure adherence to existing codes. We would develop financial data on the cost of alternate systems and accumulate facts to support proposed revenues for these systems.

Phase Three: Analysis and Final Systems Design

Phase three begins when all of the necessary data could be assembled and analyzed as a unit.

At this time, the assumptions of the proposed systems would be tested and changes made in the tentative system design. Errors would be determined and corrections built into the new design. Simulation would test and improve the system design. Development of current systems and anticipated extensions or revisions to proposed systems would be tested.

Technical advisers would recommend the best system for each selected time period in this phase. Actual routes would be identified and a total area plan, incorporating the necessary rapid transit requirements, would be submitted.

Summary

Design of a mass rapid transit system requires a variety of technical skills. Before costly decisions are made, large quantities of data must be accumulated and analyzed. A. B. Fleet and Company has successful experience in the coordination and integration of complex programs such as this, and has developed a method of operation specifically designed to support systems installations. As technical adviser, A. B. Fleet would prepare a plan of action geared to the requirements of this city's Transit Authority and the needs of this city. This activity would progress through three phases: *organization, preliminary systems design,* and *analysis and final systems design.* The end result would be the determination of area mass rapid transit requirements, based upon current factors, and projected into the future, based upon scientifically analyzed trends.

Conclusion

The problems of unifying present surface systems and determining future mass rapid transit requirements require a set of special talents. A. B. Fleet and Company would attack these issues on two fronts:

1. A. B. Fleet proposes to add the elements of science and electronics to assist in solving complex problems, such as the selection of rapid transit routes.

2. A. B. Fleet proposes to become the technical adviser to our Transit Authority because of its qualifications and recognition as a leader in the field of systems coordination and integration.

QUESTIONS

1. What is the system under study? What are the major subsystems?
2. What are the objectives or outputs at the various system and subsystem levels?
3. Who are the systems purchasers at the various system and subsystem levels?
4. What kinds of criteria might be developed to measure the effectiveness of one rapid transit system over another?
5. Compare the two programs. How does the Fleet memorandom stand up as a communication tool?
6. What is the problem?

18

Wesley Engineering, Inc.

Wesley Engineering[1] was a multi-division organization performing contract engineering work for a number of industries. Divisions were specialized for work in the fields of aircraft, shipbuilding civil engineering, plant construction, and atomic energy. Each division was autonomous and was staffed to operate as an independent entity. Administration, sales, and technical work were tailored to the requirements of each division. Contacts between the operating staffs of divisions were rare except when large projects demanded the formation of teams to work on the same contracts. At the time of this case, in 1958, each division employed about 200 engineers and technicians. In each division, about 50 administrative, non-technical personnel supplied the services which were required. Total dollar volume was $21,000,000 per year.

Like most firms in this field, Wesley saw its most spectacular growth starting in 1940. As the need to meet more complex and profitable opportunities arose, teams of specialists were formed from within and outside the organization. With each new contract in some specialized field, the size of a team would grow and its interests become more foreign to existing divisions. The result of this was the creation of new divisions and the development of supporting services which invariably paralleled the other divisions.

Fredrick Wesley advocated divisional autonomy because he recognized the need to nurture the individual interests and ambitions of his division managers and their staffs. Moreover, he found that the conflicts which customarily arose in closely held, non-autonomous divisions, were absent under his organization. Since

[1] See Chapter 5, page 81.

each division was on an individual profit and loss basis, its independence assured the minimum of shared costs, except for the charges for corporate staff management. The Wesley organization chart (Figure 18–1) is shown as Exhibit One.

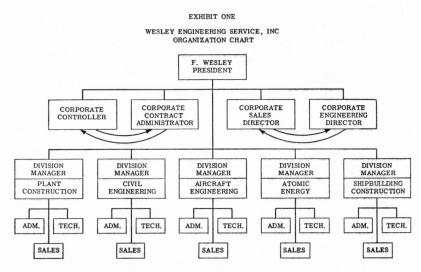

EXHIBIT ONE

WESLEY ENGINEERING SERVICE, INC
ORGANIZATION CHART

Fig. 18–1.

The corporate structure was maintained to provide control over policy matters. Once monthly, the division managers met with Wesley and his four man staff as the corporate steering committee. Likewise, as shown in Exhibit Two (Figure 18–2), three of the four

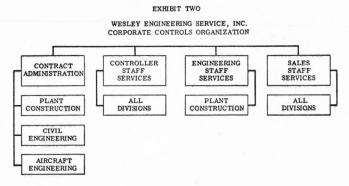

EXHIBIT TWO

WESLEY ENGINEERING SERVICE, INC.
CORPORATE CONTROLS ORGANIZATION

Fig. 18–2.

corporate staff officers met with the divisional executives whose activities were under their nominal control. Four divisions were free of even this control in the engineering area, because of highly specialized problems beyond the corporate engineering staff's ability to give effective supervision. The shipbuilding and atomic energy divisions were also independent of Corporate Contract Administration because their work was entirely in the research and development area. These departures from the format of control, as it was originally conceived, were difficult to obtain and were under constant surveillance.

The methods of keeping costs and handling Contract Administration were not identical in each division. The need to meet circumstances unique to each division had created the opportunity for each division to solve its problems in its own way. Thus, there were five cost systems, five contract administration systems, and so on, each of which were supervised at the corporate level to conform to some generalized model acceptable to top management.

Typical of this situation was the forecasting process. Each Division had a unique method of doing its advance planning. Semi-annual reports were prepared by the administrative directors of each division indicating the forecasted manpower requirements by project and by each six month period into the future for two years. Using standard rates of pay for the various job classifications and calculating the productive work hours in each period, they calculated the direct labor hours. Overhead accounts were projected, based upon history and anticipated changes in cost. From these figures, overhead rates were calculated to provide a method of quoting on new contracts. From this same information, sales, cost of sales, and profit were projected.

There were many difficult problems associated with these calculations. Productive hours depended upon several variables, such as vacations, holidays, anticipated overtime, sick leave, and transfers in and out of a division. To bring net total hours down to a conservative estimate of productive hours, the employee structure on a department and section basis had to be analyzed. This proved to be an exhaustive process which was difficult to update.

The analysis of average wage rates was time consuming. The process of obtaining raw data on the number of employees in each job classification came from section heads and received the approval of department heads. But each set of wage rates required modification for anticipated rate changes over this extended period. Furthermore, frequent changes in contract requirements would force sections to be reconstituted on a different personnel base. As a result, very gross measures were used in the determinations of average wage rates, and reports were never an accurate reflection of the status quo—or of the future.

Forecasts were done in each division on a manual basis. About three months were required to prepare a forecast from new headcounts. Material from each division required extensive revision before the preparation of a corporate forecast was possible, since information was not parallel. Among many problems were those occasioned by layoffs in one division while costly hiring was taking place in another.

In June of 1957, at the suggestion of the corporate controller, Wesley decided the time had come to tighten up the forecasting area of control because of changes that were taking place in many industries. He put the problem up to his division managers at their regular meeting, stating four principle needs:

1. Reduce personnel pools, particularly administrative.
2. Reconstitute technical sections on minimum levels.
3. Develop a reporting system sensitive to quarterly changes.
4. Simplify method of forecasting, so interim forecasts are possible.

Division managers conferred with their administrative staffs immediately, in anticipation of another meeting to discuss what steps should be taken to implement Wesley's suggestions. When the second meeting was called, the division managers presented an additional series of problems for discussion:

1. Division autonomy was being invaded.
2. Corporate forecasts were unnecessary.
3. Divisional problems precluded a uniform forecasting system.
4. There were no known methods of mechanizing forecasting.
5. Accuracy and reliability of forecasts could be questioned, but whether they were inaccurate or unreliable to any significant amount was unknown.

6. The value of forecasts was considerably diminished unless they were used in a gross way.

Wesley agreed to make no decision regarding how each division must forecast, but obtained agreement that, even if the methods were not uniform, a better model was essential. Accordingly, he asked the corporate controller to monitor a study to be undertaken by his staff on the problem of forecasting. He was asked to start at the earliest moment and to advise Wesley as soon as he had a plan to present to the division managers.

About four months after this date, the division managers and the corporate staff members heard a talk given by John Wills, the project leader on the forecasting study. The talk is reproduced as Exhibit Three.

EXHIBIT THREE

PROPOSED FORECASTING SYSTEM—

A TALK BY JOHN WILLS

The study of forecasting at Wesley began with the examination of the questions, "Why is it necessary to forecast? What is a forecast?" I will answer these questions in terms of the functions of forecasting.

A basic function is to project sales and expenses so the flow of funds and financial requirements can be anticipated. Equally important, the projection of sales and expenses previews the expected profit. Contract Administration requires forecast information to prepare proposals and bids. Budgeting and future planning are made simpler and more effective if Management is working from adequate information. Facilities and equipment planning will be enhanced if forecasting procedures provide reliable information when it is needed. From this we can conclude a working definition of forecasting: *Forecasting is the process of assembling current information and relating it to the future needs and requirements of a company.*

As a result of investigating these basic questions, we learned the symptoms of our inadequate system. Prominent among these symptoms was the problem of how long it takes to produce a complete forecast. It is obvious that the rapid growth of this company has made the production of forecast information more difficult and time consuming. This problem in its most acute stage is typified by recent forecasts which were invalid by the time they were completed—because personnel mix and sales requirements had changed markedly while the forecasting computations were in process. A second symptom was obvious because

the week-to-week changes in sales requirements could not be successfully incorporated in the forecasts without indefinitely delaying their
completion. It is therefore necessary to take the position that the
present system is incapable of producing current, valid information.

A number of symptoms can be grouped under the current method of
producing the forecast information. First among these, the corporate
controller finds it increasingly difficult to maintain the total work load
due to the large volume of man-days consumed in forecasting. We have
a completely manual system which requires large volumes of simple
arithmetic computations. An enormous variety of source documents
are required to produce the forecast. The necessity of maintaining a
high level of accuracy dictates an excessive amount of double checking,
verifying, recapping, and rearranging.

The time required to make a complete forecast can be laid out in
seven steps: Department headcount and direct costs require five days.
Division wage dollars and overhead expenses require ten days. Corporate allocated overhead expenses require fifteen days. The computation of division cost of sales and overhead rates take an additional
five days. Corporate general and administrative expenses require fifteen
days. To digest this load of data and obtain division sales and profits
takes five days. To produce the final document, the corporate forecast,
requires an additional five days. It therefore appears that forecasts
cannot be produced in less than sixty working days or twelve weeks.
Clearly what is needed is a simple, more rapid way of doing this job!

The first look at the current forecasting procedures was aimed at
identifying the problem area. To do this, we began a step-by-step process
of assembling the information that would describe the present system.
If we had correctly assessed the symptoms, it was now time to explore
the causes and get to the root of the problem. We asked, "What is it we
are trying to forecast?" It is clear we are trying to build a forecast from
the most elemental data. We want to know how many personnel are
required for each project that is either in-work or anticipated, so we can
allocate a specific personnel mix to each forecasting period in the future.
In addition to predicting the headcount, the present system is allocating divisional overhead and corporate overhead to each forecasting
period, so the overhead rates can be used to determine cost of sales and
profits.

If there is any single factor that makes the forecasting problem difficult, it is the problem of how to obtain the proper average wage rate by
job classification for each project in each forecasting period. These
figures are critical in the forecasting procedure because they are used in
the later computation of overhead rates. Let me lead you through the
present method of computing average wage rates and overhead rates.

What is immediately clear is that there are four factors that affect each and every project for which manpower is to be allocated. Present wage rates must be modified by anticipated merit increases. Present headcount by job classification must be amended by the anticipated headcount in each job classification. When all of the data are accumulated, it is possible to assess for each project in each forecasting period the average wage rates by job classification. Note, however, that each project requires a wealth of data, and each project, has to be added into the total picture, a piece at a time, on a completely manual basis. It is no wonder that it requires three months to complete a forecast, and that errors creep into the maze of arithmetic calculations. But now we can proceed to the next example: Given the average wage rates, how is the overhead rate computed?

You will remember that to make a successful forecast we allocate sales and expenses to each project in each forecasting period. This means that the various overhead items, such as indirect labor, non-labor expenses, and payroll expenses must also be accumulated in a similar fashion. In fact, this is being done on the same laborious manual basis we observed earlier. The corporate controller allocates dollars to each project in each forecasting period to spread properly the overhead costs that are anticipated in the future forecasting periods. However, before overhead rates can be obtained, the average wage rates must be multiplied by the anticipated direct headcount, project by project. This produces the total direct labor wage dollars for each project in each forecasting period.

With all the pertinent overhead costs assembled for each forecast period, the final computation is to divide total overhead dollars by the total direct labor wage dollars for the identical periods. The resulting overhead rates are now ready for use in allocating overhead dollars to each project in each forecasting period, with the intent of determining the cost of sales and potential profit. This is not the sum total of what is required in a new system. There are other inputs, such as productive work hours which require extensive computation, which we will not explore this afternoon. But, in summary, we can say that the system that exists today has been completely outgrown by Wesley, and that it is altogether inadequate for the present and future purposes of Management. What is the next step?

A computer application is indicated by the volume of data that requires processing. Current requirements are set at 7,500 input entries and over 40,000 output entries. It is estimated that by 1960, there will be over 50,000 input entries, and over 250,000 output entries, if Management does not require additional information or increased frequency of reporting. This conclusion is reinforced by the need for faster reporting without increasing, if possible, the cost per unit of operation. If information could be made available faster, it is obvious we would obtain many of the advantages as they were outlined at the outset of this report: current and reliable information on cost of sales and profits to guide Management in its decision making. However, in making a computer application, we have several alternatives. The first of these is to make a one-for-one changeover and to go through each of the processing steps as they are being done—but to do them faster. This does not seem practical in view of the large volume of data to be processed and does not satisfy the criteria of a more simple system.

We were fortunate to obtain the services of one of our technical staff experienced in the use of management statistical tools and techniques. Working closely with him, we reviewed the present state of the art of forecasting and pointed out the weaknesses that existed. A detailed examination of the data was begun, and soon it appeared that there was a novel approach to the problem of simplifying the computational tasks. Trial and error eventually revealed that the statistical technique of regression analysis could be applied successfully to this problem, with improved results. The techniques of regression analysis reveal that, as headcount increases, there is a fixed relationship with total wage dollars per hour. Points can be plotted on a chart to represent the relationship between headcount and total wage dollars per hour in different months. The line drawn between the points on the chart is represented by an equation. The value of being able to write an equation representing this regression line is, of course, convenience. With the equation, a person can quickly do the arithmetic computation to obtain total wage dollars per hour, without referring to the chart at all. This equation,

$$\$85 + \$2.623\ (HC) = \textit{Total wage dollars per hour,}$$
$$\textit{where, } HC = \text{Headcount,}$$

appears to satisfy our system requirements. It was now necessary to test this equation to determine its reliability. To do this we checked the coefficient of correlation, which proved to be .95. You will be interested to hear what the regression formula revealed when it was compared to the actual costs of the periods tested. We tested six past monthly periods. For each of these periods we moved from the headcount to the total wage dollars which we would have forecasted by our regression line. This deviation was found to be well within the requirements of the system for accuracy.

It is proper for us to ask the question, "Exactly what advantage does the regression analysis technique give the proposed forecasting system?" It is clear that the regression technique simplifies the computation of total wage dollars per hour. What formerly had to be computed by lengthy, tedious, manual means, requiring many inputs, is now produceable with only two inputs. The elimination of a cumbersome technique has, in addition, created the possibility that the new system might operate more economically. Accordingly, this technique will be used elsewhere in the system to determine overhead dollars. The other improvement is the increased speed with which computations can be made. Even though the new system is still on a manual basis, it is estimated that the reduction in time is 30 per cent. What the computer might add in terms of additional speed remains to be seen.

You have heard the important details of the proposed forecasting system. Now we can look at the "big picture" of the new system and see how it can function on a more simplified basis. You will observe that we now need only two basic inputs—headcount and total available hours. In the old system, we needed not only these two inputs but also a considerable number of other basic inputs. From only headcount and available hours, we are now able to arrive quickly at direct and indirect wage dollars and all the overhead expense dollars. Once this information has been obtained for each project in each forecasting period, it is a simple matter to compute future overhead rates, cost of sales, total cost of sales, and sales dollars.

To determine the reliability of the systems design, the proposed system has been operated manually. In this way, each step of the data processing was checked to be certain of its effectiveness in the preparation of the forecast. If this system is acceptable, the final phase of our study will be divided into four activities. The first activity will be the writing of a program in anticipation of leasing time on a computer. The second activity will be concerned with the design of new input documents and output reports to accommodate a more simplified presentation of forecasting results. The third activity will surround the preparation of written procedures to describe adequately all phases of the new forecasting procedure. The fourth activity will be centered about the development of computer routines for controlling and checking the equations used in the regression technique. In addition, we will undertake the development of routines so the computer can develop the regression formulas without human intervention.

We were given a general problem. The problem was *to reduce the clerical and administrative man hours required to prepare a forecast.* As a result of our study and planning, the forecast for forecast preparation time may be reduced from 12 weeks to 2 weeks. In effect, the computational bottleneck will be broken and the goal of the study will be reached by the use of a computer. However, there will be some additional benefits that can be classed as unanticipated by-products. A savings of $80,000 is estimated over the next four year period. Reliable, accurate, and current information will be available. The new system is flexible enough to expand and contract with changing business needs and conditions. These studies have opened up new areas where the regression technique can be used. Additional data can now be obtained at a very small marginal expense. We now have a simple and quick method for obtaining revised forecasts. Finally, proposals can now be prepared on a more competitive basis.

QUESTIONS

1. How would the systems analyst state the problem of Wesley Engineering, Inc.?

2. How well does the proposed forecasting system fill the needs of the corporation?

3. What are the systems aspects of this case?

19

Davis Engineering Company

C. R. Davis started in the business of making tools and dies in 1907. With Henry Russell, he gradually built a small, successful company, over a period of years. In 1927 Russell died, and Davis bought out his interest. The business continued to grow.

Davis Engineering Company built tooling from small die sets to large press dies to accommodate the largest hydraulic presses. Davis put his efforts into the operation of the shop and the supervision of the engineering efforts. His pride was in the reputation for skill and quality for which his firm was known. The emphasis was not heavy in administration and organization. Older employees voiced the well-accepted attitude that the firm's steadily rising dollar volume and profit were reflections of confidence of old customers.

In 1932, Davis became interested in the potential offered by the air-frame industry. He saw not only large volumes of tools of all kinds, but vast possibilities in jigs and fixtures. Always on the alert for a new technical challenge, Davis was able to obtain contracts because of his excellent reputation. The first few contracts were very costly and heavy losses pulled him farther and farther into the shop operation.

Customer contact was shifted from Davis to experienced office and engineering personnel who took on the job of liaison between the Davis organization and the customer's engineering department. Gradually, these part-time liaison men had to be replaced in the organization, because they found more and more to do to keep the new customers well satisfied. When this shift in personnel took effect in 1936, the two men, Joe Hardy and Andy White, were given the title of sales manager. They were given separate offices, secretarial help, and their duties were officially recognized. The sales organization had officially come to life.

By 1940, Davis Engineering Company was no longer the same, small business of the early thirties. They had moved into a 100,000 square foot building and their backlog with large manufacturing companies was almost $10,000,000. Hardy and White were regarded as the high powered salesmen who had "made" Davis Engineering, although Davis himself was the major factor in decision making and the final authority. There was no disputing with Davis why it was possible to get repeat orders. As a consequence, the sales organization did not grow, and the place of sales in the organization was never well defined.

When World War II ended, Davis was operating an organization of twelve hundred, and was considered among the most successful in the country. Prior to the Korean War, there was a severe drop in business. But because of certain manufacturing contracts which Davis obtained through his connections, the recession was short lived. With the resumption of defense activities, Davis again built its volume substantially. In the meantime, rising overhead had increased their break-even point. The manufacturing business was continued on a small scale.

In 1955, Hardy was forced to resign because of poor health. White continued in his former role without assistance, since the backlog was at an all-time high of $22,000,000. This was regarded as a two year load, with no apparent letup of business in sight.

In the summer of 1956, abrupt cancellation notices rocked the Davis organization. Overnight, nine major projects were halted by prime contractors who had received cancellations from the government. The backlog dropped to $5,000,000. It was clear that there would be additional business, but White did not think the expanded operation could wait for new contracts to be let. A substantial layoff was in prospect.

Davis was bitter over what he termed "customers that blew hot and cold." He determined to do something that would insure business volume and insulate his operation from being completely devoted to industries that were dependent on the armed services. He studied the situation briefly, and announced a new policy where military business would be only 60 per cent of the total sales volume.

As a first step to diversify the range of possible customers, Davis directed White to develop a "Road Show." He explained his idea in this way:

> What we need are more customers! What we want are less military customers! The problem is really not very complicated. We have to let the commercial customers know we're alive, and we'll get our share of whatever business we can handle. Now, I think the military contracts we've been working on are a fine recommendation. If we can get this message across to commercial customers, we're back in business in a big way! What could be a better way of doing this than to write letters to the biggest manufacturers all over the country, and tell them we'll bring our bag of tricks to their own back door for them to see? I've told Andy White to organize a Road Show for us to look at, and we'll start the performance rolling in thirty days.

White began the process of assembling a Road Show. However, shortly after he began work on this project, it appeared to raise many questions. The further he went, the more it became obvious that the Road Show was one facet of a many-sided issue. He finally decided that before he went any further, he would have to call a halt and report his findings, despite the fact that they would be greeted with some scepticism. This report is attached as Exhibit One.

White was surprised when Davis reacted to this report by commissioning a consulting firm to look into the sales problem. The consultants made a survey and submitted a report which has been abstracted as Exhibit Two.

EXHIBIT ONE

OUTLINE OF INVESTIGATION BY ANDY WHITE

   I. What are the essentials of a Road Show?

  II. Questions posed by the Road Show

 III. Tentative conclusions regarding Road Show problems

 IV. General conclusions and definition

   I. *What are the essentials of a Road Show?*
     A. A format or program tailored for each presentation
       1. Scope (many alternates depending on audience and location)
         a. A.M. through Luncheon
           (1) Semi-technical talks
           (2) High level luncheon speaker

b. A.M. through P.M.

    (1) Semi-technical talks in A.M.
    (2) High level luncheon speaker
    (3) Activity with accent on audience participation in P.M.

c. Dinner and evening presentation

    (1) High level guest speaker
    (2) Semi-technical talks
    (3) Social period

2. Content (dependent upon scope)

    a. Written material

        (1) Specially edited documentation of program
        (2) Brochure of activities
        (3) Give-aways

    b. Oral presentations

        (1) Talks
        (2) Discussion groups
        (3) Question and answer sessions

    c. Demonstrations

B. Support necessary to make a Road Show successful

1. Visual aids

    a. Films
    b. Slides
    c. Charts
    d. Exhibits

2. Literature

    a. Non-technical and technical material
    b. Brochures, invitations, ads

3. Publicity

    a. Before and after Road Shows
    b. Newspapers, magazines, and so on
    c. Direct mail

4. Promotion

    a. Personal letter campaigns
    b. Personal contact campaigns
    c. Group contact campaigns
    d. Direct mail campaigns

5. Follow-up

    a. Direct mail
    b. Personal calls
    c. Social or semi-social activities

II. *What are some of the problems posed by the Road Show?*

A. Audience

1. How can we be sure the audience contains potential customers?

    2. Where do we put on the show? West Coast? Nationally?

    3. Mixed groups? Special groups? Individual firms?

    4. What impressions do we wish potential customers to have after we leave? What levels of management are we trying to reach?

    5. Can Road Shows be used as a means of generating good will and interest in groups who may not be direct, potential customers?

B. Company operation

    1. How does the content emphasize our experience and capabilities?

    2. How do the technical personnel and techniques we employ support the Road Show?

    3. What tools do we need?

    4. How do we follow up and close a sale?

C. Why a Road Show?

    1. What is the fundamental purpose?

    2. What is the budget?

    3. Who will put on the show?

    4. Why do we do this in preference to something else?

    5. What other things might we do?

    6. What is the theme?

III. *What tentative conclusions can we make regarding the Road Show?*

A. Audience

    1. We need the "rifle" approach as opposed to the "shotgun."

       a. Mixed groups have mixed interests

       b. The more specialized the group, the better is our chance of creating an impression

       c. The ideal audience is one which is interested and has invited us in; no door opener required and existence of a need already established.

       d. Road Shows are a slow, expensive way to make contacts, as opposed to ads, letter campaigns, and other personal means.

       e. If the Road Show is put on in response to a request for more information, reasonable, tastefully stated, selling points will not be objectionable.

    2. Attendance at a Road Show will be poor if it is used as a sales pitch.

       a. High level executives will not attend to be "sold."

       b. Attendance will be based upon their need to know.

       c. We must satisfy a real need in our show.

    3. The audience becomes our salesmen if the Road Show is successful.

a. The needs of each group or potential customer must be analyzed.
b. A concerted, organized, well-timed plan must be developed to turn the potential into a sale.
c. The Road Show must be a smooth, professional, well-organized sales effort calculated to leave a strong impression of good-will and confidence in our ability.
d. Our Road Show contacts will die on the vine if we don't continually supply them with ammunition and point them more and more toward a specific goal.
4. Analysis of contacts in 1955 indicates we have a larger audience in the East than on the West Coast.
a. We must create a suitable means for operating in the East, to overcome most of the current objections.
b. If we cannot set up suitable means of operating nationally, expensive national advertising should not be considered.
c. Pursuit of business in the eleven western states alone, reduces our chances of obtaining our optimum volume by 66 per cent.
d. Organization modifications should accompany adoption of a sales policy.
e. Competitive considerations are effected by the selection of a policy.
5. The Road Show idea must be used in as many ways as its flexibility will permit.
a. Community or trade groups
b. Non-competitive professionals and consultants
c. Interested, but non-client industrial groups
B. Technical Groups
1. We can only talk about work we have done or work we are prepared to do.
a. Material must be specially tailored to the potential client's or group's needs, from some basic format.
b. To the extent that we have specialized portfolio, this will have a bearing on the type of personnel we hire.
c. There must be some assurance that the potential customer has a real interest in what we have to sell.
2. Technical groups must support the Road Show.
a. Members of the staff must be used where necessary to make the shows more effective.
b. Articles, talks, and personal contacts with existing or potential clients must consider the necessity of endorsing and promoting the Road Show.

    c. Additional permanent or semi-permanent assignments to the sales effort will increase amount of activity.

    d. Every staff member must understand the sales strategy, his role in sales, and how to conduct himself in the sales situation.

  3. How will plans for a Road Show be laid?

    a. Principal areas of customer interest must be built into basic formats of talks, written material, and exhibits.

    b. Some appreciation of actual customer-Davis relationships must be built into the Road Show by personnel preparing the program.

    c. Special visual aids will supplement standard types of sales tools which explain our underlying philosophy and general services.

    d. A sales strategy must be conceived for each potential customer in which the Road Show may be a critical opening wedge, but not an end in itself.

    e. A team of men will be assigned to a potential client until the prospect is realized or put aside.

    f. Individual sales strategies must be approved and integrated into over-all plans.

  4. What will happen to maintain enthusiasm or interest after the Road Show?

    a. Periodic mailings of literature of all types.

    b. Invitations to be present at programs, where our speakers are appearing.

    c. Solicit invitations to make examinations and proposals.

    d. Cooperative ventures in areas that can produce business.

    e. Consistent effort to activate potential customers in some program of ours.

    f. Frequent social, personal, and business contacts calculated to build a bridge of confidence in our ability, and find out where the jobs are and who can assist us in getting them.

    g. Availability to the potential customer, sensitivity to his needs, and awareness of when is the right time to press for a decision.

C. Road Show

  1. What is the fundamental purpose of the Road Show?

    a. To be a part of a general sales strategy leading step by step to a situation where we can make a proposal.

    b. Tell what we do; create confidence in our ability to do it.

   c. Create interest, good will, and meet customers face to face.

   d. Strengthen our sales approach by activating staff.

   e. Provide an antidote for machinery manufacturers' opinions about our role in industry.

2. What is the budget?

   a. Each out of town show will require two to five days (including travel).

   b. Only a portion of the written or visual material will be reusable.

   c. The average Road Show will cost

(1) Time preparing	$1,000.00
(2) Time away	1,200.00
(3) Sales aids and amortization	400.00
(4) Rent, food, etc., (25 people)	650.00
	$3,250.00

   d. Twenty shows per year per sales-technical team is a conservative estimate of annual capability, if more personnel are added to the sales organization.

   e. We need about 22 new jobs in 1957 to support the proposed annual budget.

3. Who will put on the Road Show?

   a. Arrangements will be a complex problem.

   b. Sales-technical staff should be active show participants.

   c. Minimum of two men are required to present a Road Show; if the job potential is good, or if the group contains very high level personnel, a principal speaker should be provided.

   d. Personnel assigned to Road Shows must be temporarily or semi-permanently disassociated from other responsibilities.

   e. Members of Road Shows must have wide experience and present mature, sound appearance to potential customers.

4. What is the suggested theme for the Road Shows?

   a. Must be tied into literature, visual aids, and so on.

5. Are we doing the Road Show in preference to some other, perhaps more effective tool?

   a. Road Shows should not replace or eliminate any existing effort.

   b. Road Shows should be one, new type of effort, the value of which can only be judged by results.

   c. The conception of the Road Show must be flexible and change as circumstances and experience require.

6. What other things might we consider now or in the future?

       a. Educational course, seminars, workshops
         (1) On Davis premises
         (2) On customer premises
       b. Cooperative efforts to find applications or solutions to industry problems
       c. Advertising program
       d. Mailing list and letter campaign
       e. Personal contact campaign

IV. *General Conclusions and Definition*

A Road Show must be a part of an enlarged sales effort, each showing specifically tailored for the potential customer.

Contact with prospective customers must be established prior to a Road Show.

The Road Show should be carried only to contacts where we are reasonably sure of having an audience we want.

Now is the time for a Road Show because we have a large repertoire of impressive jobs.

We define a Road Show as a tour of sales-technical personnel who meet the potential customer face to face, and use a pre-determined format to present our sales story.

EXHIBIT TWO

ABSTRACT OF CONSULTANT REPORT

  I. What steps were taken to conduct this study?

 II. What came out of investigations?

III. Conclusions with reference to assignment.

IV. What are the alternatives?
    A. Pursue the Road Show idea with support up to maximum budget will allow.
    B. Pursue a Road Show on a national scale with exploitation of existing contacts.
    C. Defer the Road Show but tailor promotional presentations for existing customer contacts.
    D. Defer the Road Show but step-up advertising and personal contact.

 V. Recommendation

What Steps Were Taken to Conduct this Study?

 I. Personal Contacts.

II. Conferences.
    A. Develop a sales strategy.
    B. Prepare recommendations.

What Came out of the Investigation?

  I. Sales strategy must grow out of experience and capabilities.

 II. Sales strategy must grow out of the potential market for these services.

III. Sales strategy must consider the necessity to be competitive.

IV. The method of operation must support the sales strategy.

 V. Sales strategy must encompass a continuing and integrated effort.

VI. The sales strategy must be compatible with company objectives.

What Is Davis' Training and Experience?

 I. Training
   A. Command of professional tools
   B. Superior understanding of tooling problems

II. Experience
   A. Large scale tooling problems
   B. Wide range of industries

What Is the Potential Market?

  I. Firms Davis is currently working for or has worked for in the past.
   A. Competition has done 74 per cent of volume on repeat business.
   B. Davis has done most of its volume on repeat business.

 II. Other contacts already established
   A. No door opener needed.
   B. Existing expression of potential customer problems or interests.
   C. Some degree of rapport in existence.

III. All other firms in need of our services
   A. No estimate of regional or national markets.
   B. No estimate of demand for some specialized tooling service.
   C. What is the desirable sales goal in terms of current budget? Development of annual volume for 1957 of $7,000,000—need about 22 new jobs to make this billing.

How Can Davis Become Competitive?

 I. Who is the competition?

II. What are the essential characteristics of competitors' operations?
   A. Sales
    1. Social persuasion.
    2. Full time, high level salesmen.

    3. Organized continuing promotional campaign.
    4. Unrelenting stimulation of customers.
    5. Build professional reputation of individual members of staff.
  B. Services
    1. Activities organized by regions which permit regular and satisfying communication with customers.
    2. Full time, permanent, well-equipped sales staff.
    3. Well-established method of project management.
    4. Draw on a wide variety and a long history of successful projects.
  C. Cost of services
    1. Initial answers generated quickly.
    2. Out of pocket expenses minimized by regional organization.

How Can the Method of Operation Support the Sales Strategy?

  I. Every staff member is a salesman.
    A. Every staff member must understand the sales strategy.
    B. Every staff member must understand his role in sales.
    C. Every staff member must understand how to conduct himself with the customer.

  II. Project work must satisfy the customer—Davis must do what it has agreed to do.
    A. Davis must do its work within the quoted time schedule.
    B. Each staff member must have an individual schedule which he is responsible for meeting.
    C. Content of a program must be compatible with what Davis has agreed to do.
    D. Staff members must be assigned only to jobs for which they have demonstrated capabilities.
    E. Davis must have records of what transpired on the job.

  III. Project work must be concluded so customer can make continued profitable use of new tools.
    A. Customer's personnel must understand what has been done.
    B. Customer's organization must be prepared to handle new tools.

Sales Strategy Must Encompass a Continuing And Integrated Effort

  I. Permanent full-time administration of sales—no lapse in personal contacts.
    A. A Steady stream of new customer contacts and proposals.
    B. Constant personal follow-up.

  II. Regularly scheduled promotional activities of varied types.
    A. Distribution of literature.
      1. Quarterly bulletin.

2. Annual Report.
3. Bi-monthly list of accomplishments.
4. Periodic special mailings.
B. Personal presentations.
1. Road Shows.
2. Professional societies and trade groups.

III. Provide for continuous revision of sales tools.
A. Measure effectiveness of sales tools—change and modify emphasis of sales program.
B. Add new tools as they are developed.

IV. There must be an underlying and general plan.
A. Objective: to get a steady stream of new contracts.
B. Central themes must have wide applicability to the potential market.
C. All parts of the plan must be compatible with central themes.
D. Take advantage of accepted and proven methods of reaching potential customers.

V. There must be basic selling techniques for handling contacts.
A. Objective: to develop a tailored sales plan for each contact.
B. There must be a scheduled step-by-step plan leading to a sale—there must be continuous revisions in light of each contact.
C. All recognized sales techniques should be used where applicable:
1. Social and business visits
2. Presentations and Road Shows
3. Demonstrations and workshops
4. Cooperative efforts
5. Promotional devices
6. Distribution of literature

Conclusions

I. The Road Show has a specific place in an integrated sales program, but has little value by itself.

II. Sales will be registered only by a well-planned, perservering program.

III. Ability to close sales rests primarily on confidence in the company generated by extensive personal contact.

IV. The market for Davis' services, in terms of past and potential contacts, indicates that the business should operate on a national scale.

QUESTIONS

1. What is the system under study?
2. What are the assumptions implicit in Davis's position?
3. If you were Davis, what would you do?
4. What are the systems aspects of the problem?

References

OPERATIONS RESEARCH

Batchelor, James H., *Operations Research: A Preliminary Annotated Bibliography*. Cleveland: The Case Institute of Technology, 1951.

Case Institute Proceedings in Operations Research.

Charnes, A., W. W. Cooper, and A. Henderson, *An Introduction to Linear Programming*. New York: John Wiley & Sons, 1953.

Churchman, C. West, Russell L. Ackoff and E. Leonard Arnoff, *Introduction to Operations Research*. New York: John Wiley & Sons, 1957.

Ireson, W. Grant, and Eugene L. Grant, *Handbook of Industrial Engineering and Management*. Englewood Cliffs, N.J.: Prentice-Hall, Inc., 1955.

Journal of the American Institute of Industrial Engineers.

Journal of the Operations Research Society of America.

McClosky, J. F., and F. N. Trefethen, *Operations Research for Management,* two vols. Baltimore: Johns Hopkins Press, 1954.

Operational Research Quarterly.

Publications of the American Management Association.

Publications of the Institute of Management Sciences.

Publications of the Management Sciences Research Project, University of California at Los Angeles.

Publications of the Office of Naval Research, Washington, D.C.

Publications of the Rand Corporation.

Vazsonyi, A., *Scientific Programming in Business and Industry*. New York: John Wiley & Sons, 1958.

ELECTRONIC DATA PROCESSING

Canning, R. G., *Cutting the Cost of Your EDP Installation*. Los Angeles: Published by the author, 1958.

Canning, R. G., *Electronic Data Processing for Business and Industry.* New York: John Wiley & Sons, 1956.

Canning, R. G., *Installing Electronic Data Processing Systems.* New York: John Wiley & Sons, 1957.

Canning, Sisson, and Associates, "Suggested Reading List," *Data Processing Digest,* February, 1957.

Handbook of Automation, Computation and Control, three vols. New York: John Wiley & Sons, 1959.

Kozmetsky, G., and P. Kircher, *Electronic Computers and Management Control.* New York: McGraw-Hill Book Company, 1956.

Publications of the Association for Computing Machinery.

Publications of the Institute of Radio Engineers.

RELATED TOPICS

Bross, I. D. F., *Design for Decision.* New York: The Macmillan Company, 1953.

Chicago Area Transportation Study, Survey Findings, Vol. I, State of Illinois, December, 1959.

Fisher, R. A., *The Design of Experiments.* New York: Hafner Publishing Co., 1951.

Goode, H. H., and R. E. Machol, *System Engineering.* New York: McGraw-Hill Book Company, 1957.

Payne, S., *The Art of Asking Questions.* Princeton, N.J.: Princeton University Press, 1951.

Publications of the Society for General Systems Research.

Wiener, Norbert, *Cybernetics.* New York: John Wiley & Sons, 1948.

Index

271